2026 교원임용시험 전공영어 대비
최신 기출문제 경향 반영

앤드류 채
멘토영어학 문제은행

LSI 영어연구소 앤드류 채 편저

Mentor Linguistics

PREFACE

멘토영어학 문제은행은 실제 시험 대비를 위한 종합적 훈련 교재이다.

2023년~2024년까지 2년간 출제된 문제를 주제별로 엄선해서 지금까지 배운 내용학 복습과 문제 적용 훈련 및 답안 작성 연습을 통해 실제 시험 대비를 위한 종합적 훈련이 가능하도록 구성했다. 임용시험 합격을 위해선 지문 분석 능력과 답안 작성의 기술적인 능력 향상이 필요하다.

효과적인 학습을 위해 아래와 같은 학습법을 제안한다.

- **수업 전** 수업 진도에 따라 반드시 미리 문제를 풀어보고, 이해되지 않는 부분을 표시한다.
- **수업 중** 강의를 통해서 이해되지 않았던 부분을 해결하고, 관련 주제의 핵심 개념을 다시 숙지한다.
- **수업 후** 모범답안을 참고하여 본인의 답안을 보완하고, 자주 쓰는 표현을 익숙하게 쓸 수 있도록 연습한다.

임용시험 준비 기간의 후반기로 접어들면서 정신적·체력적으로 지쳐가는 시기이다. 7~8월 무더운 날씨에 건강에 유의하여 체력관리를 잘하는 것도 시험 준비에 있어서 중요한 부분이다. 같은 시간이라도 집중력 있게 공부하고 출제 빈도가 높은 주제에 좀 더 시간을 투자해서 학습의 효과를 극대화하길 바란다.

부디, 수험생 예비교사 여러분의 임용시험 합격에 본 교재가 조금이나마 도움이 되었으면 한다.

효과적인 학습전략

1 비중이 높은 영역을 공략하라.

통사론·학교문법·음운론의 비중이 높고, 기타 형태론·의미론·화용론이 비중이 상대적으로 낮으므로 효율적인 학습계획과 학습전략을 수립하는 것이 필요하다.

2 개념이해와 용어정리를 확실히 하라.

주어진 지문을 정확하게 읽고 이해하기 위해서는 영어학의 개념과 용어를 정확히 숙지하고 있어야 한다.

3 주어진 자료를 문제 지시내용에 따라 정확하게 분석하라.

영어학 문제는 주어진 자료(data)에 한정하여 출제자의 의도를 파악하고 지시내용(directions)을 토대로 분석해야만 출제자가 원하는 답을 도출할 수 있다. 지시내용을 무시하고 관련 주제에 관해 자신이 아는 내용을 함부로 적용해서는 안 된다.

4 기입형 대비: 지문 흐름 따라가기 훈련과 정확한 용어정리를 하라.

출제자가 요구하는 답은 지문에 정해져 있으므로 평소 지문이 말하고자 하는 바를 파악하는 훈련이 필요하다.

5 서술형 대비: 주어진 자료를 분석하고 지시내용을 토대로 서술하는 훈련을 하라.

서술형은 지문을 이해하고 지시내용에 따라 주어진 자료를 분류·분석하여 서술하는 문제로 출제된다. 따라서 답안에 포함되어야 할 핵심 용어(key terms)를 찾고 이것들을 정돈해 깔끔하게 기술하는 연습이 필요하다. 자신의 지식이나 생각보다 출제자가 의도하고 요구하는 답을 도출하는 연습이 필요하다.

수험생 예비교사 여러분의 합격을 진심으로 기원하며

2025년 6월

Andrew Chai

Mentor Linguistics
CONTENTS

Part 01   Syntax   ··· 8

Unit 01.	Raising	··· 8
Unit 02.	Complements & Adjuncts	··· 16
Unit 03.	Substitution	··· 33
Unit 04.	Case Theory	··· 45
Unit 05.	Binding Theory	··· 49
Unit 06.	Control Theory	··· 57
Unit 07.	Theta Theory	··· 61
Unit 08.	Constituency	··· 64
Unit 09.	Verbs	··· 78
Unit 10.	Syntactic Structures	··· 85
Unit 11.	Additional Tests	··· 94

Part 02   Grammar   ··· 126

Part 03   Phonetics & Phonology   ··· 186

Part 04	Morphology	... 326

Part 05	Semantics	... 336

Part 06	Pragmatics	... 352

모범 답안

Unit 01 Raising

Unit 02 Complements & Adjuncts

Unit 03 Substitution

Unit 04 Case Theory

Unit 05 Binding Theory

Unit 06 Control Theory

Unit 07 Theta Theory

Unit 08 Constituency

Unit 09 Verbs

Unit 10 Syntactic Structures

Unit 11 Additional Tests

멘토영어학
문제은행

Part 01

Syntax

Unit 01 Raising

• Answer Key p.03

01 Read the passage and fill in each blank with the ONE most appropriate word. Write your answers in the correct order. [2 points]

> There are four distinct types of embedded non-finite constructions: subject-to-subject raising, subject-to-object raising, subject control, and object control. It should be noted that some verbs allow more than one type of construction. For example, the verb *want* allows either subject control or subject-to-object raising:
>
> (1) a. Jean$_i$ wants [PRO$_i$ to leave].   *subject control*
>   b. Jean wants Bill$_i$ [t$_i$ to leave].   *subject-to-object raising*
>
> We can see four types of embedded non-finite constructions and their properties below:
>
> (2) Jean is likely to leave.
>   (a) Main clause predicate assigns one theta role (to the proposition) and no external (subject) theta role.
>   (b) DP movement of embedded subject to the specifier of TP for EPP and Case.
>   (c) Allows idiomatic readings and extraposition.
>
> (3) Jean prefers Robert to leave.
>   (a) Main clause predicate assigns ____①____ theta roles.
>   (b) Main clause predicate has an Accusative [ACC] Case feature.
>   (c) Allows idiomatic readings.

Part 01 Syntax

(4) Jean is reluctant to leave.

　　(a) Main clause predicate assigns two theta roles.

　　(b) No DP movement for Case.

　　(c) Does not allow idiomatic readings or extraposition.

(5) Jean ordered Robert to leave.

　　(a) Main clause predicate assigns _____②_____ theta roles.

　　(b) No DP movement for Case.

　　(c) Does not allow idiomatic readings or extraposition.

02 Read the passage <A> and the sentences in <B>, and follow the directions.

[4 points]

Consider the following examples:

(1) a. To understand this lesson is difficult.
　　b. → It is difficult to understand this lesson.
　　c. → This lesson is difficult to understand.

In English, there are adjectives which allow the transformation of sentences like the examples given in (1). The adjective *difficult* in (1) has to do mainly with the ease or difficulty of the situation described in the infinitival clause or with one's emotional attitude to it.

However, the adjective *ready* in (2) is semantically and syntactically less homogeneous. A number of adjectives used in this construction are collocationally quite restricted.

(2) a. *To sign the document is now ready.
　　b. *It is now ready to sign the document.
　　c. The document is now ready for you to sign.

As shown in (2c), in *ready*-type, the subject of the main clause is identified with the object of the infinitive clause. But unlike *difficult*-type in (1), *ready*-type cannot allow the construction with an infinitive clause subject shown in (2a) and an extraposed construction shown in (2b).

The adjectives like *essential* can allow the transformation of sentences in (3).

(3) a. To spray the trees every year is essential.
　　b. It is essential (for you) to spray the trees every year.

The infinitive clause is an extraposed subject. Adjectives in this type express volition, modality, or emotion.

B

(a) John is wonderful to work with.
(b) John is impossible to live with.
(c) It is free to borrow these toys.
(d) It is crucial for us to take three meals a day.
(e) To breathe the air was frosty.
(f) To follow this direction is awkward.

In <B>, identify TWO ungrammatical sentences, and explain why, specifying the type of the adjective, based on the description in <A>.

03 Read the passage and fill in each blank with ONE word from the passage. Write your answers in the correct order. [2 points]

How can we account for the differences between raising and control verbs or adjectives? A simple traditional analysis is to derive a surface structure via a derivational process, for example, from (1a) to (1b):

(1) a. Deep structure: △ seems [Stephen to be irritating].
　　b. Surface structure: Stephen seems [t] to be irritating.

To derive (1b), the subject of the infinitival VP in (1a) moves to the matrix subject position. The movement of the subject *Stephen* to the higher subject position will correctly generate (1b). This kind of movement to the subject position can be triggered by the requirement that each English declarative have a surface ___①___. A similar movement process can be applied to the ___②___ raising cases:

(2) a. Deep structure: Tom believes [Stephen to be irritating].
　　b. Surface structure: Tom believes Stephen to be irritating.

Here the embedded subject *Stephen* moves not to the matrix subject but to the matrix object position.
　Consider the following tree diagram, focusing on the NP movement (*Mary*):

(3)
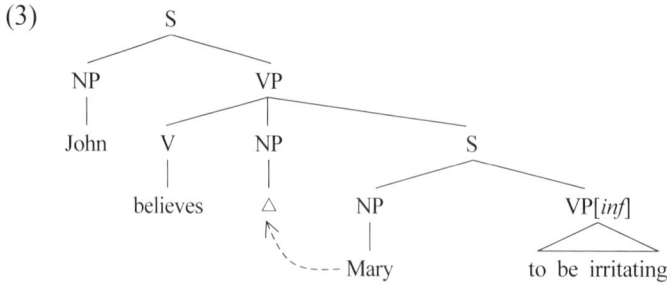

Control constructions are different: there is no movement operation involved. Instead, it is the lower subject position which has special properties. Consider the examples in (4):

(4) a. John tried to please Stephen.
　　b. John persuaded Stephen to be more careful.

Since *try* and *persuade* assign a semantic role to their subjects and objects, an unfilled position of the kind designated above by △ cannot be allowed. Instead, it is posited that there is an unexpressed _____①_____ of the infinitival VP *to please Stephen* and *to be more careful*. This is traditionally represented as the element called 'PRO' (a silent 'pro'noun).

04 Read the passage and fill in each blank with ONE word from the passage. (Use the SAME answer for both blanks.) [2 points]

In raising constructions, the subject of the raising predicate is selected as the subject of the complement VP. Observe the following contrast:

(1) a. Stephen seemed [to be intelligent].
 b. It seems [to be easy to fool Ben].
 c. There is likely [to be a letter in the mailbox].
 d. Tabs are likely [to be kept on participants].
(2) a. *There seemed [to be intelligent].
 b. *John seems [to be easy to fool Ben].
 c. *John is likely [to be a letter in the mailbox].
 d. *John is likely [to be kept on participants].

For example, the VP *to be intelligent* requires an animate subject, and this is why (1a) is fine but (2a) is not. Meanwhile, the VP *to be easy to fool Ben* requires the expletive *it* as its subject. This is why *John* cannot be the subject in (2b). The contrast in (c) and (d) is similar. The VP *to be a letter in the mailbox* allows its subject to be *there* (cf. *There is a letter in the mailbox*) but not *John*. The VP *to be kept on participants* requires a subject which must be the word *tabs* in order to induce an idiomatic meaning.

In raising constructions, whatever category is required as the subject of the infinitival VP is also required as the subject by the higher VP—hence the intuition of 'raising' is as follows: the requirement for the subject passes up to the higher predicate.

However, for control verbs, there is no direct selectional relation between the _____ of the main verb and that of the infinitival VP. It is the control verb or adjective itself which fully determines the properties of the _____:

(3) a. Sandy tried [to eat oysters].
    b. *There tried [to be riots in Seoul].
    c. *It tried [to bother me that Chris lied].
    d. *Tabs try [to be kept on Bob by the FBI].
    e. *That he is clever is eager [to be obvious].

Unit 02 Complements & Adjuncts

• Answer Key p.05

01 Read the passage and fill in each blank with the ONE word from the passage. Write your answers in the correct order. [2 points]

> Complements have to be licensed by the head noun. Consider the following examples:
>
> (1) a. the attack <u>on the Prime Minister</u>
>   b. the abolition <u>of taxes</u>
>   c. the fact <u>that she's alive</u>
>
> Subordinate clauses may be finite or non-finite, and both types are found as complements to nouns, as in (2)—(3):
>
> (2) a. the claim <u>that he was ill</u>   FINITE
>   b. a suspicion <u>that it was a hoax</u>   FINITE
> (3) a. her ability <u>to complete the task</u>   NON-FINITE
>   b. his eagerness <u>to redeem himself</u>   NON-FINITE
>
> Consider now the following examples, where brackets enclose the NP and underlining marks the complement.
>
> (4) a. We had to put up with [a longer delay <u>than we had bargained for</u>].
>   b. He gave [so complicated an explanation <u>that I was completely baffled</u>].
>   c. It was [too serious a problem <u>for us to ignore</u>].

We call these indirect complements because although they follow the head noun, it is not the head noun that licenses them. In (4a) the complement is licensed by the word ____①____: if we drop this the NP becomes ungrammatical. Similarly, in (4b) the complement is licensed by the word ____②____. In (4c) it is licensed by the word *too*. This time we could drop *too serious* without loss of grammaticality—but it would have a dramatic effect on the interpretation of the infinitival clause. *A problem for us to ignore* means "a problem that we can/should ignore", whereas the NP in (4c) means "a problem that was so serious that we could/should not ignore it".

02 Read the passage <A> and the sentences in <B>, and follow the directions.

[4 points]

A

The dependents of the predicator in the VP are of two main kinds: complements and adjuncts. The admissibility of a complement depends on the predicator belonging to a particular subclass of verbs. The term we use for this is licensing: complements have to be licensed by their head, V, N, A, etc.

The object is one kind of complement, and we can illustrate the concept of licensing by considering the occurrence of an object with the following three verbs:

(1) a. Sue used the cheese.
  b. *Sue used. [object obligatory]
(2) a. Sue ate the cheese.
  b. Sue ate. [object optional]
(3) a. *Sue disappeared the cheese.
  b. Sue disappeared. [object excluded]

An object such as *the cheese* is admissible with, hence licensed by, the verbs *use* and *eat,* but not *disappear*: (3a) is ungrammatical. There is a further difference between *use* and *eat*. With *eat* the object is optional whereas with *use* it is obligatory: (2b) is grammatical, but (1b) is not. The status of a dependent as a complement is most obvious when it is obligatory for at least some heads. But this is not essential: the crucial feature of licensing is that the admissibility of the element depends on the presence of an appropriate head.

The occurrence of adjuncts is not restricted in this way. They occur more freely, essentially without regard to what the predicator is. The examples in (4) illustrate the difference between complements (the italicized phrase) and adjuncts (single underlining).

(4) a. I saw *your father* this morning.
  b. They still think *they were right*.

In (4a), *your father* is a complement licensed by *see*. If *see* were replaced by *fall*, we would have an ungrammatical sentence. *This morning* in (4a), by contrast, is an adjunct; a temporal NP of this kind is compatible with any verb. In (4b), *still* is an adjunct, again because it is compatible with any verb. But the subordinate clause *they were right* is a complement, licensed by *think*. Again it is easy to find verbs like *alter* or *lose* or *work* that are incompatible with a subordinate clause of this kind, whatever its particular semantic content.

───┤ B ├───

Consider the following examples focusing on the underlined PPs:

(a) I cut it <u>with a razor-blade</u>.
(b) She regularly gives us very useful advice <u>on financial matters</u>.
(c) John blamed the incident <u>on Mary</u>.
(d) He declaimed <u>against Syntax</u>.
(e) Max glanced <u>at the falling acrobat</u>.
(f) He will work <u>at the office</u>.

In <B>, identify TWO sentences where the underlined PP has the different function from the rest (i.e., only the two PPs have the same function), and state the function of each PP, based on the description in <A>.

03 Read the passage and fill in the blank with the appropriate TWO words.
[2 points]

> A phrase normally consists of a head, alone or accompanied by one or more dependents. The category of the phrase depends on that of the head: a phrase with a noun as head is a noun phrase, and so on.
>
> The object is a kind of complement since it satisfies the licensing requirement. The subject is rather different: all canonical clauses contain a subject, so in a sense subjects are compatible with any verb. However, certain syntactic kinds of subject are restricted to occurrence with particular kinds of verb, so the concept of licensing applies here too. Take, for example, the subject of (1a):
>
> (1) a. <u>Whether we will finish on time</u> depends primarily on the weather.
>   b. *<u>Whether we will finish on time</u> ruined the afternoon.
>
> The underlined expression in (1a) is a subordinate clause functioning as subject of the larger clause that forms the whole sentence. It is, more specifically, a subordinate interrogative clause: the main clause counterpart is *Will we finish on time?* A subject of this syntactic form has to be licensed by the verb (or VP). It is admissible with *depend*, but there are innumerable other verbs such as *ruin, see, think, yearn*, etc., that do not accept subjects of this form; so (1b), for example, is ungrammatical.
>
> Therefore, subjects do satisfy the condition for being complements. But they are different from other types of complement in an obvious way: they are not positioned within the VP. We will refer to the subject as a/an _____. The other complements that are internal to the VP will be referred to as internal complements.

04 Read the passage <A> and the sentences in <B>, and follow the directions.
[4 points]

― A ―

Not all syntactic ambiguity can be explained in terms of hierarchical structure. Some ambiguities arise in sentences in which material is missing but nevertheless understood. Phrase structure helps us explain why we understand such sentences the way we do.

The following sentence is ambiguous:

(1) The crab is too hot to eat.

Do you understand the sentence as having two meanings? There are no lexical ambiguities here; the noun *crab*, whether the living creature or your dinner, has the same meaning; *hot* indicates temperature, and *eat* means *consume*. In syntactic terms, the ambiguity can be stated in this way: who or what is the subject of *eat* —the crab or someone else? And who or what is the complement of *eat*—crab food or the crab itself? Complements are phrases that combine with heads to form (or "complete") a larger phrase. So, *eat* is a verb that typically is followed by an NP complement because we typically eat *something*. Here, the complement is understood but not overt or pronounced.

What all this boils down to is that in order to interpret this sentence, we must assume that there is an unpronounced subject of the (infinitival) verb *eat* and also an unpronounced complement of that verb. These two "invisible" NPs are represented by the delta symbol, Δ.

(2) The crab is too hot [Δ to eat Δ].
(3) The crab is too hot (for someone) to eat (the crab).
(4) The crab is too hot (for the crab) to eat (something).

We explain the syntactic ambiguity of this sentence by proposing not that the sentence could have two different structures but that there is an "understood" or "silent" subject of *eat* and also a silent complement of *eat*.

Other ambiguities arise in a sentence due to the difference of functions (complement vs. adjunct), of grammatical forms (NP, AP, etc.) or of scope.

B

(a) George wants the presidency more than Martha.

(b) Tell me when you are ready.

(c) Liz bought a pen.

(d) Nicole saw the people with binoculars.

(e) The tuna can hit the boat.

(f) John couldn't explain last night.

In <B>, identify TWO ambiguous sentences due to the difference of functions (*complement* vs. *adjunct*), and explain why, stating the phrase or clause which involves a complement or adjunct interpretation, based on the description in <A>.

05 Read the passage and fill in each blank with the appropriate preposition. Write your answers in the correct order. [2 points]

One striking difference between nouns and verbs is that nouns don't take objects. With nouns that are morphologically related to transitive verbs, as *criticism* is related to *criticise*, the complement of the noun that corresponds to the object of the verb has the form of a PP:

(1) a. I *criticised her decision.*
    b. my *criticism of her decision*
(2) a. He *abandoned his ship.*
    b. his *abandonment of his ship*
(3) a. Sandy *married Pat.*
    b. Sandy's *marriage to Pat*

The preposition is usually *of*, as in (1b) and (2b), but with certain nouns other prepositions are selected, as in (3b).

Dependents with the form of PPs qualify as complements when they are licensed by the particular head noun. The clearest cases have one or more of the following properties.

They correspond to object or subject NPs in clause structure. The object case has been illustrated in (1)—(3), while correspondence with a subject is seen in (4)—(5):

(4) a. The warriors returned.
    b. the return of the warriors
(5) a. The premier attacked.
    b. an attack by the premier

The choice of preposition is specified by the head noun. Many nouns take complements headed by a particular preposition:

(6) a. their belief *in* God
    b. your reply *to* my letter
    c. secession ___①___ the alliance
    d. his disillusionment ___②___ Linguistics

The PP is obligatory because the noun makes little sense without it:

(7) a. the advent of the steam engine
    b. the abandonment of sensible budgetary policies
    c. the feasibility of the proposal
    d. a dearth of new ideas

06 Read the passages and follow the directions. [4 points]

── A ──

All phrases have something in common, namely the fact that they must minimally contain a Head. In the bracketed phrases in the sentences below, the Heads are shown in bold type:

(1) The defendants denied the charge: they claim that they did [VP not **destroy** the garden]

(2) She proposed [NP an **analysis** of the sentence]

(3) Jack is [AP so **fond** of coffee]

Notice that apart from the obligatory presence of the Heads, there are further similarities between these phrases. First of all, there appears to be a strong bond between the Head and the constituent that follows it in each case. Thus, in (1) the verb *destroy* requires the presence of a Noun Phrase that refers to an entity that is destroyable. Similarly, in (2) the PP *of the sentence* complements the noun *analysis* in that it specifies what is being analysed. We briefly introduced the notion Complement as a general term to denote any constituent whose presence is required by another element.

The phrases we have looked at so far contained only a Specifier, a Head and a Complement. Phrases can, however, be structurally more complicated. Consider first the bracketed VP below:

(4) The defendants denied the charge: they claim that they did [VP not destroy the garden deliberately]

In this sentence the AdvP *deliberately* modifies the sequence *destroy the garden*, and is positioned after the Head *destroy* and its Complement *the garden*. This AdvP functions as an Adjunct. In tree diagrams, the Complement *the garden* is closer to the Head *destroy* than the Adjunct *deliberately*: the Complement is a sister of V, whereas the Adjunct is a sister of the V' that immediately dominates V.

B

Draw the tree for each sentence or phrase below in your mind, and then decide whether the statements for each sentence or phrase are true or false.

(a) *their realisation that all is lost*: the underlined clause is the Complement and is a sister of N.

(b) *her question whether the expense was worth it*: the underlined clause is the adjunct and is a sister of the N'.

(c) *I served as secretary*: the underlined PP is the complement and is a sister of V.

(d) *He looked at the picture*: the underlined PP is the complement and is a sister of V.

(e) *The tiles on the floor are ancient*: the underlined PP is the complement and is a sister of N.

Identify TWO false statements in <B>, and correct the statements, based on the description in <A>.

07 Read the passage and follow the directions. [4 points]

A

Like verbs, certain adjectives can also select CPs as their complements. For example, *insistent* selects a finite CP, whereas *eager* selects an infinitival CP:

(1) a. Tom is insistent [that the witnesses be truthful].
　　b. Tom seems eager [for her brother to catch a cold].

We can easily find more adjectives which select a CP complement:

(2) a. I am ashamed that I neglected you.
　　b. I am delighted that Mary finished his thesis.

Nouns can also select a CP complement, for example, *eagerness*:

(3) (John's) eagerness [for Harry to win the election]

One pattern that we can observe is that when a verb selects a CP complement, if there is a corresponding noun, it also selects a CP, as shown in (4):

(4) a. We believe that the directors were present.
　　b. the belief that the directors were present

This shows us that the derivational process which derives a noun from a verb preserves the COMPS (complements) value of that verb. A caution here is that not all nouns can of course select a CP complement:

(5) a. *his attention that the earth is round
　　b. *the expertise that she knows how to bake croissants

These nouns cannot combine with a CP complement, indicating that they do not have CP in the value of COMPS.

┌─────────────────── B ───────────────────┐
(a) Tom is confident that the elephants respect him.

(b) We are content for the cleaners to return the drapes next week.

(c) his conviction that the operation is safe

(d) the allegation that Fred signed the check

(e) the ignorance that James can play the flute

(f) his article that the earth is flat
└───┘

In <B>, identify TWO ungrammatical sentences or phrases, and explain why, based on the description in <A>.

08
Read the passage and fill in each blank with ONE word from the passage. Write your answers in the correct order. [2 points]

X-bar theory is a very simple and general theory of phrase structure. Using only three rules, this theory explains the distinction in function between adjuncts, complements, and specifiers.

(1) a. Specifier rule: XP → (YP) X'
    b. Adjunct rule: X' → X' (ZP) or X' → (ZP) X'
    c. Complement rule: X' → X (WP)

X is a head, WP is a complement, ZP is an adjunct, and YP is a specifier. The complement rule stipulates that the complement should always be more _____①_____ to the head than the adjunct, as seen in the following tree:

(2)
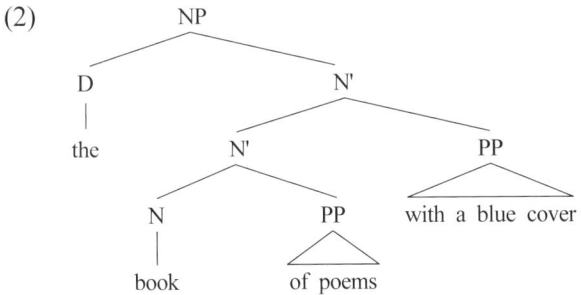

The adjunct rule takes an X-bar level category and generates another X-bar category. Since lines can't cross, it will always be higher in the tree than the output of the complement rule. Consider the following sentences:

(3) a. *She likes the book from the MIT press of poems.
   b. *She likes the book from the MIT press and of poems.

The sentence in (3a) is ungrammatical since the complement *of poems* is not more adjacent to the head than the adjunct *from the MIT press* violating the complement rule. The sentence in (3b) is ungrammatical since it violates the following conjunction principle: the conjoined elements must belong to the same category in terms of ____②____; in other words, the conjoined elements must be the same adjuncts or they must be the same complements.

09 Read the passage <A> and the phrases in <B>, and follow the directions.

[4 points]

A

There are three structurally distinct classes of nominal premodifier, namely (i) Determiners, (ii) Complements, and (iii) Attributes. These three different classes of premodifier have the different structural properties described in (1) below:

(1) (i) Determiners expand N-bar into N-double-bar (or NP)
    (ii) Attributes recursively expand N-bar into N-bar
    (iii) Complements expand N into N-bar

Since both *Attributes* and *Adjuncts* recursively expand N-bar into N-bar, it seems clear that the two have essentially the same function, so that Attributes are simply prenominal Adjuncts. For the time being, we shall concentrate on the distinction between Complement NPs and Attribute NPs. In this connection, consider the following Noun Phrase:

(2) a [Cambridge] [Physics] student

Clearly, (2) is ambiguous; the structural symmetry principle would suggest that (2) should be assigned the structure (3) below:

(3)
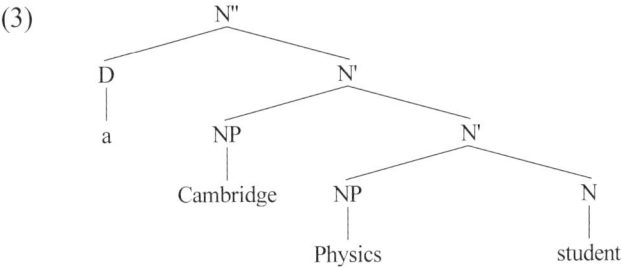

Now, consider the following ambiguous phrase:

(4) a French professor

(5) a. a professor of French (a professor who teaches French)
    b. a professor from France (a professor who is from France)

(4) has the meaning of (5a) when the NP *French* is interpreted as a complement; (4) has the meaning of (5b) when the NP is used as an adjunct. The ambiguity arises according to whether the lexical item *France* is interpreted as an adjunct or a complement. Be careful that when an adjunct or a complement occurs post-nominally, it must be a post-nominal PP.

B

(a) the proportional representation campaign
(b) the fraud investigations
(c) famine relief
(d) the fight after the match
(e) the advertisement on the television
(f) a student of high moral principles

In <B>, identify ONE ambiguous phrase, and then explain why the phrase is ambiguous, stating each interpretation, based on the description in <A>.

Unit 03 Substitution

• Answer Key p.09

01 Read the passage <A> and the sentences in <B>, and follow the directions.

[4 points]

---- A ----

English possesses a word that can replace less than a full NP, and this is the proform *one*. The proform *one* replaces N'-constituents. Consider the following sentence:

(1) Mark is a dedicated teacher of language, but Paul is an indifferent one.

In this sentence, *one* replaces *teacher of language*. This proform cannot be a full NP because it is preceded by the determinative *an* and the AP *indifferent*. We can show this more clearly in a tree diagram.

(2)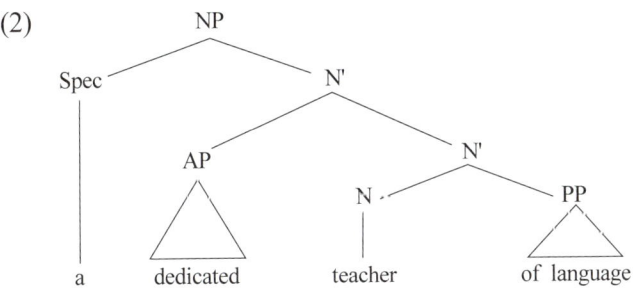

(3)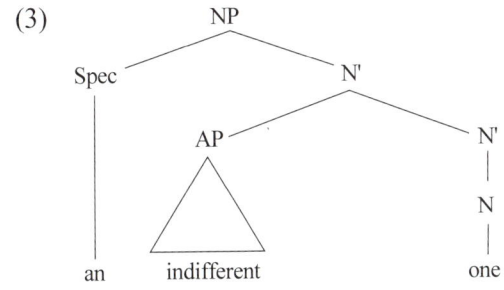

As *one* in (3) replaces *teacher of language* in (2), it must be replacing an N' (N-bar). *One* is a pro-N'. It cannot replace an N by itself unless an N is the constituent of an N'. Consider (4):

(4) *Ben likes the Italian student of English, but not the Spanish one of literature.

─┤ B ├─

(a) Frank believed the claim that Mary made, and he believed another one.
(b) Frank believed the claim that Mary made, and he believed another one that she put forward recently.
(c) Frank believed the claim that Mary made a mistake, and he believed another one.
(d) Frank believed the claim that Mary made a mistake, and he believed another one that she solved the problem.

Identify ONE ungrammatical sentence in <B>, and explain why, stating the corresponding word(s) for the proform *one*, based on the description in <A>.

02 Read the passage <A> and the sentences in <B>, and follow the directions.

[4 points]

A

The fact that complements are more closely related to the verb than adjuncts is reflected in the scope of certain anaphoric expressions, notably *do so*. Anaphoric expressions are those which derive their interpretation from an antecedent. Compare, for example, *Jill signed the petition and Pam did so too* with *Jill visited my mother and Pam did so too*, where the first instance of *did so* is interpreted as "signed the petition" and the second as "visited my mother". The relevance of *do so* to the distinction between complements and adjuncts is seen in the following examples:

(1) a. *Jill keeps her car in the garage but Pam does so in the road.
   b. Jill washes her car in the garage but Pam does so in the road.

The antecedent for *do so* must embrace all internal complements of the verb: it therefore cannot itself combine with such a complement. In (1a) *in the garage* is a complement of *keep* (it is obligatory when *keep* has the sense it has here), and therefore must be included in the antecedent for *do so*. This means that *Pam does so* has to be interpreted as "Pam keeps her car in the garage"; we can't add *in the road* as another complement in the second clause. The inclusion of *in the road* to contrast with *in the garage* in the first clause requires the interpretation "Pam keeps her car": the ungrammaticality results from this conflict. But in (1b) *in the garage* is an adjunct in the *wash*-clause, and hence need not be included in the antecedent of *does so*: we interpret it as "Pam washes her car"; with *in the road* added as an adjunct contrasting with *in the garage* in the first clause.

Note that the data in (1) lend support to the position adopted in (1b) above, namely that certain kinds of element can be either complements or adjuncts: locative *in the road*, for example, is a complement in (1a) and an adjunct in (1b). Moreover, in certain case, the added phrase in the second clause does not contrast with anything in the first clause because the added phrase can consist of another complement; it cannot combine with *do so* in the second clause.

━━━━━━━━━━━━━━━━━━━━━ B ━━━━━━━━━━━━━━━━━━━━━

(a) I didn't read all the reports but I did so most of them.

(b) I didn't cover this topic last time but I shall do so on Tuesday.

(c) She rode her bicycle and she did so to school.

(d) She performed all the tasks and she did so remarkably well.

(e) Mary treated us remarkably well and John did so too.

Identify ALL and ONLY ungrammatical sentence(s), and explain why, specifying the antecedent for do so, ONLY based on the description in <A>.

03 Read the passages and follow the directions. [4 points]

A

According to the X-bar theory, determiners expand N-bar into NP, adjuncts recursively expand N-bar into N-bar, and complements expand N into N-bar.

(1)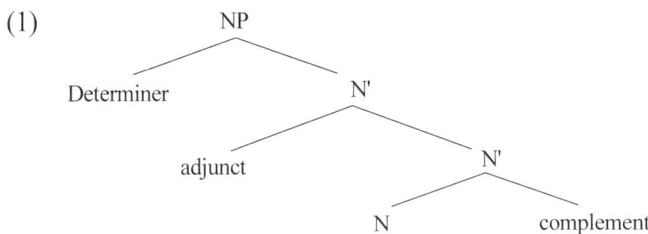

Consider the following Noun Phrase:

(2) an English teacher

(2) is ambiguous; this phrase can be paraphrased as in (3) below:

(3) a. a teacher of English (a teacher who teaches English)
    b. a teacher from English (a teacher who is from English)

On one reading, (2) has the meaning of (3a) when *English* is interpreted as an NP complement. On the other reading, (2) has the meaning of (3b) when *English* is used as an AP adjunct. The ambiguity arises according to whether the lexical item *English* is interpreted as a complement or an adjunct in terms of function, and the categorial status (form) of *English* can either be a prenominal NP or a prenominal AP in (2).

B

The proform *one* replaces N'-constituents; it cannot replace an N. All the words *French* in (4) have the same meaning, and in (5) also have the same meaning.

(4) a. Frank is a French professor and Steve is another one.
    b. Frank is a French professor and Steve is an English one.
    c. a [typically French] professor
(5) a. Frank is a French professor and Steve is another one.
    b. *Frank is a French professor and Steve is an English one.
    c. an [old French] professor

Note: '*' *indicates the ungrammaticality of the sentence.*

In <B>, first, state the function AND form of the word *French* in (4b) and (5b), respectively. Second, identify the form of *French* in (4c) and in (5c), respectively, based on the description in <A>.

04 Read the passage and fill in the blank ① with TWO words from the passage, and the blank ② with the appropriate phrase. Write your answers in the correct order. [2 points]

The constituency of a particular sequence of words can be established by replacing it with a proform. Substitution by proforms is thus a useful test for constituency. Consider (1) below:

(1) *My father* admires *my mother*.

Notice now that *my father* can be replaced by *he*, and *my mother* by *her*:

(2) *He* admires *her*.

The pronouns *he* and *her* function as proforms here because they stand in for the noun phrases *my father* and *my mother*.

Other phrase types, and even clauses, can be replaced by proforms too, as the following sentences demonstrate:

(3) Bill is *unhappy* and *so* she is.

(4) He said *that the operation will be successful*. I certainly hope *so*.

In (3) the AP *unhappy* has been replaced by *so*, and in (4) *so* replaces the clause.

It can also be useful for determining the categorial status of a particular constituent (i.e. what type of phrase it is). To see how this works, consider the italicised portion of the following sentence:

(5) *The French* are hospitable people.

At first sight it may appear that we are dealing with an Adjective Phrase here because the Head of this string is clearly an adjective (cf. *a French village, the French President,* etc.). There are, however, quite a few reasons for saying that *the French* is not an AP. One reason is that it occurs in Subject position. Another is that the phrase is introduced by the definite article *the*. Third, here Substitution plays a role. We can replace *the French* by a pronoun: 'They are hospitable people'. We conclude that phrases such as *the French, the Dutch, the Portuguese,* etc. are _____①_____.

English also possesses a word that can replace less than a full NP, and this is the proform *one*. Consider (6):

(6) Mark is a dedicated teacher of language, but Paul is an indifferent *one*.

In this sentence, *one* replaces _____②_____. This proform cannot be a full NP.

05 Read the passage <A> and the sentences in <B>, and follow the directions. [4 points]

--- A ---

There is a similar process to *one*-replacement in the syntax of VPs. This is the process of *do-so*-replacement. Consider first the VP in the following sentence, which has both an NP and a PP in it.

(1) I [eat beans with a fork].

(2)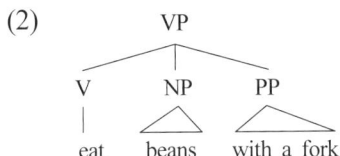

Consider the flat tree in (2). In this tree, there is no constituent that groups together the V and NP and excludes the PP. However, *do-so*-replacement targets exactly this unit, as shown in (3).

(3) I [eat beans] with a fork but Janet [does (so)] with a spoon.

Let's formalize this rule as:

(4) *Do-so*-replacement: Replace a V-bar (V') constituent with *do so*.

The tree structure for the VP in (1) will look like (5).

(5)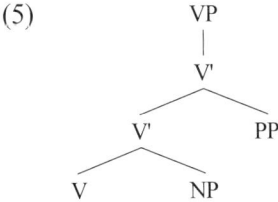

The rule of *do-so*-replacement seen in (4) targets the lower V' and replaces it with *do so*. Evidence for the higher V' comes from sentences like (6):

(6) Kevin [ate spaghetti with a spoon] and Geordie [did so] too.

In this sentence, *did so* replaces the higher V' (which includes the V, the lower V', the NP, and the PP).

┤ B ├

(a) John carried her on his back and Max did so on his shoulders.

(b) John mended his car in the garage and Max did so in the garden.

(c) Peter drove his car on the left in France but Max did so his sports car on the right in the States.

(d) Peter drove his car on the left in France but Max did so on the right in the States.

(e) John will buy the book on Tuesday and Paul will do so on Thursday.

Identify TWO ungrammatical sentences in <B>, and explain why, discussing the word(s) which do so replaces, based on the passage in <A>.

06 Read the passage <A> and the sentences in <B>, and follow the directions. [4 points]

A

The definition of a constituent states that it is a group of words that functions as a unit. If this is the case, then we should find instances where groups of words behave as single units.

The smallest constituent is a single word, so it follows that if you can replace a group of words with a single word then we know that group forms a constituent. Consider the italicized NP in (1). It can be replaced with a single word (in this case a pronoun which can replace a full NP). This is the replacement test:

(1) a. *The man from NY* flew only ultra-light planes.
　　b. *He* flew only ultra-light planes.

There is one important caveat to the test of replacement. There are many cases in our rules of optional items (those things marked in parentheses like the AdjP in NP → (D) (AdjP) N). When we replace a string of words with a single word, how do we know that we aren't just leaving off the optional items? To avoid this problem, we have to keep the meaning as closely related to the original as possible. This requires some judgment on your part.

There is another replacement test. The existence and role of the intermediate phrase N', which is a larger than a lexical category but still not a fully-fledged phrase, can be supported from the pronoun substitution examples in (2):

(2) a. The present king of country music is more popular than the last *one*.
　　b. *The king of Rock and Roll is more popular than the *one* of country music.

Why do we have the contrast here? One simple answer is that the pronoun *one* here replaces an N' but not an N or an NP. In (2b), the pronoun *one* replaces the N *king*; it is ungrammatical.

─┤ B ├─

(a) I bought the big book of poems with the blue cover, not the small one.

(b) I bought the big book of poems with the blue cover, not the small one with the red cover.

(c) I want this big book of poems with the blue cover, not that one.

(d) The book that I reviewed is longer than the one that you reviewed.

(e) The student of physics with long hair is more intelligent than the one of chemistry with short hair.

(f) The king of England is taller than the one of Spain.

Identify TWO ungrammatical sentences in <B>, and explain why, based on the description in <A>.

Unit 04 Case Theory

• Answer Key p.12

01 Read the passage <A> and the sentences in <B>, and follow the directions.

[4 points]

A

Consider the following examples:

(1) Frank kicked a tiger.
(2) *Frank disappeared a tiger.

The contrast between (1) and (2) can be accounted for by Case Filter: Every overt Noun Phrase (NP) must be assigned (abstract) case. Case is assigned to every NP by case assigners, either inherently or structurally.

(3) Nominative case is assigned by [+ Tense]:
 Mary finish**ed** the assignment.

(4) Accusative case is assigned by a Transitive Verb or a Preposition:
 John **kill**ed *a dog*.
 The child stood **near** *the fence*.

(5) Genitive case is assigned by the frame [____'s]:
 John's father

(6) Inherent case is assigned to the direct object of the ditransitive verb structure:
 Mary **gave** me *a book*.

Notice that the case assignment is concerned with Noun Phrases only. (1) is grammatical because the subject NP is nominative case-assigned by [+ past tense] of the verb *kicked*, and the object NP is accusative case-assigned by the transitive verb *kicked*. However, (2) is ungrammatical because the NP *a tiger* cannot be accusative case-assigned by the intransitive verb 'disappeared', violating the case filter.

┤ B ├

(a) John believed sincerely that Mary is smart.

(b) Constantly reading novels makes me feel alive.

(c) The river ran dry.

(d) John is envious Mary.

(e) It is vital that we act to stop the destruction the rainforests.

In <B>, identify TWO ungrammatical sentences, and explain why, discussing a caseless NP and a case assigner, based on the description in <A>.

02 Read the passage and fill in each blank with the ONE most appropriate word. Write your answers in the correct order. [2 points]

Case theory accounts for some of the formal properties of overt NPs and integrates the traditional notion of case into the grammar. Consider the examples in (1):

(1) a. The butler attacked the robber.
    b. [That the butler attacked the robber] is surprising.
    c. [For the butler to attack the robber] would be surprising.

(1a) is a simple sentence, containing two NPs, *the butler* and *the robber*. In (1b), the simple sentence (1a) is used as the subject clause of an adjectival predicate (*surprising*). In (1c), we find the non-finite parallel of (1a) used as the subject of the adjectival predicate.

Let us replace the argument NPs in (1) by the corresponding pronouns:

(2) a. *He* attacked *him*.
    b. That *he* attacked *him* is surprising.
    c. For *him* to attack *him* would be surprising.

Depending on their positions in the sentences, the third person pronouns appear in different forms. When the pronoun is the internal argument of *attack*, it takes the form *him*. Adopting the terminology of traditional grammar, we call this form the ACCUSATIVE case. When the third person pronoun is the ____①____ argument of *attack*, it takes either the form *he* or the form *him*. The latter form is again the ACCUSATIVE case of the pronoun; the form *he* will be called the NOMINATIVE case. Pronouns thus can be seen to have different case forms: *he* is NOMINATIVE, *him* is ACCUSATIVE. A third case form found in English NPs is the GENITIVE, illustrated in (3a) and (3b).

(3) a. *The butler's* coat was too big.
    b. *His* coat was too big.

As can be seen in (2), the NOMINATIVE case (*he*) is reserved for the NP in the subject position of finite clauses. The ACCUSATIVE case (*him*) is used both for the object NP of a transitive verb in (2a)—(2c) and for the subject NP of an infinitival subordinate clause in (2c). We also find ACCUSATIVE case realized on the NP complement of a/an _____②_____, as in (4):

(4) Jeeves moved towards *him/*he*.

Adopting the concepts of traditional grammar, we can say that subjects of finite clauses have NOMINATIVE case and that NPs that are complements of prepositions or verbs as well as NPs that are subjects of infinitival clauses appear in the ACCUSATIVE.

Unit 05 Binding Theory

• Answer Key p.13

01 Read the passage <A> and the sentences in <B>, and follow the directions.

[4 points]

A

Let us consider the binding principles:

(1) Principle A: An anaphor (reflexives or reciprocal) must be bound (c-commanded) by its antecedent within its smallest binding domain (clause or noun phrase).

(2) Principle B: An pronominal must not be bound (c-commanded) by its antecedent within its smallest binding domain (clause or noun phrase).

(3) C-command: α c-commands β if the first branching node dominating α dominates β, and if neither α nor β dominates the other.

Consider the following examples:

(4) a. *Mary said that herself discoed with John.
  b. *Mary said that John's mother loved himself.
  c. Mary said that John discoed with himself.
  d. Mary said that John's mother loved herself.
  e. John said that Mary discoed with him.

The binding principles above can explain the (un)grammaticality of the sentences in (4). Sentences (4a) and (4b) violate the binding principle A. (4a) is ungrammatical because the anaphor *herself* is not bound by its antecedent *Mary* within its smallest binding domain *that herself discoed with John*. (4b) is also ungrammatical because the anaphor *himself* cannot be c-commanded by its antecedent *John* although the anaphor and its antecedent are in the same binding domain. On the other hand, sentences (4c)—(4e) observe the binding principles.

B

(a) Frank promised Sally to feed himself.
(b) Frank persuaded Sally to behave himself.
(c) Frank persuaded Sally to behave herself.
(d) Frank ordered Sally to gather evidence about himself.
(e) Frank ordered Sally to gather evidence about herself.
(f) Frank ordered Sally to gather evidence about him.

Identify TWO ungrammatical sentences in <B>, and explain why, stating the antecedent and the binding domain, based on the description in <A>.

02 Read the passage <A> and the sentences in <B>, and follow the directions.

[4 points]

A

Consider the case of the NP *herself* in the following sentence:

(1) Heidi bopped *herself* on the head with a zucchini.
(2) Art said that *he* played basketball.

In (1), this kind of NP, one that obligatorily gets its meaning from another NP in the sentence, is called an anaphor. There is yet another kind of NP. These are NPs that can optionally get their meaning from another NP in the sentence, but may also optionally get it from somewhere else (including context or previous sentences in the discourse). These NPs are called pronouns, as shown in (2). In this sentence, the word *he* can optionally refer to *Art* or it can refer to someone else.

We can postulate the following Binding Principle to explain (un)grammaticality of the sentences:

(3) Binding Principle A (revised): An anaphor must be bound in its binding domain.
(4) Binding Principle B: A pronoun must be free in its binding domain.
(5) Binds: A binds B if and only if A c-commands B and A and B are coindexed.
(6) Binding domain: The clause or NP containing the NP (anaphor or pronoun)

Consider the following examples:

(7) a. *[Heidi$_i$'s mother]$_j$ bopped herself$_i$ on the head with a zucchini.
    b. *Heidi$_i$ bopped her$_i$ on the head with the zucchini.

In (7a) the anaphor *herself* is not bound by the potential antecedent *Heidi* in its binding domain; it violates Binding Principle A. In (7b) the pronoun *her* is not free in its binding domain. It is bound by the potential antecedent *Heidi* in its binding domain; it violates Binding Principle B.

〈 B 〉

(a) The girl who likes John bopped himself.
(b) Mary believes a description of herself.
(c) Bill believes Mary's description of herself.
(d) Bill's brother believes that John kicked him.
(e) Bill's mother-in-law admires himself.

Identify TWO ungrammatical sentences in <B>, and explain why, specifying the potential antecedent, based on the description in <A>.

03 Read the passage <A> and the sentences in <B>, and follow the directions. [4 points]

| A |

The c-command relation plays an important role in accounting for the use of reflexive and reciprocal anaphors. The same can be argued to be true of another type of expression, namely non-anaphoric pronominals like *he/him/her/it,* etc. Now we see the development of a Theory of Binding which incorporated the two binding principles outlined informally below:

(1) Principle A: an anaphor must be bound within its local domain.
(2) Principle B: a (non-anaphoric) pronominal (expression) must be free within its local domain.

Although there is controversy about how best to define the notion of local domain in relation to binding, for present purposes assume that this corresponds to the notion of the closest clause, and that the two binding principles in (1) and (2) thus amount to the following:

(3) Principle A: An anaphor must be bound by (i.e. must refer to) a c-commanding constituent within the closest clause containing it.
(4) Principle B: A pronominal must not be bound by (i.e. must not refer to) any c-commanding constituent within the closest clause containing it.

Consider the following examples:

(5) a. John thought [that Mary$_i$ loved herself$_i$].
    b. *John$_i$ thought [that Mary loved himself$_i$].
    c. John$_i$ thought [that Mary loved him$_i$].
    d. *John thought [that Mary$_i$ loved her$_i$].

(5a) is grammatical because the anaphor *herself* is bound by the c-commanding constituent *Mary* within the closest clause *that Mary loved herself*. However, (5b) is ungrammatical; the anaphor *himself* cannot be bound by the c-commanding constituent *John* within the closest clause (i.e., the embedded clause). (5c) is grammatical because the pronominal *him* is free within the closest clause *that Mary loved him*. (5d), however, is ungrammatical. The pronominal *her* is bound by the c-commanding constituent *Mary* within the closest clause *that Mary loved her*, violating Principle B.

┤ B ├

(a) Mary$_i$ urged Anne to be loyal to her$_i$.
(b) Kevin urged Anne$_i$ to be loyal to herself$_i$.
(c) We$_i$ persuaded the dentist to examine us$_i$.
(d) We$_i$ persuaded the dentist to examine ourselves$_i$.
(e) We persuaded patients$_i$ to examine themselves$_i$.
(f) We persuaded patients$_i$ to examine them$_i$.

Identify TWO ungrammatical sentences in <B>, and explain why, ONLY based on the description in <A>.

04 Read the passage and fill in each blank with ONE word from the passage. Write your answers in the correct order. [2 points]

> Let us consider the relation between the reflexive and its antecedent.
>
> (1) a. Poirot$_i$ hurt himself$_i$.
>   b. *Poirot$_i$ thinks that Mary hurt himself$_i$.
>   c. Mary thinks that Poirot$_i$ has hurt himself$_i$.
>
> In (1a), *himself* is bound by *Poirot*, as indicated by coindexation. In (1b), binding is apparently not possible. Consider the grammatical (1c) where *Poirot* and the reflexive are closer to each other and where the NP *Poirot* can bind the reflexive. We conclude that reflexives need an antecedent and that the antecedent must not be too far away from the reflexive. In a sense to be made more precise, the antecedent must be found in some local domain, the binding domain. The reflexive must be locally bound. From the examples in (1), we might provisionally conclude that reflexive and antecedent must be in the same clause.
>
> Let us extend our data base now to check whether the locality constraint we have set up is adequate to account for all the data. Consider (2a):
>
> (2) a. *I expect [$_{IP}$ himself$_i$ to invite Poirot$_i$].
>   b. Poirot$_i$ invited himself$_i$.
>   c. *Poirot$_i$'s sister invited himself$_i$.
>   d. [$_{IP}$ [$_{NPj}$ [$_{NPi}$ Poirot]'s brother] invited himself$_j$].
>
> (2a) shows that the clause-mate condition is not sufficient to allow for binding of a reflexive. In (2a), both the reflexive and the antecedent appear in the nonfinite clause (IP), but the reflexive cannot be bound. We might propose that in addition to being a clause-mate, the antecedent must precede the reflexive. This would entail that (2a) is ungrammatical and (2b) is grammatical. This also predicts that (2c) is grammatical, but it is not. In both (2b) and (2c), the reflexive and the antecedent are clause-mates, they are inside the same local domain of the clause. But the reflexive *himself* in (2c) cannot be successfully bound by the presumed

antecedent *Poirot*. Compare the ungrammatical (2c) and the grammatical (2d). As shown by the indexation the antecedent of *himself* in (2d) is not NPi, *Poirot*, but rather NPj, *Poirot's brother*, which contains NPi. A careful comparison of the structural relations in the tree diagram between antecedents and reflexives in the sentences above leads us to the conclusion that the ____①____ must c-command the ____②____ .

Unit 06 Control Theory

• Answer Key p.15

01 Read the passage and fill in each blank with ONE word from the passage. Write your answers in the correct order. [2 points]

> Let's observe that some parts of control are sensitive to syntactic structure. Consider what can control PRO in (1):
>
> (1) [Jean$_i$'s father]$_j$ is reluctant PRO$_{j/*i}$ to leave.
>
> If you draw the tree for (1), you'll see that while the whole DP *Jean's father* c-commands PRO, *Jean* by itself does not. The fact that *Jean* cannot control PRO strongly suggests that there is a c-command requirement on obligatory control. This said, the structure of the sentence doesn't seem to be the only thing that comes into play with control. Compare now a subject control sentence to an object control one:
>
> (2) a. Robert$_i$ is reluctant [PRO$_i$ to behave].
>   *subject control*
>   b. Susan$_j$ ordered Robert$_i$ [PRO$_{i/*j}$ to behave].
>   *object control*
>
> In both these sentences PRO must be controlled by *Robert*. PRO in (2b) cannot refer to *Susan*. This would seem to suggest that the closest DP that c-commands PRO must control it. In (2a), *Robert* is the only possible controller, so it controls PRO. In (2b), there are two possible controllers: *Susan* and *Robert*. But only *Robert*, which is structurally closer to PRO, can control it. This hypothesis works well in most cases, but the following example shows it must be wrong:

(3) Jean_i promised Susan_j [PRO_i/*j to behave].
    subject control

In this sentence it is *Jean* doing the behaving, not *Susan*. PRO must be controlled by the subject *Jean*, even though *Susan* is structurally closer. So structure doesn't seem to be the only thing determining which DP does the controlling.

The sentences in (4) all use the verb *beg*, which is traditionally viewed as an object control verb.

(4) a. Louis begged Kate PRO to leave her job.
    b. Louis begged Kate PRO to be allowed PRO to shave himself.

Considering the position of the controller, sentence (4a) shows ____①____ control; Sentence (4b) shows ____②____ control. Examples like these might be used to argue that control is not entirely syntactic or thematic, but may also rely on our knowledge of the way the world works. This kind of knowledge, often referred to as pragmatic knowledge, lies outside the syntactic system we're developing.

02 Read the passage <A> and the sentences in <B>, and follow the directions. [4 points]

A

For raising verbs like *seem* and *believe*, the subject and object respectively is dependent for its semantic properties solely upon the type of VP complement. This fact is borne out by the examples in (1):

(1) a. There/*It/*John seems [to be a fountain in the park].
 b. We believed there/*it/*John [to be a fountain in the park].

Control verbs are different, directly assigning a semantic role to the subject or object. Hence expletives cannot appear (illustrated here for the subject of *try*):

(2) a. *There/*It/John tries to leave the country.
 b. We believed *there/*it/John to try to leave the country.

In a raising example such as (3a), the idiomatic reading can be preserved, but not in a control example like (3b):

(3) a. The cat seems to be out of the bag.
 b. The cat tries to be out of the bag.

This is once again because the subject of *seems* does not have any semantic role: its subject is identical with the subject of its VP complement *to be out of the bag*, whereas the subject of *tries* has its own agent role.

Exactly the same explanation applies to the following contrast:

(4) a. The dentist is likely to examine Pat.
 b. Pat is likely to be examined by the dentist.

Since *likely* is a raising predicate, as long as the expressions *The dentist examines Pat* and *Pat is examined by the dentist* have roughly the same meaning, the two raising examples will also have roughly the same meaning.

However, control examples are different:

(5) a. The dentist is eager to examine Pat.

   b. Pat is eager to be examined by the dentist.

The control adjective *eager* assigns a semantic role to its subject independent of the VP complement.

| B |

(a) Under the bed seems to be a fun place to hide.
(b) Gregory appears to have wanted to be loyal to the company.
(c) There coaxed his brother to give him the candy.
(d) Frank hopes to persuade Harry to make the cook wash the dishes.
(e) There seems likely to be a strike.
(f) The captain ordered there to proceed.

Identify TWO ungrammatical sentences in <B>, and explain why, specifying the types of verb, based on the description in <A>.

Unit 07 Theta Theory

• Answer Key p.16

01 Read the passage and fill in each blank with ONE word from the passage. Write your answers in the correct order. [2 points]

> Some linguists have attempted to devise a universal typology of the semantic roles played by arguments in relation to their predicates. In the table in (1) below are listed a number of terms used to describe some of these roles (the convention being that terms denoting semantic roles are CAPITALISED), and for each role an informal gloss is given, together with an illustrative example in which the italicized expression has the semantic role specified:
>
> (1) List of roles played by arguments with respect to their predicates
>
> | Role | Gloss |
> |---|---|
> | THEME | Entity undergoing the effect of some action
The FBI arrested *Larry Luckless* |
> | AGENT | Entity instigating some action
Debbie killed Harry |
> | EXPERIENCER | Entity experiencing some psychological state
I like syntax |
> | LOCATIVE | Place in which something is situated or takes place
He hid it *under the bed* |
> | GOAL | Entity representing the destination of some other entity
John went *home* |
> | SOURCE | Entity from which something moves
He returned *from Paris* |
> | INSTRUMENT | Means used to perform some action
He hit it *with a hammer* |

We can illustrate how the terminology in (1) can be used to describe the semantic roles played by arguments in terms of the following examples:

(2) *The audience* enjoyed *the play*.
(3) *The suspect* received *a caution*.
(4) *They* stayed *in a hotel*.

Using this terminology, we can say that in (2) *the audience* is the ____①____ argument of the predicate *enjoyed*, and that *the play* is the THEME argument of *enjoyed*. In (3) *the suspect* is the ____②____ argument of the predicate *received*, and *a caution* is the THEME argument of *received*. In (4) *they* is the THEME argument of the predicate *stayed*, and *in a hotel* is the LOCATIVE argument of *stayed*.

02 Read the passage and fill in each blank with ONE word from the passage. Write your answers in the correct order. [2 points]

Every argument Noun Phrase is concerned with the assignment of the thematic roles (theta-roles). Linguists don't agree exactly how many there are, nor do they agree exactly which roles we should recognise. However, the following thematic roles are widely accepted:

- Agent: The person or thing carrying out the action
- Theme: The person or thing affected by the action
- Experiencer: Entity experiencing some psychological state
- Instrument: Means by which the action or event is carried out
- Goal: The recipient of the object of the action or entity toward which something moves
- Source: Entity from which something moves

Consider the sentences below and determine which thematic roles the italicized phrases can be said to carry.

(1) a. *Mary* killed a dog. (*Mary* = Agent)
　　b. Mary bought *a book*. (*a book* = Theme)
　　c. *John* saw the accident. (*John* = Experiencer)
　　d. *The brick* smashed the window. (*The brick* = Instrument)

Other examples can be seen in (2):

(2) a. His mother sent David a letter.
　　b. The mayor died.
　　c. A hammer broke the window.
　　d. John strikes Mary as pompous.

In (2a) the Subject Noun Phrase carries the role of Agent, the indirect object *David* is the Goal of the act of sending, and the direct object NP *a letter* carries the role of Theme. The subject in (2b) carries the role of ____①____, whereas the object in (2d) has the role of ____②____. In (2c) the Subject Noun Phrase carries the role of Instrument.

Unit 08 Constituency

• Answer Key p.17

01 Read the passage <A> and the sentences in <B>, and follow the directions.

[4 points]

─┤ A ├─

In a large majority of the coordinate structures, the coordinates belong to the same category as in (1).

(1) a. John wrote to Mary and to Fred.   [PP + PP]
　　b. John wrote a letter and a postcard.   [NP + NP]

But coordinates do not have to be of the same category. Other examples are given in (2):

(2) a. I'll be back [next week or at the end of the month].   [NP + PP]
　　b. John is [a banker and extremely rich].   [NP + AP]

What makes the coordinations in (2) acceptable despite the differences of category is that each coordinate could occur alone with the same function.

(3) a. I'll be back next week.
　　b. I'll be back at the end of the month.
(4) a. John is a banker.
　　b. John is extremely rich.

In each pair here the underlined element in (b) has the same function as that in (a): time adjunct in (3), complement of the verb in (4).
　Now consider the following example:

(5) *We're leaving [Rome and next week].   [NP + NP]

Here the coordinates belong to the same category, but don't satisfy the requirement of functional likeness. In (5) the NP *Rome* is a complement, but the NP *next week* is an adjunct; the functions would be different. Therefore, the different functions cannot be conjoined.

> **B**
>
> (a) You can bring these and those books.
> (b) He acted selfishly and with no thought for the consequences.
> (c) I ran to the park and for health reasons.
> (d) He won't reveal the nature of the threat or where it came from.
> (e) He is a very shy and rather inarticulate man.
> (f) The discussion of the riots and in the bar was full and frank.

Identify TWO ungrammatical sentences in <B>, and explain why, discussing each coordinate, based on the description in <A>.

02 Read the passage <A> and the sentences in <B>, and follow the directions.

[4 points]

A

Constituency tests involve so-called Cleft (*It*-Cleft) and Pseudocleft (*Wh*-Cleft) sentences, examples of which are given below:

(1) Frank washed his shirts yesterday.   'Regular' sentence
(2) It was *Frank* who washed his shirts yesterday.   *Cleft*
(3) It was *his shirts* that Frank washed yesterday.   *Cleft*
(4) It was *yesterday* that Frank washed his shirts.   *Cleft*
(5) What Frank washed yesterday was *his shirts*.   *Pseudocleft*
(6) What Frank did yesterday was *wash his shirts*.   *Pseudocleft*
(7) What Frank did was *wash his shirts yesterday*.   *Pseudocleft*

Clefts and Pseudoclefts are special constructions in English which enable language users to highlight a particular string of words in a sentence. Clefts and Pseudoclefts are easily recognisable because they have a typical structure. They always start with the same word: *it* in the case of the Cleft construction and *what* (and a few other *wh*-items) in the case of the Pseudocleft. Both Clefts and Pseudoclefts always contain a form of the copular verb *be* (is/was/were). The position following this copular verb is called the focus position (italicised in the examples above). The elements that occur here receive special prominence. Different elements are able to occupy the focus position in Clefts and Pseudoclefts, and for this reason a sentence can have more than one Cleft or Pseudocleft version, as the examples in (2)—(7).

For current purposes the following principle is important: Only constituents can occur in the focus position of a Cleft or Pseudocleft. In addition, we can explain the restrictions on *it*-cleft and *wh*-cleft sentences. VP and AP cannot be in the focus position of a *it*-cleft sentence, and TP cannot be in the focus position of a *wh*-cleft sentence, as shown in (8).

(8) a. *It is *go home* that I will.
    b. *It was *happy* that I made her.
    c. *What they believe is *him to be right*.

───┤ B ├───

(a) What Arni wanted was for Karim to be quiet.
(b) What he promised was to have it today.
(c) What John considered was them to be conscientious.
(d) What Bill does is sell cars.
(e) It is not to make life easier for us that they are changing the rules.
(f) It is very pretty that she is.

Identify TWO ungrammatical sentences in <B>, and explain why, based on the description in <A>.

03
Read the passage <A> and the sentences in <B>, and follow the directions. [4 points]

─┤ A ├─

　Coordination involves the linking of two or more strings by a coordinating conjunction, typically *and, or* or *but*, e.g [*very clever*] and [*extremely eager*], [*in the box*] or [*on the floor*], [*that Mary likes poems*] and [*that John likes novels*], etc. AP can conjoin with another AP, PP with another PP, TP with another TP, and CP with another CP. The claim now is the following: only identical categories can be coordinated, but the different categories cannot be coordinated.

　Let's see if coordination facts can confirm the constituent structure of Verb Phrases. Consider the following sentence:

(1) Frank washed his shirts yesterday.

For (1) we posited a structure like (2):

(2)
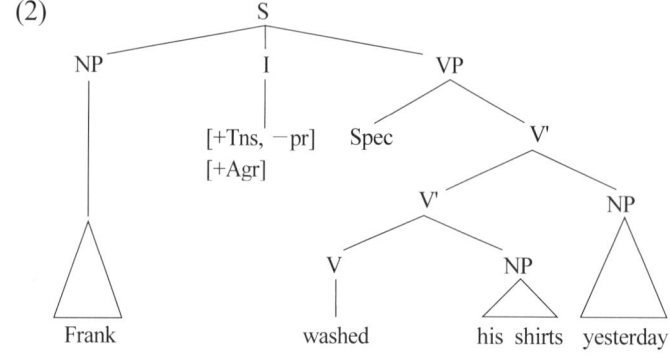

The constituents inside the VP of (2) are the (empty) Specifier position, the higher V-bar, the lower V-bar, the main verb and the Direct Object NP, as well as the Adjunct NP. The constituent status of all of these is confirmed by the fact that they can be coordinated with other similar units:

(3) Frank *washed* and *ironed* his shirts yesterday. (coordinated main verbs)
(4) Frank *washed his shirts* and *polished his shoes* yesterday. (coordinated lower V-bars)
(5) Frank washed his shirts *yesterday* and *last week*. (coordinated adjunct NPs)
(6) Frank *washed his shirts yesterday* and *polished his shoes last week*.
　　　　　　　　　　　　　　　　　　　　　　　　　(coordinated higher V-bars)

─┤ B ├─

(a) I wonder whether John likes fish and Mary meat.
(b) I wonder whether John likes fish and whether Mary likes meat.
(c) Anna loudly announced the election victory and cheerfully gave an interview to the press.
(d) They reported that John made a mistake and him to be in great pain.
(e) I would prefer there to be fried squid at the reception and for John to stay.

Identify TWO ungrammatical sentences in <B>, and explain why, discussing the grammatical category of each coordinate, based on the description in <A>.

04 Read the passage <A> and the sentences in <B>, and follow the directions. [4 points]

A

From a syntactic point of view, there are two different classes of Adverbials: VP-adverbs and Sentence-adverbs. What is important about VP-Preposing is that we can use it as a test to see whether a particular element or string of elements is part of VP. Adjuncts like *carefully* are sisters of V′ inside VP, as in the tree in (1):

(1)
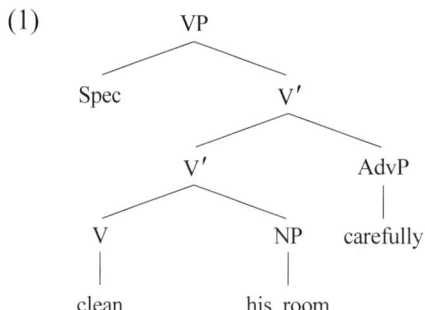

We now want to know whether we can show that the AdvP in (1) is indeed part of the VP or not. Let us apply VP-Preposing and see:

(2) a. Ralph says that he will clean his room carefully, and [clean his room carefully] he will _____.
　　b. *Ralph says that he will clean his room carefully, and [clean his room] he will _____ carefully.

The result of preposing the VP is that the AdvP *carefully* must be moved along with the main verb *clean* and its Direct Object *his room*, and is therefore inside VP, as shown in (2a). Leaving this VP-adverb *carefully* behind, as in (2b), leads to an ungrammatical result. On the other hand, the sentence-adverb does not need to move along with the preposing of the VP; it is not part of the VP.

┌──────────────────────── B ────────────────────────┐
(a) John says that he will probably clean his garage, and clean his garage he will probably.

(b) Ray says that he certainly will get off the bus, and get off the bus he certainly will.

(c) Dawn will clean the windows diligently, and clean the windows diligently he will.

(d) Ray says that he will interrupt the speaker politely, and interrupt the speaker he will politely.

(e) Clean his garage meticulously though Ralph will, he'd rather watch TV.

(f) Clean his garage though Ralph will meticulously, he'd rather watch TV.
└───┘

Identify TWO ungrammatical sentences in <B>, and explain why, discussing the VP-adverb or the sentence-adverb, based on the description in <A>.

05 Read the passage <A> and the sentences in <B>, and follow the directions. [4 points]

⊣ A ⊢

Linguists have argued that one way of finding out whether a particular sequence of words behaves like a unit is by trying to move it to another position in the sentence. If we can move a particular string of words in a sentence from one position to another, then it behaves as a constituent.

(1) a. I like Belgian beer, but I hate Belgian wine.
  b. Belgian beer I like -, but Belgian wine I hate -.
  c. *Beer I like Belgian -, but wine I hate Belgian -.

We can move NPs to the sentence-initial position. This movement process is called *Topicalisation*. Notice that we cannot leave behind any of the component parts of the moved NP, as in (1c).

Like movement, substitution can affect full phrases, but it can affect clauses and bar-level constituents or zero-level constituents, too. A particular string of words is a constituent if it can be substituted by a suitable proform.

(2) a. They say that Wayne is *very unhappy* and *so* he is.
  b. Our neighbours will go on holiday *on Sunday*, and we will leave *then* too.
  c. Tim sat *on the couch* and stayed *there*.
  d. Janet drove her car *too fast*, and Sam rode his bike *likewise*.

In (2a) the AP *very unhappy* has been replaced by *so*, while in (2b) and (2c) *then* and *there* replace the PPs *on Sunday* and *on the couch*, respectively. In (2d) *likewise* replaces the AdvP *too fast*. We can see that the constituency of a particular sequence of words can be established by replacing it with a proform. Substitution by proforms is thus a useful test for constituency.

┌──────────── B ────────────┐
(a) Nobody liked <u>the books about New York</u> that she bought.
(b) Six women <u>with yellow hats</u> on their heads appeared.
(c) I like <u>those funny people who eat with their hands and sing at the dinner table</u>.
(d) Lenny <u>sent a post card</u> to Mary.
(e) John moved <u>a big table</u> with small legs into the dining room.
(f) Ben likes the Italian <u>student of English</u>.
└───────────────────────────┘

In <B>, choose ONE sentence where the underlined part qualifies as a constituent. Then explain how both *movement* AND *substitution* can be applied to verify the constituency of the string of words. Your answer must include the types of phrase and provide the example sentences using the constituency tests, as shown in <A>.

06 Read the passages and follow the directions. [4 points]

─┤ A ├─

How do we determine whether a given sequence of words is a constituent of a given type? We might propose the following diagnostics for determining whether a given set of words in a sentence is a constituent or not:

(1) a. Can it undergo movement (i.e., preposing or postposing)?
   If so, it is a phrase of some sort. Only full phrases can undergo movement.
 b. Can it undergo Ordinary Coordination with another string?
   If so, it is a constituent of the same type as the one with which it is coordinated.
 c. Can it be replaced by, or serve as the antecedent of an appropriate proform?
   If so, it is a phrase of the same type as the proform.

Having outlined our structural diagnostics, let's see how we might apply them to help us determine the constituent structure of the following pair of sentences:

(2) a. Drunks would [get off the bus].
 b. Drunks would [put off the customers].

The sequences [*get off the bus*] in (2a) and [*put off the customers*] in (2b) are Verb Phrase constituents. For example, note that the VP in either case can undergo 'preposing' for emphasis in an appropriate discourse setting:

(3) a. If the driver told the drunks that they had to get off the bus, then [get off the bus] they would.
 b. The restaurant manager thinks that drunks would put off the customers, and [put off the customers] they undoubtedly would.

> **B**
>
> However, the elements of the bracketed phrases in (2) behave differently in certain sentences. Consider the following examples:
>
> (4) If, whenever they needed to heed the call of nature, drunks would get off the bus—which they obviously would—then we ought not to allow them on in the first place.
>
> (5) If drunks would put off the customers—which they obviously would—then we ought not to allow them in the restaurant in the first place.
>
> (6) Every afternoon, the big red bus would stop in front of the village clock, and off the bus would get a dear old lady carrying a shopping bag.
>
> (7) The manager suspects that drunks would put off the customers, and off the customers they certainly would put.
>
> (8) Drunks would get off the bus and the train.
>
> (9) Drunks would put off the customers and the waitresses.

Identify ALL and ONLY ungrammatical sentence(s) in <B>, and explain why, specifying the types of the target verb (i.e., a prepositional verb or a phrasal verb), based on the passage in <A>.

07 Read the passage <A> and the sentences in <B>, and follow the directions. [4 points]

⊢ A ⊢

Consider the following example:

(1) a. Darin will [eat a squid sandwich], but Raiza won't.
   b. Darin will [eat a squid sandwich]$_i$, but Raiza won't [eat a squid sandwich]$_i$.

The second CP in (1a) *Raiza won't* is obviously missing the VP [*eat a squid sandwich*], and the auxiliary verb cannot be elided but must be left behind. The ellipsis in (1) appears to be the deletion of the VP under identity with the VP in the preceding clause, and is called *VP ellipsis*.

Simple VP ellipsis always targets an entire VP, and typically does so under coordination of two clauses where there is an equivalent VP in the other clause. A specialized form of VP ellipsis that does not use coordination is called *antecedent-contained deletion* (or ACD). ACD finds a VP elided that corresponds to a VP that dominates it. Take (2) as an example. What is elided out of the clause *that Megan read every book* is the VP [*read every book*].

(2) Brandon [$_{VP}$ read every book that Megan did [$_{VP}$ ⋯]].

There is another kind of ellipsis that appears not to target whole VPs, but only parts of them. This kind of ellipsis is called *Pseudogapping*. The most generally acceptable versions of pseudogapping are found in comparative constructions (and are called *comparative subdeletion*). An example of a comparative subdeletion case of pseudogapping is in (3a), where the missing item in the second clause is the non-constituent *been reading*, but the DP *short stories* survives the ellipsis. Similar to pseudogapping is *Gapping*, where apparent non-constituents are missing from the structure, as in (3b). Gapping allows, among other things, the omission of modals and auxiliaries as well as the verb. When the verb is omitted in the gapping construction, all auxiliary verbs must be omitted.

(3) a. Brandon has been reading more novels than he has _____ short stories.
   b. Jeff can play the piano, and Sylvia _____ the mandolin.

The last kind of ellipsis is called *Sluicing*. Sluicing appears to be the deletion of a TP rather than a VP, because the missing constituent includes any subject DP or auxiliary that might be in the missing string as well: but it does not elide a CP, as it requires that a *wh*-phrase remain. An example is given in (4), where the elided phrase is *he could bake*.

(4) John could bake something, but I'm not sure what _____.

B

(a) Could John close the window, and Mary the door?
(b) John would get off the bus, and Mary off the taxi.
(c) I could never have formulated the argument as clearly as Susan has.
(d) Ernie has been courting the French girl, and Bert has been the Russian girl.
(e) If Mary gives buns to the elephant, then John, too.
(f) Calvin will fire someone today, but I don't know who.

Identify TWO ungrammatical sentences in <B>, and explain why, specifying the types of ellipsis, based on the description in <A>.

Unit 09 Verbs

• Answer Key p.21

01 Read the passage <A> and the sentences in <B>, and follow the directions. [4 points]

─┤ A ├─

Consider the following examples:

(1) Barnett *seemed* to understand the formula.
(2) Barnett *tried* to understand the formula.

The surface strings in (1) and (2) are identical. The sole surface difference is the choice of the matrix verb, *seem* vs. *try*. In the Raising construction in (1), the subject *Barnett* is semantically linked only to the embedded verb *understand*, while in (2) it is semantically linked to both the matrix verb *try* and the embedded verb. For this reason, the subject in (2) is said to "control" the reference of the subject of the embedded clause and the construction has come to be referred to as "Subject Control."

Parallel data are found with transitive matrix verbs where the locus of these differences is the immediate postverbal NP.

(3) Barnett believed the doctor to have examined Tilman.
(4) Barnett persuaded the doctor to examine Tilman.

Again, the surface strings are identical, but there are fundamental differences in the characteristics of the NPs immediately following the matrix verbs. In (3), *the doctor* is semantically linked only with the embedded verb *examine*, while in (4) *the doctor* is semantically linked to both the matrix verb *persuade* and the embedded verb. The construction in (3) is referred to as Raising-to-Object and that in (4) as Object Control.

When the matrix clause is passivized, these two constructions are different.

(5) The flood was believed to have destroyed the town.
(6) *The flood was persuaded to destroy the town.

The contrast indicates that the subject *the flood* in (5) is not selected by the verb *believe*, while that in (6) must selected by the verb *persuade*; thus, this sentence is semantically ill-formed. In *persuade*-type, the matrix passive is not always possible because of thematic relation between the matrix verb and the subject of the matrix passive.

― B ―

(a) There proved to be toxins in the soap.
(b) There threatens to be a famine in Bulgaria.
(c) Mice are claimed to be afraid of cats.
(d) The avalanche was told to hit the town.
(e) The painting was declared to be a forgery.
(f) The key was asked to open the door.

Identify TWO ungrammatical sentences in <B>, and explain why, ONLY based on the description in <A>.

02 Read the passage and fill in each blank with ONE word from the passage. (Use the SAME answer for both blanks.) [2 points]

> A large number of verbs that include *hope, like, promise,* and *want,* either can or must occur without a following NP, as shown in (1).
>
> (1) Joan *wanted* to write a letter to the mayor.
>
> The bracketing in (2) reflects our intuition that the missing subject of the complement is identical to the main clause subject. What Joan wanted was that she herself write a letter to the mayor.
>
> (2) *Joan* wanted [(*Joan*) to write a letter to the mayor].
>
> Some verbs in this group, including *expect, need, promise,* and *want,* can also have a following NP, as shown in (3).
>
> (3) Joan *wanted Bill* to write a letter to the mayor.
>
> What is the status of the NP following the verb *wanted*? Notice that if we ask the question *What did Joan want ?*, we get the answer *for Bill to write a letter to the mayor*. Thus, the NP *Bill* is the _____ of the infinitive complement, as shown in the bracketing in (4).
>
> (4) Joan *wanted* [*Bill* to write a letter to the mayor].
>
> Passivization supports this conclusion. The only way to apply the passive rule to (3) is within the infinitive complement, so that the complement object, *a letter*, is moved into _____ position, as is shown in (5a). If *Bill* were the object of *want*, the passive in (5b) would be grammatical, but it clearly is not.
>
> (5) a. Joan wanted [a letter to be written to the mayor (by Bill)].
>   b. *Bill was wanted (by Joan) [to write a letter to the mayor].
>
> The passive test thus allows us to confirm whether the postverbal NP is the object of the main verb or the subject of the infinitive complement.

03 Read the passage <A> and the sentences in <B>, and follow the directions.

[4 points]

| A |

There are two tests to determine whether a phrase is a complement or a modifier.

First, complements are strictly-required phrases whereas modifiers are not. The examples in (1)—(3) show that the verb *placed* requires an NP and a PP as its complements, *kept* an NP and an AP, and *stayed* a PP.

(1) a. John placed Kim behind the garage.
　　b. John kept him behind the garage.
　　c. *John stayed Kim behind the garage.
(2) a. *John placed him busy.
　　b. John kept him busy.
　　c. *John stayed him busy.
(3) a. *John placed behind the counter.
　　b. *John kept behind the counter.
　　c. John stayed behind the counter.

In contrast, modifiers are optional. Their presence is not required by the grammar:

(4) a. John deposited some money in the bank.
　　b. John deposited some money in the bank on Friday.

In (4b), the PP *on Friday* is optional here, serving as a modifier.

Second, the possibility of iterating identical types of phrase can also distinguish between complements and modifiers. In general two or more instances of the same modifier type can occur with the same head, but this is impossible for complements.

(5) a. *John placed Kim [behind the garage] [in the room].
　　b. Kim and Sandy met [in Seoul] [in the lobby of the Lotte Hotel] in March.

In (5a) the PP *behind the garage* is a complement and thus the same type of PP *in the room* cannot co-occur. Yet in (5b) the PP *in Seoul* is a modifier and we can repeatedly have the same type of PP.

> **B**
>
> (a) This is an analysis of the sentence with tree diagrams.
> (b) The UN blamed global warming on humans on natural causes.
> (c) He is much faster than me by far.
> (d) I never argue with anyone about anything.
> (e) There is an advocate of the abolition of indirect taxation.
> (f) She regularly gives us very useful advice on financial matters on etiquette.

Identify TWO ungrammatical sentences in <B>, and explain why, based on the description in <A>.

04
Read the passage <A> and the sentences in <B>, and follow the directions. [4 points]

─┤ A ├─

Among the verbs selecting a sentential complement, there also exist verbs requiring an indirect question:

(1) a. John inquired [which book [he should read __]].
    b. He told me [how many employees [Karen introduced __ to the visitors]].

Notice that not all verbs allow such indirection questions as their complements:

(2) a. Tom denied (that) he had been reading that article.
    b. *Tom denied which book he had been reading.

Verbs like *deny* cannot combine with an indirect question; only a finite CP can function as their complement. Verbs selecting an indirect question as their complement can be in general classified by the meaning:

(3) a. interrogative verbs: *ask, inquire*
    b. verbs of knowledge: *know, learn*
    c. verbs of increased knowledge: *teach, tell, inform*
    d. decision verbs/verbs of concern: *decide, care*

The complement CP of these verbs cannot be a canonical CP: it must be an indirect question. Unlike verbs such as *inquire*, those like *tell* can select either a declarative CP or an indirect question:

(4) a. *John inquired that he should read it.
    b. He told me that he had been to America.
(5) a. John inquired which book he should read.
    b. He told me how many employees Karen introduced to the visitors.

This means that verbs like *inquire* will be different from those like *deny* in that the former's CP complement is specified with the feature [QUE +] (Question).

B

(a) Tom claimed how much money she had spent.

(b) We doubt whether you're capable.

(c) John has forgotten which player his son shouted at.

(d) Kim has wondered that Gary stayed in the room.

(e) They debated whether conclusive evidence had been presented.

Identify TWO ungrammatical sentences in <B>, and explain why, based on the description in <A>.

Unit 10 Syntactic Structures

• Answer Key p.23

01 Read the passage and fill in each blank with ONE word from the passage. Write your answers in the correct order. [2 points]

> The largest unit of syntactic analysis is the sentence. Sentences typically consist of an NP (often called 'the subject') and a VP that are linked together by an abstract category dubbed 'T' (for 'tense'). As illustrated in figure 1, T serves as the head of the sentence, taking the VP as its complement and the subject NP as its specifier. What we think of as a sentence or a sentential phrase, then, is really a TP.
>
> Figure 1
>
>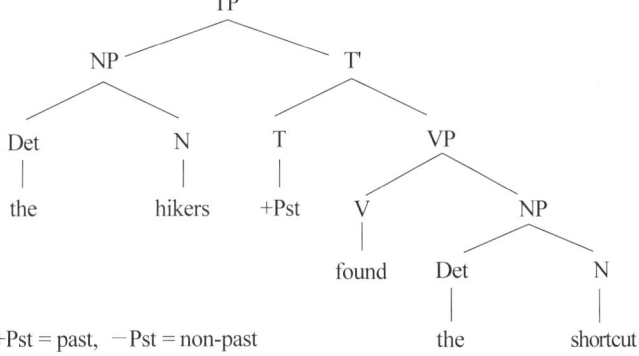
>
> +Pst = past, −Pst = non-past
>
> The tense feature in T must be compatible with the form of the verb. So a sentence like the one above, whose head contains the feature +Pst, must contain a verb marked for the past tense (hence, *found* rather than *find*).
>
> Although somewhat abstract, this analysis has the advantage of giving sentences the same internal structure as other phrases (with a specifier, a head, and a complement), making them consistent with the X' Schema. Moreover, because T, like all heads, is obligatory, we also account for the fact that all sentences have _____①_____ (i.e., they are all past or non-past).

The TP structure also provides us with a natural place to locate modal auxiliaries such as *can, may, will,* and *must*, most of which are inherently ____② ____, as shown by their incompatibility with time adverbs such as *yesterday*: *He can/will/must work yesterday.* The modals *could* and *would* can be either past or non-past: *He could swim when he was three/He could swim tomorrow.* Because modals are themselves markers of tense, we will assume that it is not necessary to have the feature ±Pst in the T position when they are used.

02 Read the passage and fill in the blank with TWO words from the passage.
[2 points]

Verb Raising (Move V to the T position) can apply in English, but only to *have* and *be*. To begin, consider the sentences in (1), which contain two auxiliaries—modal and non-modal.

(1) a. The students should have finished the project.
　b. The children could be playing in the yard.

Modal auxiliaries occur under T, but what about non-modal auxiliaries? They are considered to be a special type of V that takes a VP complement.

As expected, only the modal auxiliary can undergo Inversion in these structures.

(2) a. The modal auxiliary verb moves to the C position (grammatical):
　　[CP Should [TP the students __t__ have finished the project]]?
　b. The non-modal auxiliary moves to the C position (ungrammatical):
　　*[CP Have [TP the students should __t__ finished the project]]?

Crucially, however, a non-modal auxiliary can undergo Inversion when there is no _____ in the sentence as shown in (3).

(3) [CP Have [TP the students __t__ finished the project]]?
　(from: The students have finished the project.)

Since Inversion involves movement from T to C, *Have* in (3) must have moved to the T position, and from there to the C position, as depicted in (4).

(4)

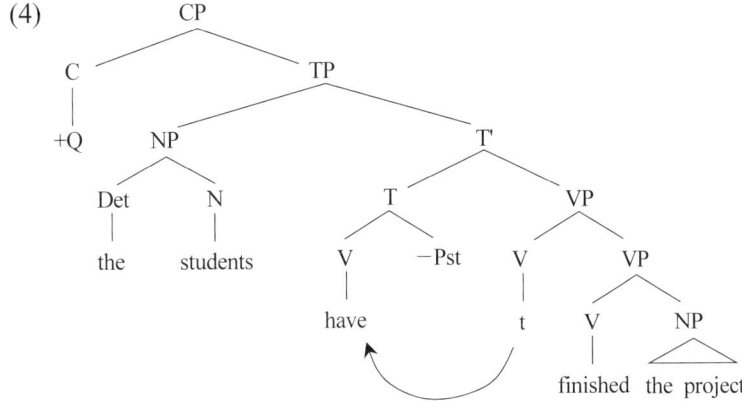

03 Read the passage and fill in the blank with ONE word from the passage.

[2 points]

The standard generalization of VP Ellipsis (VPE) is that it is possible only after an auxiliary verb as shown in the contrast (1) and (2).

(1) a. Kim can dance, and Sandy can ___, too.
   b. Kim has danced, and Sandy has ___, too.
   c. Kim was dancing, and Sandy was ___, too.
(2) a. *Kim considered joining the navy, but I never considered ___.
   b. *Kim got arrested by the CIA, and Sandy got ___, also.
   c. *Kim wanted to go and Sandy wanted ___, too.

The data means that the VP complement of an auxiliary can undergo VP ellipsis as long as the context provides its interpretation.
  Consider the following data:

(3) Kim must have been dancing and
   a. Sandy must have been ___, too.
   b. Sandy must have ___, too.
   c. Sandy must ___, too.

The elided VP is all the complement of the auxiliary verbs *been, have,* and *must*.
  The analysis predicts the behavior VPE after the infinitival marker *to*:

(4) a. Tom wanted to go home, but Peter didn't want to ___.
   b. Lee voted for Bill because his father told him to ___.
(5) a. Because John persuaded Sally to ___, he didn't have to talk to the reporters.
   b. Mary likes to tour art galleries, but Bill hates to ___.

Based on the given data above, the infinitival marker *to* is a type of _____ verb. This means that its complement can be freely elided.

04 Read the passage and fill in the blank with ONE word from the passage.

[2 points]

The syntactic structure includes the following two rules:

(1) a. XP → Specifier, X' (Head-Specifier Rule)
    b. XP → X, YP (Head-Complement Rule)

These Head-Specifier and Head-Complement Rules, which form the central part of 'X'-theory', account for the core structure of NP as well as that of S. In fact, these two general rules can also represent most of the PS rules. In addition to these two, we just need one more rule:

(2) XP → Modifier, X' (Head-Modifier Rule)

One thing to notice in the Head-Complement Rule is that the head must be a lexical element. This in turn means that we cannot apply the Head-Modifier Rule first and then the Head-Complement Rule. This explains the following contrast:

(3) a. the king [of Rock and Roll] [with a hat]
    b. *the king [with a hat] [of Rock and Roll]

The badness of (3b) is due to the fact that the modifier *with a hat* is combined with the head *king* first.

(4) a. 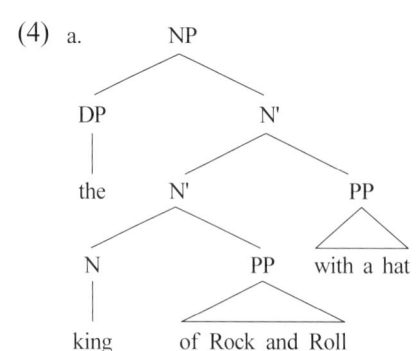 b.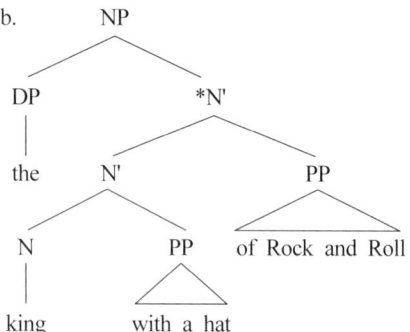

We can observe in (4b) that the combination of *king* with *with a hat* forms an N', but the combination of the complement *of Rock and Roll* with this N' will not satisfy the _____ Rule.

05 Read the passage <A> and the sentences in <B>, and follow the directions. [4 points]

― A ―

Consider the subject NP in the sentence in (1):

(1) [The big book of poems with the blue cover] is on the table.

(2)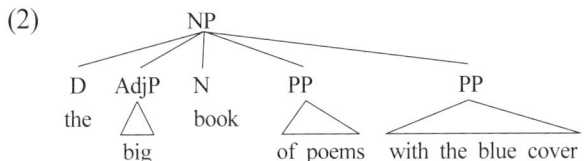

We can call this *a flat structure*, as shown in (2). The PP *of poems* and the PP *with the blue cover* are on the same level hierarchically; there is no distinction between them in terms of dominance or c-command. From the point of view of constituency, we can see a more complicated structure. Consider the constituency test of conjunction.

(3) Give me [the [blue book] and [red binder]].

We need an "intermediate" N' category to explain the items that are conjoined in the sentence.

Similarly, conjunction seems to show an intermediate A' projection:

(4) the [very [[bright blue] and [dull green]]] gown

In this NP, *bright* clearly modifies *blue*, and *dull* clearly modifies *green*. One possible interpretation of this phrase allows *very* to modify both *bright blue* and *dull green*. If this is the case then the structure must minimally look like (5).

(5)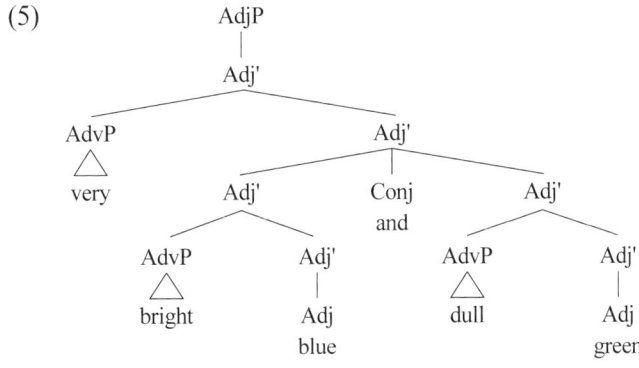

| A |

All the major phrase types have a level that is intermediate between the phrase XP and the Head X.

| B |

(a) Bob is very <u>serious about Mary</u>, but less <u>so</u> than Paul.
(b) I am <u>afraid of tigers</u> and <u>fond of clowns</u> without exception.
(c) Susanna was utterly <u>in love</u>, but Louis was only partly <u>so</u>.
(d) The chef <u>eats beans</u> and <u>serves salads</u> with forks.
(e) If you can <u>speak French fluently</u>—<u>which</u> we all know he can—why is he shy with French girls?
(f) Paul won't <u>finish the assignment</u>, and <u>so</u> will Mary.

Identify TWO sentences in which the underlined parts are NOT an intermediate category, and then state the types of constituent for both TWO underlined parts of each sentence, based on the description in <A>.

06 Read the passage and fill in each blank with ONE word from the passage. (Use the SAME answer for both blanks.) [2 points]

Consider the following three rules:

(1) a. XP → Specifier, X' (Head-Specifier Rule)
  b. XP → X, YP (Head-Complement Rule)
  c. XP → Modifier, X' (Head-Modifier Rule)

These Head-Specifier and Head-Complement Rules, which form the central part of 'X'-theory', account for the core structure of NP as well as that of S.

There exist several more welcoming consequences that the three X' rules bring to us. The grammar rules can account for the same structures as all the PS rules: with those rules we can identify phrases whose daughters are a head and its complement(s), or a head and its specifier, or a head and its modifier. The three X' rules thereby greatly minimize the number of PS rules that need to characterize well-formed English sentences.

In addition, these X' rules directly solve the endocentricity issue, for they refer to 'Head'. Assume that X is N, then we will have N, N', and NP structures. We can formalize this more precisely by introducing the feature POS (part of speech), which has values such as *noun, verb, adjective*. The structure (2) shows how the values of the features in different parts of a structure are related:

(2)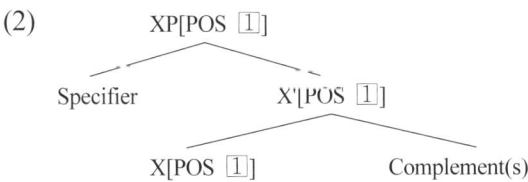

The notation $\boxed{1}$ shows that whatever value the feature has in one place in the structure, it has the same value somewhere else. This is a representational tag, in which the number $\boxed{1}$ has no significance: it could as easily be $\boxed{7}$ or $\boxed{439}$. So (2) indicates that the phrase's POS value is identical to its _____, capturing the headedness of each phrase: the grammar just does not allow any phrase without a/an _____.

Unit 11 Additional Tests

• Answer Key p.25

01 Read the passage and fill in each blank with ONE word from the passage. Write your answers in the correct order. [2 points]

> Prototypical adjectives have comparative and superlative forms and take degree modifiers such as *very, too* ("excessively") and *pretty*. Adjectives of this kind are said to be gradable. They denote scalar properties that can apply in varying degrees. *Good, old, big* and so on denote properties of this kind—and one can ask about the degree to which the property applies with *how*: *How big is it?*, etc.
>
> Not all adjectives are of this kind. There are also non-gradable adjectives, as in *an alphabetical list*. It makes no sense to ask how alphabetical a list is, or to say that one list is more alphabetical than another. *Alphabetical* thus denotes a non-scalar property. Other examples of non-gradable adjectives are seen in (1):
>
> (1) the <u>chief</u> difficulty <u>federal</u> taxes
>   <u>glandular</u> fever my <u>left</u> arm
>   a <u>medical</u> problem <u>phonetic</u> symbols
>   <u>pubic</u> hair their <u>tenth</u> attempt
>
> Some adjectives can be used in either way: like the distinction between count and non-count in nouns, the gradable vs. non-gradable distinction applies to uses rather than lexemes as such. Compare:
>
> (2) a. in the <u>public</u> interest
>   b. the <u>British</u> government
>   c. The motorway is now <u>open</u>.
> (3) a. a very <u>public</u> quarrel
>   b. a very <u>British</u> response
>   c. He was more <u>open</u> with us than the boss.

Typically, as in these examples, the non-gradable sense is the basic one, with the gradable sense representing an extended use. Therefore, the adjectives in (2) are ____①____, and the adjectives in (3) are ____②____.

02 Read the passage and fill in each blank with ONE word from the passage. Write your answers in the correct order. [2 points]

Adverbs do not normally occur as dependents of nouns: in related adjective-adverb pairs it is the adjective that appears in this function. No such restriction applies to prepositions. Compare:

(1) a. She criticised them with tact.
    b. She criticised them tactfully.
(2) a. [A manager with tact] is needed.
    b. *[A manager tactfully] is needed.

The underlined expressions in (1) modify the ____①____, and we see that both PP and Adverb are admissible. In (2), however, they modify the noun *manager* and here the PP is admissible but the adverb is not; instead we need an adjective in (2b): *a tactful manager*.

Adverbs cannot normally function as complement to the verb *be*: here we again have adjectives, in their predicative use. Compare:

(3) a. The key is under the mat.
    b. The meeting is on Tuesday.
(4) a. *Lucy was enthusiastically today.
    b. *Rain is again.

The examples in (3), with a PP functioning as complement of *be*, are impeccable, but the ones in (4), with an adverb in this function, are ungrammatical.

However, it has often been suggested that the traditional adverb category has something of the character of a classificatory wastebasket. Now consider the following examples:

(5) a. She went <u>aboard</u> the liner.

　　b. He sat <u>outside</u> her bedroom.

(6) a. She went <u>aboard</u>.

　　b. He sat <u>outside</u>.

The words *aboard, outside* are traditionally analysed as prepositions when they have an NP complement but as adverbs when they have no complement. The best way to remove this inconsistency is to amend the definition of prepositions so that they are no longer required to have an NP complement. *Aboard, outside* and similar words will then be _____②_____ both when they have NP complements and when they occur alone. This revision simultaneously gets rid of the complication of a dual classification for these words.

03 Read the passage and fill in each blank with TWO words from the passage. Write your answers in the correct order. [2 points]

The two functions a predicative complement (PC) and a direct object (DO) are distinguished syntactically in a number of ways.

Both DO and PC can have the form of an ordinary NP, but only PC can also have the form of an adjective phrase (AdjP):

(1) a. He seemed *a very nice guy*.
   b. He seemed *very nice*.
(2) a. He met *a very nice guy*.
   b. *He met *very nice*.

In (1) with *seem*, *a very nice guy* is a predicative complement and hence can be replaced by the AdjP *very nice*. In (2) with *meet*, no such replacement is possible because *a very nice guy* is a direct object.

A bare role NP is a singular NP that is 'bare' in the sense of lacking the determiner which would elsewhere be required, and that denotes some kind of role, office, or position. A predicative complement can have the form of a bare role NP, but an object (O) can't:

(3) a. She became *the treasurer*.
   b. She knew *the treasurer*.
(4) a. She became *treasurer*.
   b. *She knew *treasurer*.

(3a) and (3b) examples are fine because an ordinary NP like *the treasurer* can be either a PC or an O. In (4), *treasurer* is a bare role NP, so it is permitted with *become*, which takes a PC, but not with *know*, which takes an object.

There is another test for these two functions. A typical object in an active clause corresponds to the subject of the passive clause that has the same meaning. A PC shows no such relationship. Consider the following examples:

(5) a. They arrested *a member of the party*.
 b. She remained *a member of the party*.

In (5a) *a member of the party* is a/an ____①____, but in (5b), *a member of the party* is a/an ____②____.

04 Read the passage and fill in each blank with ONE word from the passage. Write your answers in the correct order. [2 points]

In their predicative use, adjectives (AdjPs) generally function as complement, not adjunct, in clause structure. Predicative complements occur in complex-intransitive and complex-transitive clauses:

(1) The suggestion is ridiculous.
    COMPLEX-INTRANSITIVE CLAUSE
(2) I consider the suggestion ridiculous.
    COMPLEX-TRANSITIVE CLAUSE

The adjective is related to a predicand (*the suggestion*), which is subject in the complex-intransitive construction, and object in the complex-transitive construction.

In addition to being a complement, licensed by the head, a predicative adjective phrase can be a/an ___①___. Compare, for example:

(3) a. Max was <u>unwilling to accept these terms</u>.
    b. <u>Unwilling to accept these terms</u>, Max resigned.

In (3a) the underlined AdjP is a complement licensed by the verb (*be*), but in (3b) it is a/an ___①___, — it is, more specifically, a supplement, detached by intonation or punctuation from the rest of the clause. It is nevertheless still ___②___, in that it is related to a predicand. We understand in (3b), no less than in (3a), that the unwillingness to accept these terms applies to *Max*.

In addition, there are two relatively minor functions in which adjectives are found. Postpositive adjectives function in NP structure as post-head internal modifier. There are three cases to consider:

(4) a. everything <u>useful</u>　　　　somebody <u>rich</u>
　　b. children <u>keen on sport</u>　　a report <u>full of errors</u>
　　c. the only modification <u>possible</u>　the ones <u>asleep</u>

The examples in (4a) have fused determiner-heads, making it impossible for the adjectives to occur in the usual pre-head position—compare *everything useful* with *every useful thing*. The modifiers in (4b) would be inadmissible in pre-head position because the adjective has its own post-head dependents; the postpositive construction provides a way of getting around the fact that such AdjPs cannot be used as attributive modifiers. A limited number of adjectives can occur postpositively without their own dependents and with a non-fused head noun, as in (4c): *possible* can also be attributive whereas *asleep* cannot.

Certain forms of AdjP occur right at the beginning of the NP, before the indefinite article *a*:

(5) a. [<u>How long</u> a delay] will there be?
　　b. He'd chosen [<u>too dark</u> a colour].
(6) a. It seemed [<u>such</u> a bargain].
　　b. [<u>What</u> a fool] I was.

05 Read the passage <A> and the sentences in <B>, and follow the directions. [4 points]

─────────── A ───────────

There are some constraints on what categories you can move out of. Compare the following two sentences:

(1) a. What_i did Bill claim [_CP_ that he read _t_i_ in the syntax book]?
   b. *What_i did Bill make [_NP_ the claim [_CP_ that he read _t_i_ in the syntax book]]?

Note: the letter 't' stands for 'trace.'

In (1a), *wh*-movement out of a complement clause is grammatical, but in (1b), movement out of a CP that is dominated by an NP is ungrammatical. This phenomenon has come to be known as the *complex NP island* phenomenon. NPs are islands. You cannot move out of an island, but you can move around within it.

The second constraint is a *wh*-island. It is possible to the specifier of the main CP as in (2a). However, in (2b), look at what happens when you try to do both (move one *wh*-phrase to the embedded specifier, and the other to the main CP specifier). This sentence is ungrammatical. Movement of both, *what* and *how*, results in terrible ungrammaticality. Once you move a *wh*-phrase into the specifier of a CP, then that CP becomes an island for further extraction.

(2) a. [_CP_ How_k do [_TP_ you think [John bought the sweater _t_k_]]]?
   b. *[_CP_ How_k do [_TP_ you wonder [_CP_ what_i [_TP_ John bought _t_i_ _t_k_]]]]?

The third constraint is a *subject condition*. Consider (3a); it has a CP in its subject position. When you try to *wh*-move the *wh*-equivalent to *several rioters* (*who* in (3b)), the sentence becomes ungrammatical. No constituent can be moved out of a sentential subject.

(3) a. [_TP_ [_CP_ That the police would arrest several rioters] was a certainty].
   b. *Who_i was [_TP_ [_CP_ that the police would arrest _t_i_] _t_was_ a certainty]?

B

(a) Whom would for Mary to kiss be strange?
(b) I wonder what John bought with the $20 bill.
(c) I wonder what John bought how.
(d) Who did you think kissed Mary?
(e) Who did you wonder what kissed?
(f) I asked what John kissed.

Identify TWO ungrammatical sentences in <B>, and explain why, stating what constraint each sentence violates, based on the description in <A>.

06 Read the passage and fill in each blank with ONE word from the passage. Write your answers in the correct order. [2 points]

> The crucial distinction between adverbs and adjectives is a matter of function. Adjectives modify nouns whereas adverbs modify other categories. But there is another functional difference that is no less important. Most adjectives can function as predicative complement as well as noun modifier, but adverbs do not normally occur in this function. Again the difference is most easily seen by taking adjective-adverb pairs related by -ly:
>
> (1) a. an *impressive* performance
>   MODIFIER
>   b. Her performance was *impressive*.
>   PREDICATIVE COMPLEMENT
> (2) a. She performed *impressively*.
>   MODIFIER
>   b. *Her performance was *impressively*.
>   PREDICATIVE COMPLEMENT
>
> *Impressive* and *impressively* can both function as modifier (here of noun and verb respectively), but only the adjective can be used predicatively. The same applies to those adverbs that are not derived from adjectives—they cannot be used as predicative complements:
>
> (3) a. She *almost* succeeded.
>   b. *Her success was *almost*.

We do find some overlap between the adjective and adverb categories—items that belong to both by virtue of occurring in both sets of functions. Compare:

(4) a. their *early* departure
　　b. They departed *early*.
(5) a. that *very* day
　　b. It's *very* good.
(6) a. I didn't play *well*.
　　b. I don't feel *well*.

With some items, such as *early*, the meaning is the same, while in others it is different. The adjective *very*, for example, means something like "particular": it emphasises the identity of the day (that one, not any other). The adverb *very*, on the other hand, means approximately "extremely". Now compare the examples in (6): In (6a) the word *well* is used as the ____①____ category, and in (6b) the word *well* is used as the ____②____ category.

07 Read the passage and fill in each blank with ONE word from the passage. Write your answers in the correct order. [2 points]

The reliable criterion for determining a word's category involves its distribution—the type of elements, especially functional categories, with which it can co-occur. For example, nouns can typically appear with a determiner, verbs with an auxiliary, and adjectives with a degree word in the patterns illustrated in (1).

(1)

Category	Distributional property	Examples
Noun	occurrence with a determiner	*a car, the wheat*
Verb	occurrence with an auxiliary	*has gone, will stay*
Adjective	occurrence with a degree word	*very rich, too big*

In contrast, a noun cannot occur with an auxiliary, and a verb cannot occur with a determiner or degree word.

(2) a. a noun with an auxiliary: *will destruction
   b. a verb with a determiner: *the destroy
   c. a verb with a degree word: *very arrive

Distributional tests for category membership are simple and highly reliable. They can be used with confidence when it is necessary to categorize unfamiliar words. Thanks to distributional and inflectional clues, it's often possible to identify a word's category without knowing its meaning. In (3), the poem "Jabberwocky," by Lewis Carroll, illustrates this point in a particularly brilliant way—it's interpretable precisely because readers are able to figure out that *gyre* is a/an ___①___ (note the auxiliary verb to its left), that *borogoves* is a/an ___②___, and so on.

(3) 'Twas brillig, and the slithy toves
   Did gyre and gimble in the wabe;
   All mimsy were the borogoves,
   And the mome raths outgrabe.

   "Beware the Jabberwock, my son!
   The jaws that bite, the claws that catch!
   Beware the Jubjub bird, and shun
   The frumious Bandersnatch!"

08 Read the passage and fill in each blank with ONE word from the passage. Use the SAME answer for both blanks. [2 points]

The head is the obligatory nucleus around which a phrase is built. For now, we will focus on four categories that can function as the head of a phrase—nouns (N), verbs (V), adjectives (A), and prepositions (P).

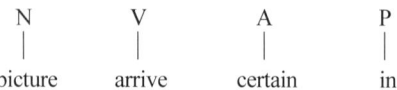

The type of specifier that appears in a particular phrase depends on the category of the _____. Determiners serve as the specifiers of Ns, while degree words serve as the specifiers of As and (some) Ps. A special class of preverbal adverbs, which we will call 'qualifiers', can function as the specifiers of Vs.

TABLE 1. Some Specifiers		
Head	Specifier	Examples
N	Determiner (Det)	
	the, a, some,	*a picture, the map,*
	this, those...	*those people, some guests*
V	Preverbal adverb (Adv)	
	never, perhaps, often,	*never quit, perhaps go,*
	always, almost...	*often failed, almost forgot*
A or P	Degree word (Deg)	
	very, quite, more,	*very smart, quite rich,*
	almost...	*almost in*

Note: Almost can be either an adverb or a degree word.

Specifiers have no single semantic function or grammatical category. Structurally, though, they are alike in that they occur at the edge of a phrase. As illustrated in table 1 above, the specifier position in English is at a phrase's left margin (the beginning). Semantically, specifiers help to make the meaning of the _____ more precise. Hence, in *the books*, the determiner *the* indicates that the speaker has in mind specific books, and in *never overeat*, the qualifier *never* indicates non-occurrence of the event.

09 Read the passage <A> and the sentences in <B>, and follow the directions. [4 points]

─┤ A ├─

The verb *recommend* can be realized at least in the following two environments:

(1) a. The UN recommended an enlarged peacekeeping force.
   b. These qualities recommended him to Oliver.
(2) a. This is the book which the teacher recommended ___.
   b. Who will they recommend ___?

The verbs *recommend* in (1) are its canonical realization whereas those in (2) are not. That is, in (1), the object of the verb is right next to it whereas in (2) its object does not occur in the adjacent position, but appears in a nonlocal position.

One thing to note here is that in English only complements can be realized as a GAP value. Unlike languages like Korean or Japanese where both subject and object can be extracted, Indo-European languages including English exhibit subject-object asymmetry in various phenomena. For example, though the object can be easily realized as a gap element, the subject is not, and also an element from the subject is not extractable.

(3) a. *I saw the car that you think that John claimed that ___ could hit the man.
   b. I saw the car that you think that John claimed that the man could hit ___.

However, complication arises from the following contrast:

(4) a. Who do you believe that Sara invited ___?
   b. *Who do you believe that ___ invited Sara?
(5) a. Who do you believe Sara invited ___?
   b. Who do you believe ___ invited Sara?

The data show us that the subject can function as a gapped element when there exists no complementizer *that*. In other words, the extraction of the subject is sensitive to the presence or absence of the complementizer *that* whereas that of the object is not. One thing to note here is that such a subject-gapped example is possible only with so-called 'parenthetical verbs' like *believe, assume* and so forth:

(6) a. Who do you believe likes Mary?
   b. *Who do you know won the prize?

| B |

(a) What did that John bought upset Jack?
(b) What did Julia think that John bought?
(c) Who is the class reading a book about?
(d) Who is a book about being read by the class?
(e) Who do you imagine likes Mary?
(f) Who do you think likes Mary?

Identify TWO ungrammatical sentences in <B>, and explain why, based on the description in <A>.

10 Read the passage <A> and the sentences in <B>, and follow the directions. [4 points]

─────────────── A ───────────────

The classical transformational grammar assumes the so-called Passive Formation Rule in terms of structural descriptions (SD) and structural change (SC):

(1) Passive Formation Rule

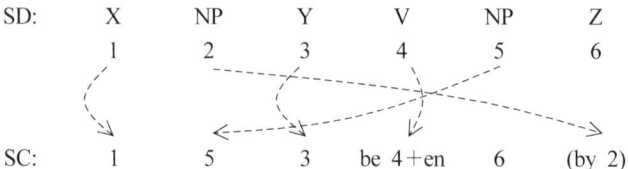

A more elaborated approach is a transformational approach assuming a passive movement operation represented in the following:

(2)
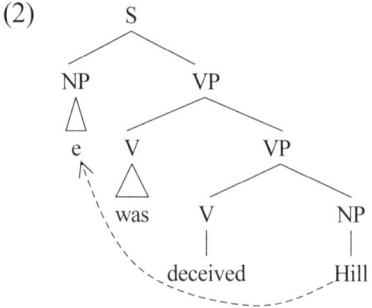

The operation basically moves the object *Hill* to the subject position. This kind of movement analysis is based on the following three basic assumptions: (a) Move anything anywhere (as long as the movement observes general principles), (b) Every NP needs to get Case (nominative (NOM) or accusative (ACC)). The subject gets NOM case from tense, and the object gets ACC from an active transitive verb, and (c) A passive participle does not license ACC case. These basic assumptions are taken to trigger the movement of *Hill*. That is, the NP *Hill* in (2) does not have ACC case since the passive participle cannot assign any case. This would violate the Case Theory requiring every NP to have a case. To salvage this case violation, the NP must be moved to the subject position whose case is assigned by the tensed verb *was*.

Unlike the movement approach that relies on the tree structure, we can resort to the lexical properties of passive verbs. We can observe that there are many exceptions to passives. For example, transitive verbs, especially, *stative verbs* like *resemble* do not have any passive counterpart, as in (3). There are also verbs like *said* used only in passive forms, as in (4).

(3) a. John resembles his father.
　　b. *His father is resembled by John.
(4) a. John is said to be rich.
　　b. *They said him to be a good teacher.

─┤ B ├─

(a) It is rumored that he is on his way out.
(b) Someone rumors that he is on his way out.
(c) He is reputed to be a good scholar.
(d) They reputed him to be a good scholar.
(e) The meeting will be held in the community center.
(f) The watering can holds two gallons of water.

Identify TWO ungrammatical sentences in <B>, and then explain why, based on the description in <A>.

11 Read the passage and fill in the blank ① with ONE word from the passage and the blank ② with the ONE most appropriate word. Write your answers in the correct order. [2 points]

> The core class of pronouns in English includes at least three main subgroups:
>
> (1) a. Personal pronouns: *I, you, he, she, it, they, we*
>   b. Reflexive pronouns: *myself, yourself, himself, herself, itself*
>   c. Reciprocal pronoun: *each other*
>
> Personal pronouns refer to specific persons or things and take different forms to indicate person, number, gender, and case. They participate in agreement relations with their antecedent, the phrase which they are understood to be referring to (indicated by the underlined parts of the examples in (2)).
>
> (2) a. After reading the pamphlet, Judy threw it/*them into the garbage can.
>   b. I got worried when the neighbors let their/*his dogs out.
>
> Reflexive pronouns are special forms which typically are used to indicate a reflexive activity or action.
>
> (3) a. After the party, I asked myself why I had faxed invitations to everyone in my office building.
>   b. Edward usually remembered to send a copy of his e-mail to himself.
>
> These personal or reflexive pronouns neither take a determiner nor combine with an adjective except in very restricted constructions. These restricted constructions involve some indefinite pronouns (e.g., *a little something, a certain someone*).
>   Since proper nouns which are non-countable usually refer to something or someone unique, they do not normally take a plural form and cannot occur with a/an ____①____, as in (4):

(4) a. John, Bill, Seoul, January, ⋯
　　b. *a John, *a Bill, *a Seoul, *a January, ⋯

　However, proper nouns can be converted into _____②_____ nouns when they refer to a particular individual or type of individual:

(5) a. No John Smiths attended the meeting.
　　b. This John Smith lives in Seoul.
　　c. There are three Davids in my class.
　　d. My brother is an Einstein at maths.

MENTOR LINGUISTICS

12 Read the passage <A> and the sentences in <B>, and follow the directions. [4 points]

───────────────── A ─────────────────

Adjectives are expressions commonly used to modify a noun. However, not all adjectives can modify nouns. Even though most adjectives can be used either as in a modifying (attributive) function or as a predicate (as in *She is tall*), certain adjectives are restricted to their usages. Adjectives such as *alive, asleep, afraid, ashamed*, can be used only predicatively, whereas others such as *wooden, drunken, golden, mere* are only used attributively:

(1) a. He is *alive*.
　　b. He is *afraid* of foxes.
(2) a. It is a *wooden* desk.
　　b. It is a *golden* hair.
(3) a. *It is an *alive* fish. (cf. living fish)
　　b. *They are *afraid* people. (cf. nervous people)

The adjective *alive* in (1a) is used only predicatively. This lexical information will prevent predicative-only adjectives from also functioning as noun modifiers, as shown in (3a).

Postnominal modifiers are basically the same as prenominal modifiers with respect to what they are modifying. The only difference is that they come after what they modify. Various phrases can function as such postnominal modifiers:

(4) a. [The boy [in the doorway]] waved to his father.
　　b. [The man [holding the bottle]] disappeared.
　　c. [The money [that you gave me]] disappeared last night.

These modifiers must modify either an N or N′, but not a complete NP.

┤ B ├

(a) She thought that he was an utter fool.
(b) This fact is key.
(c) How long have you been awake?
(d) John in the doorway waved to his father.
(e) The man eager to start the meeting is John's sister.
(f) The papers removed from the safe have not been found.

Identify TWO ungrammatical sentences in <B>, and explain why, based on the description in <A>.

13 Read the passage and fill in the blank with the ONE FEATURE from the passage. [2 points]

In forming questions, it is essential to invert the subject and the auxiliary:

(1) Are you studying English syntax?

The canonical movement approach is to assume that the auxiliary verb is moved in the sentential front position.

However, there are certain exceptions that present problems for the analysis of inverted interrogatives via movement transformation. Observe the following contrast:

(2) a. I shall go downtown.
    b. Shall I go downtown?

Here there is a semantic difference between the auxiliary verb *shall* in (2a) and the one in (2b): the former conveys futurity whereas the latter has a deontic sense.

Further, there are inflected forms that only occur in inversion constructions, e.g. the first person singular negative contracted form of the copula illustrated in (3):

(3) a. *I aren't going.
    b. Aren't I going?

Notice that English has various Subject-Aux inversion constructions:

(4) a. Wish: May she live forever!
   b. Matrix Polar Interrogative: Boy, was I stupid!
   c. Negative Imperative: Don't you even touch that!
   d. Subjunctive: Had they been here now, we wouldn't have this problem.
   e. Exclamative: Am I tired!

Each of these constructions has its own constraints that can hardly be predicted from other constructions. For example, in 'wish' constructions, only the modal auxiliary *may* is possible. In negative imperative, only *don't* allows the subject to follow.

This analysis hints that there are two types of finite auxiliary verbs in terms of the feature [INV] (i.e., Inverted): [+ INV] and [− INV]. This then means that as discussed in (2) and (3), the [+ INV] *shall* will only a deontic sense and the [+ INV] *aren't* can select the first person singular as its subject. Meanwhile, even though the word *better* is an auxiliary verb, it always carries _____ as attested by the following contrast:

(5) a. You better not drink.
   b. *Better you not drink.

14 Read the passage and fill in the blank with TWO words from the passage.

[2 points]

> Consider the following measure noun phrases:
>
> (1) a. A can of tomatoes is/*are added.
>   b. Two cans of tomatoes are/*is added.
>
> We can see here that it is the head noun *can* or *cans* which determines the number (NUM) value of the whole NP. The inner NP in the PP does not affect the NUM value at all.
>
> There is one set of words whose behavior leaves them somewhere between quantity words and measure nouns. These are words such as *dozen, hundred*, and *thousand*:
>
> (2) a. three hundred of your friends
>   b. *three hundreds of your friends
>   c. *three hundreds of friends
>   d. three hundred friends
>   e. hundreds of friends/*hundreds friends
>
> Consider the behavior of *hundred* and *hundreds* here. The singular *hundred*, when used as noun, obligatorily requires a PP [of] complement as well as a numeral specifier, as in (2a). The plural *hundreds* requires no _____ although it also selects a PP complement. Not surprisingly, similar behavior can be observed with *thousand* and *thousands*:
>
> (3) a. several thousand of Bill's supporters
>   b. *several thousands of Bill's supporters
>   c. *several thousands of supporters
>   d. several thousand supporters
>   e. thousands of supports/*thousands supports

15 Read the passage and fill in the blank ① with the ONE most appropriate word and the blank ② with TWO words from the passage. Write your answers in the correct order. [2 points]

> Like other languages, English also distinguishes a set of clause types that are characteristically used to perform different kinds of speech acts:
>
> (1) a. Declarative: John is clever.
>   b. Interrogative: Is John clever? Who is clever?
>   c. Exclamative: How clever you are!
>   d. Imperative: Be very clever.
>
> Each clause type in general has its own functions to represent speech acts. For example, declarative makes a statement, interrogative asks a question, exclamative makes an exclamatory statement, and imperative issues a directive.
>
> Meanwhile, *wh*-questions, in addition to the subject-auxiliary inversion, introduce one of the interrogative words *who, whom, whose, what, which, when, where, why,* and *how*. These *wh*-phrases have a variety of functions in the clause. For example, they can be subject, _____①_____, as well as subject complement:
>
> (2) a. [Who] called the police?
>   b. [Which version] did they recommend?
>   c. [What] are they?
>   d. [What] did John give to Bill?
>
> The syntactic category of the *wh*-questioned phrase need not be an NP. It also can be a PP, AP, or AdvP:
>
> (3) a. [NP Which man] [did you talk to ___]?
>   b. [PP To which man] [did you talk ___]?
>   c. [AP How ill] [has Hobbs been ___]?
>   d. [AdvP How frequently] [did Hobbs see Rhodes ___]?

As noted here, in terms of the structure, *wh*-questions consist of two parts: a *wh*-phrase and an inverted sentence with a missing phrase which is linked to the *wh*-phrase. The filler *wh*-phrase must be identical with the gap with respect to the ____②____ :

(4) a. *[PP To which man] [did you talk to [NP ___]]?
    b. *[NP Which man] [did you talk [PP ___]]?

멘토영어학
문제은행

Part 02

Grammar

PART 02 Grammar

• Answer Key p.32

01 Read the passage <A> and the sentences in <B>, and follow the directions. [4 points]

A

A predicative complement (PC) commonly has the form of an NP, and in that case it contrasts directly with an object (O).

(1) a. Stacy *was* <u>a good speaker</u>.　　*predicative complement*
　　b. Stacy *found* <u>a good speaker</u>.　　*object*
(2) a. Lee *became* <u>a friend of mine</u>.　　*predicative complement*
　　b. Lee *insulted* <u>a friend of mine</u>.　　*object*

There is a sharp semantic distinction in elementary examples of this kind. The object NPs refer to participants in the situation: in each of (1b) and (2b) there are two people involved. The predicative NPs, however, do not refer to participants like this. There is only a single person involved in the (a) examples, the one referred to by the subject NP. The predicative complement NP denotes a property that is ascribed to this person.

PCs are most clearly illustrated by examples like (1a). The verb *be* here has basically no semantic content. The most important thing that *be* does in this example is to carry the preterite tense inflection that indicates reference to past time. The meaning of the clause is really just that Stacy spoke in an entertaining manner. So although *a good speaker* is syntactically an NP complement, it is semantically comparable to a predicate like *spoke well*. This is the basis for the term 'predicative complement': the complement typically represents what is predicated of the subject-referent in a way that is similar to that in which a whole predicate does.

A few verbs can take either a PC or an O, but with obvious differences in meaning as shown in (3) and (4):

126　Part 02 Grammar

(3) a. This *proved* a great asset.

　　b. This *proved* my point.

(4) a. He *sounded* a decent guy.

　　b. He *sounded* the gong.

Again, the objects denote participants but the predicative complements don't.

―――――――――――――――| B |―――――――――――――――

(a) Honestly, I felt a fool standing there alone on the platform.

(b) Suddenly, I felt a fool pushing in front of me on the platform.

Identify whether the NP *a fool* is a predicative complement or an object in each sentence in <B>, and explain why, discussing participants, based on the description in <A>.

02 Read the passage <A> and the sentences in <B>, and follow the directions. [4 points]

— A —

Phrases linked by the coordinator *and* may express combinatory or segregatory meaning. The distinction is clearest with noun phrases. When the coordination is segregatory, we can paraphrase it by clause coordination as shown in (1).

(1) a. *John and Mary* know the answer.
　　b. = John knows the answer, and Mary knows the answer.

When it is combinatory we cannot do so, because the conjoins function in combination with respect to the rest of the clause, as in (2).

(2) a. *John and Mary* make a pleasant couple.
　　b. ≠ *John makes a pleasant couple, and Mary makes a pleasant couple.

Many conjoint noun phrases are in fact ambiguous between the two interpretations:

(3) *John and Mary* won a prize.

This may mean that they each won a prize or that the prize was awarded to them jointly.

Certain markers explicitly indicate that the coordination is segregatory. The adverb *respectively* indicates which constituents go with which in the two parallel sets of conjoint phrases. Sentence (4a) has only the segregatory meaning:

(4) a. *Thomas Arnold and his son Matthew* were *respectively* the greatest educator and the greatest critic of the Victorian age.
　　b. = Thomas Arnold was the greatest educator of the Victorian age, and his son Matthew was the greatest critic of the Victorian age.

Further examples of combinatory meaning are shown in (5).

(5) a. *Peter and Bob* separated (from each other).
　　b. *Mary and Paul* are just good friends.
　　c. *Paula and her brother* look alike.
　　d. *Law and order* is a primary concern of the new administration.

> **B**
>
> (a) Jill and Ben visited their uncles.
> (b) Both John and Mary have won a prize.
> (c) old and new furniture
> (d) old and valuable books

Identify TWO unambiguous sentences or phrases in <B>, and stating the type of coordination (i.e., the combinatory or segregatory meaning), based on the description in <A>.

03 Read the passage <A> and the sentences in <B>, and follow the directions. [4 points]

A

Positive and negative clauses differ in the way they combine with other expressions in the structure of larger units. Here are the three major differences.

First, after a negative clause we can add a constituent introduced by *not even*, and it makes sense. This is not possible with positive clauses:

(1) a. *I have read your book, *not even* the introduction.
    POSITIVE CLAUSE
 b. I haven't read your book, *not even* the introduction.
    NEGATIVE CLAUSE

The addition in (1b) is interpreted as "*I haven't even read the introduction*". The *not* isn't obligatory (cf. *I haven't read your book, even the introduction*) but the crucial point is that it can occur in the negative clause (1b) but is impossible in the positive as in (1a).

Second, when we add a related clause of the same polarity, the positive pair may be linked by *so*, the negative pair by *neither* or *nor*:

(2) a. I have read your book, and *so* have my students.
    POSITIVE CLAUSE
 b. I haven't read your book, and *neither* have my students.
    NEGATIVE CLAUSE

Switching the connectives leads to ungrammaticality: *I have read your book and neither have my students; *I haven't read your book and so have my students.*

A common device for seeking confirmation of what one says is to add a truncated interrogative clause known as a tag (*reversed polarity tags*). It generally consists of just an auxiliary verb + personal pronoun subject, and its polarity is the reverse of that of the clause to which it is attached:

(3) a. They have read my book, *haven't they*?
    POSITIVE CLAUSE + NEGATIVE TAG
 b. They haven't read my book, *have they*?
    NEGATIVE CLAUSE + POSITIVE TAG

In (3a) the negative tag *haven't they?* attaches to the positive clause, while in (3b) the positive tag *have they?* attaches to the negative clause.

┤ B ├

(a) He was unkind, and so was Sue.
(b) He wasn't kind, and neither was Sue.
(c) He was unkind, not even to me.
(d) He wasn't kind, not even to me.
(e) Few of them realised it was a hoax, didn't they?
(f) There's scarcely any food left, is there?

Identify TWO ungrammatical sentences in <B>, and explain why, based on the description in <A>.

04 Read the passage <A> and the sentences in <B>, and follow the directions. [4 points]

A

Several form criteria distinguish nonrestrictive relative clauses from their restrictive counterparts.

Nonrestrictive relative clauses have commas around them, as in (1a). Restrictive relative clauses must not be separated by commas, as shown in (1b).

(1) a. My sister, *who lives in Seoul*, is a chemist.
  b. My sister *who lives in Seoul* is a chemist.

Nonrestrictive relative clauses may modify an entire sentence, that is, a preceding independent clause, and must be set off from the main clause by a comma, as in (2a). Restrictive relative like (2b) cannot modify an entire sentence, and may only modify noun phrases.

(2) a. Professor Fish gave everyone an A, *which was just fine with Alice*.
  b. *Professor Fish gave everyone an A *which was just fine with Alice*.

Nonrestrictive relative clauses may not modify *any, every,* or *no* + noun or indefinite pronouns such as *anyone, everyone,* or *no one*, as shown by (3a); restrictive relatives may, as shown in (3b).

(3) a. *Any man, *who goes back on his word*, is no friend of mine.
  b. Any man *who goes back on his word* is no friend of mine.

Nonrestrictive relative clauses cannot be stacked. Stacking results in ungrammatical sentences like (4a). Restrictive relatives can be stacked, as in (4b).

(4) a. *They gave job to Rob, *who is very qualified, who starts next month*.
  b. I really like that car *that you have that your wife is always zipping around town in*.

───── B ─────

(a) Bill, who is a lawyer, was not impressed by Professor Fish's arguments.

(b) Triangles, which have three sides, are fascinating.

(c) Susan is afraid of dogs which doesn't surprise me at all.

(d) The 2022 winners for Literature, whose books have sold well, who everyone likes, are all from Oxford.

(e) The books which John has consulted are out of date.

(f) The tornado which struck the town destroyed several homes.

First, identify TWO ungrammatical sentences in <B>, and explain why, based on the description in <A>.

05
Read the passage <A> and the sentences in <B>, and follow the directions. [4 points]

A

There are some syntactic circumstances that can make preposition stranding almost or completely impossible.

(1) a. *This is the safe [which the key to was stolen].   STRANDED
    b. This is the safe [to which the key was stolen].   FRONTED
(2) a. *I have a lecture ending at two [which I'll be free all day after].   STRANDED
    b. I have a lecture ending at two [after which I'll be free all day].   FRONTED
(3) a. *What way am I annoying you in?   STRANDED
    b. In what way am I annoying you?   FRONTED

In (1a) the stranded preposition occurs within a subject NP (the subject of *was stolen*). That is fairly clearly ungrammatical. In (2) the PP is in adjunct rather than complement function, specifically an adjunct of time. There is a tendency for the stranding construction to be avoided in adjuncts generally. With adjuncts of place it is not so strong, so you may hear sentences like ?*That's the town [which I first met her in]*; but the tendency is quite strong for many other adjuncts, like adjuncts of time or duration. In (3) this is more than just a tendency with some fixed adjunct expressions: the manner adjunct *in what way*, as in (3b), can never be split up by stranding.

There are also syntactic circumstances that make the nonstranded version, with preposition fronting, almost or completely impossible.

(4) a. That depends on [who I give it to].   STRANDED
    b. *That depends on [to whom I give it].   FRONTED
(5) a. What did you hit me for?   STRANDED
    b. *For what did you hit me?   FRONTED
(6) a. Which metals does it consist of?   STRANDED
    b. ?Of which metals does it consist?   FRONTED

In (4) the bracketed clause containing the preposition is a subordinate interrogative clause functioning as complement to a preposition (*on*); here stranding is obligatory. In (5) we have the idiom *what for* meaning "why", where *for* is never fronted. The verb *consist* in (6) is one of those that license a PP complement with a specified preposition, and there is a fairly strong preference for the stranding construction with such verbs. The (3b) version isn't grammatically forbidden, but it sounds very stiff and formal.

B

(a) What circumstances would you do a thing like that under?
(b) We can't agree on for which grant we should apply.
(c) That wasn't the one which we were looking out for.
(d) This is the sort of English which I will not put up with.
(e) What are you asking for?

Identify TWO ungrammatical sentences in <B>, and explain why, based on the description in <A>.

06
Read the passage <A> and the sentences in <B>, and follow the directions. [4 points]

┤ A ├

Declarative content clauses mostly function as complement of a verb, noun, adjective, or preposition. The range of complement functions is illustrated in (1):

(1) a. <u>That they refused</u> didn't surprise us.   SUBJECT
    b. It didn't surprise us <u>that they refused</u>.   EXTRAPOSED SUBJECT
    c. I realise <u>that you feel insulted</u>.   INTERNAL COMP OF VERB
    d. You can't ignore the fact <u>that he was drunk</u>.   COMP OF NOUN
    e. I'm glad <u>that you could come</u>.   COMP OF ADJECTIVE
    f. You can go provided <u>that you are careful</u>.   COMP OF PREPOSITION

In (1a), the content clause is subject. It is licensed by *surprise*. In (1b), we see a much more frequent kind of case than (1a), but synonymous with it: the subordinate clause is extraposed. In (1c), the content clause is internal complement to the verb *realise* of a clause. In the next two, the content clause is complement to the noun *fact* in (1d) and the adjective *glad* in (1e). Finally, in (1f), the content clause is complement of a preposition.

Like declaratives, interrogative content clauses usually function as complements, as illustrated in (2):

(2) a. <u>What caused the delay</u> remains unclear.   SUBJECT
    b. It remains unclear <u>what caused the delay</u>.   EXTRAPOSED SUBJECT
    c. I've discovered <u>where they keep the key</u>.   INTERNAL COMP OF VERB
    d. The question <u>whether it's legal</u> was ignored.   COMP OF NOUN
    e. I'm uncertain <u>what we can do about it</u>.   COMP OF ADJECTIVE
    f. That depends on <u>how much time we have</u>.   COMP OF PREPOSITION

The range of functions is almost like that illustrated for declaratives in (1). One difference from declaratives, however, is that prepositions are often optional; for example, we could add *of* after *question* in (2d), and we could omit *on* in (2f). There is only partial overlap between the items that license declaratives and those that license interrogatives. For example, some verbs accept both declaratives and interrogatives, and others accept only declaratives or only interrogatives.

> **B**
>
> (a) I know she's right.
> (b) I know what he did.
> (c) I insist that she's right.
> (d) I insist what he did.
> (e) I inquire that he's ill.
> (f) I inquired what he did.

In <B>, identify TWO ungrammatical sentences, and explain why, based on the description in <A>.

_____
_____
_____
_____
_____

07 Read the passage <A> and the sentences in <B>, and follow the directions. [4 points]

| A |

Adverbs that modify verbs can occur in several positions in a sentence but never between a verb and its object, as the comparison in (1) show.

(1) a. He *often* takes the metro.
　　b. *He takes *often* the metro.

The possible positions that an adverb that modifies a verb can occupy are the following: sentence initial, before a main verb (including between an auxiliary or modal and a main verb), between the main verb and a following element such as a PP, and sentence final.

Fewer types of adverbs are acceptable in sentence-initial position. Prominent among them are time adverbs, as in (2a), and certain frequency adverbs, as in (2b). But others, such as *always*, cannot appear in initial position, as shown by (2c).

(2) a. *Earlier* he told us a different story.
　　b. *Sometimes* she comes in over an hour late.
　　c. **Always* she speaks English to her mother.

Adverbs of a given type may differ considerably in the positions in which they can occur. For example, although many degree adverbs occur in sentence-final position, others, such as *almost*, cannot occur sentence finally, as shown in (3a). This variation is especially evident with frequency adverbs. *sometimes* can occur in sentence finally and sentence initially. In contrast, *always* cannot appear in initial position, as shown by (2c), except in imperative sentences, as in (3b), and sounds odd in sentence-final position, as in (3c).

(3) a. *He fainted *almost*.
　　b. *Always* remember to call your mother once a week.
　　c. ?She speaks English to her mother *always*.

Particularly worth mentioning in this context are negative frequency adverbs. When a negative frequency adverb appears sentence initially, the rule of subject-aux inversion must be applied, as shown in (4).

(4) a. *Never have I* seen anything as brilliant as that.
　　b. **Never I have* seen anything as brilliant as that.

B

(a) She caught up nearly.
(b) She enjoyed the party tremendously.
(c) The price of stocks rose enormously in the late 1990s.
(d) Not long ago there was a rainstorm.
(e) Seldom John forgets to do his taxes on time.
(f) Hardly had he arrived when she started complaining.

Identify TWO ungrammatical sentences in <B>, and explain why, stating the type of adverbs, based on the description in <A>.

08 Read the passage <A> and follow the directions. [4 points]

--- A ---

In general, there is little difficulty in distinguishing verbs from prepositions. Verbs usually function as predicator in clause structure, and in finite or infinitival clauses they are easily recognizable as verbs by this function. There is, for example, no doubt about the status of *follow* as a verb in (1):

(1) a. We always *follow* the manual.
　　b. I advise you to *follow* the manual.

There are, however, a number of prepositions which have the same shape as the gerund-participle or past participle forms of verbs. These are cases where historical change led to a word taking on the properties of a preposition in addition to its original verbal properties, so that it now belongs to both categories. Two examples, with the relevant word underlined, are given in (2) and (3):

(2) a. <u>Following</u> the meeting, there will be a reception.
　　b. Liz did remarkably well, <u>given</u> her inexperience.
(3) a. <u>Following</u> the manual, we tried to figure out how to assemble the unit.
　　b. Liz was <u>given</u> only three months to live.

Predicative adjectives have to be related to a predicand, and verbs in predicator function have to be related to a subject, either overt or understood. In (3a) *following* is predicator in a gerund-participial clause functioning as adjunct; this clause itself has no overt subject, but an understood subject is retrievable from the subject of the main clause: the sentence implies that *WE* were following the manual. Example (3b) is a passive clause, and *Liz* is the subject—compare the active version *They gave Liz only three months to live*.

　However, in (2), there is no such predicational relationship to a subject. The underlined words derive historically from verbs, but they have developed meanings distinct from the verbal ones, and in this use these words belong to the preposition category. *Following* means "after", and *given X* means roughly "if we take X into account".

Identify whether each underlined word in <B> below is a preposition or a verb, and explain why, based on the description in <A>.

―――――――――――――| B |―――――――――――

(4) Owing so much to the bank, farmers can't afford any luxuries.

(5) Owing to the drought, many farms are going bankrupt.

09 Read the passage <A> and follow the directions. [4 points]

┤ A ├

Although most adjectives can be used both attributively and predicatively, there are nevertheless many that are restricted to one or other of these two uses:

(1) a. a *huge* hole
   b. *utter* nonsense
   c. *the *asleep* children
(2) a. The hole was *huge*.
   b. *That nonsense was *utter*.
   c. The children were *asleep*.

Huge illustrates the default case, where the adjective appears both attributively and predicatively. *Utter* is an exceptional case: an attributive-only adjective, which can't be used predicatively, as shown in (2b). *Asleep* is the opposite kind of exception; it can occur predicatively but not attributively: it is a never-attributive adjective.

NPs containing a sample of other adjectives that are attributive-only are given in (3):

(3) the *sole* survivor   the *eventual* winner   her *former* husband
    our *future* prospects   the *main* problem   a *mere* child
    the *only* drawback   their *own* fault   the *principal* advantage

Here are some further examples of predicative uses of never-attributive adjectives:

(4) a. The house was *ablaze*.
   b. Something was *amiss*.
   c. It is *liable* to flood.
   d. I was utterly *bereft*.

┌──────────────────── B ────────────────────┐
│   │
│ (a) Corruption was rife.   │
│ (b) The heir is lawful.   │
│ (c) It was devoid of interest.   │
│ (d) the content baby   │
│ (e) a veritable jungle   │
│ (f) the putative father   │
│   │
└──┘

Identify TWO ungrammatical sentences or phrases in <B>, and explain why, specifying the type of adjectives, based on the description in <A>.

_____

_____

_____

_____

_____

10 Read the passage and follow the directions. [4 points]

A

Two information-structuring principles help determine the choice of pattern in sentences with an indirect object. According to the given-new contract, information that has been mentioned in the previous context and is therefore given, or old, generally comes before new information in a sentence. In sentences with an indirect object, if the indirect object is given information, the dative movement pattern is preferred; otherwise it is inappropriate.

(1) Susan: You know, I can't figure out what to get John for his birthday. Any ideas?
Ann: <u>Give him a CD</u>. You know how much he likes music.

If the direct object is given information, the prepositional pattern is preferred.

(2) I have two pistols here, a Colt .45 and a German Luger. Here are the rules of the duel. I'm going to <u>give the Colt to Fred and the Luger to Alex</u>. They will then walk in opposite directions for 20 paces, turn, and wait for my command to fire.

According to the end weight principle, a long, complex ("heavy") noun phrase can be moved to the end of the sentence to increase comprehension and avoid ambiguity as in (3b). However, in (3a), in the prepositional pattern, the heavy direct object NP in the middle of the sentence is inappropriate.

(3) a. ?Abby gave <u>foot-long frankfurters that had been roasted over an open hickory fire</u> to the kids.
b. Abby gave the kids <u>foot-long frankfurters that had been roasted over an open hickory fire</u>.

| B |

(a) When Alice arrived at the auditorium, she saw that hall was packed. But she wasn't worried about finding somewhere to sit because she was sure that John had saved a seat for her.

(b) A: There were two more items on the table, a package and a letter. Do you remember who you sent them to?
B: We sent the package to a Mr. Green and the letter to a Mrs. Harrison.

(c) John reported to the police the theft of his new sky-blue BMW convertible with the heated leather seats and the yellow fog lights.

(d) The mediator recommended an alternative solution for eliminating the barriers to a negotiated settlement of the dispute to the strikers.

In <B>, identify TWO inappropriate discourses or sentences due to the information-structuring principles, and explain why, based on the description in <A>.

11 Read the passage <A> and the sentences in <B>, and follow the directions. [4 points]

⊣ A ⊢

A fair number of words or larger expressions are polarity-sensitive in the sense that they occur readily in clauses of one polarity but not of the other.

(1) a. I have *some* objections to make.
    b. *I don't have *some* objections to make.
(2) a. *I have *any* objections to make.
    b. I don't have *any* objections to make.

Some is by no means wholly excluded from negative clauses; it has positive orientation. Conversely *any* has negative orientation; it occurs freely in negatives but is excluded from positives. What excludes *any* from (2a) is not just that the clause is positive; it is also declarative. If we look instead at an interrogative clause, we find it is freely admitted:

(3) a. Have you *any* objections to make?
    b. Who has *any* objections to make?

We refer to items like *any*, therefore, as non-affirmatives. The verb *affirm* contrasts with question and hence suggests declarative; the adjective *affirmative* is a synonym of positive. In general, then, the restriction on non-affirmative items is that they cannot occur in clauses that are both declarative and positive.

It is not only negatives and interrogatives that allow non-affirmative items to appear. They are also found in a number of other constructions, as illustrated in (4). Sentence (4) has a semantic affinity with negation. Because of the *too* in (4), we understand that she did NOT say anything.

(4) She was too taken aback to say *anything*.

In addition, the versions with nonverbal negation can often be paraphrased using verbal negation, as illustrated in (5).

(5) Nonverbal Negation   Verbal Negation
    a. We found *no* mistakes.   We *didn't* find *any* mistakes.
    b. There is *no one* here.   There *isn't anyone* here.

> **B**
>
> (i) a. She ran faster than she had ever run before.
> b. We slipped away without anyone noticing.
> c. He denies I ever told him.
> d. We were unaware of some hostility.
> (ii) a. We knew neither of them.
> b. He never apologises.

In <B>, first, identify ONE ungrammatical sentence in (i), and explain why. Second, in (ii), for each sentence with nonverbal negation, provide an equivalent sentence with verbal negation, based on the description in <A>.

12 Read the passage <A> and the sentences in <B>, and follow the directions. [4 points]

┤ A ├

There is, in fact, a "middle voice," intermediate between active and passive voices. The middle voice allows the subject of a sentence to be nonagentive, as in the passive voice, but the morphology of the verb to be in the active voice.

(1) a. Her high C shattered the glass. (active voice)
　　b. The glass was shattered by her high C. (passive voice)
　　c. The glass shattered. (middle voice)

English uses special verbs to express spontaneous occurrences. Such verbs, which allow the object of a transitive clause to be a subject of an intransitive clause without changing voice, are called *ergative*, or *change-of-state verbs*. Ergative verbs, such as *shatter*, can appear in all three voices and thus take either agents or undergoers of the action (sometimes called patients or themes) as subjects. The idea of an ergative verb is new for ESL/EFL students.

(2) The window broke.

The students argue that windows can't break themselves, and thus they feel obliged to use the passive or express an agent, as shown in (3).

(3) a. The window was broken.
　　b. Someone broke the window.

While such sentences are not wrong, of course, the active voice sentence with a nonagentive subject is perfectly permissible in English with ergative verbs. The difference between the two options is that the passive sentence suggests the existence of an agent, even if the agent is not explicit. The verb used ergatively does not permit an agent; thus, it cannot be used with a by-phrase. The following are situations in which ergative sentences are needed: (a) when the focus is on the change of state, and the agent is irrelevant; (b) when it is natural to expect change to occur (i.e., physical, social, or psychological "laws" seem to be involved); (c) when there are so many possible causes for a change of state that it would be misleading to imply a single agent, and so on.

| B |

(a) The expression on her face suddenly changed from sadness to rage.
(b) The name of the company was changed to avoid confusion with another company.
(c) The weather suddenly changed.
(d) The ice on the pond was melted earlier than usual.
(e) It is ridiculous that most women in developing countries suffered from extreme poverty.
(f) The window broke by the gang.

In <B>, identify TWO inappropriate sentences, and explain why, based on the description in <A>.

13 Read the passage and follow the directions. [4 points]

─┤ A ├─

There are many verbs that take a PP complement. They are called *prepositional verbs*, and occur in a range of constructions, as illustrated in (1):

(1) a. He asked for water.
    b. We came across some errors.
(2) He'll treat me to lunch.
(3) That counts as satisfactory.
(4) They rated it as a success.

The examples in (1) are all intransitive. The example in (2) is transitive—the PP complement follows an NP object. In (3)—(4) the complement of the preposition is predicative.

Some verb + preposition combinations are *fossilised*, in the sense that they don't permit any variation in their relative positions. Now consider the following examples:

(5) NON-FOSSILISED
    a. I <u>asked for</u> some information.
    b. the information [which I <u>asked for</u>]
    c. the information [<u>for</u> which I <u>asked</u>]
(6) FOSSILISED
    a. I <u>came across</u> some letters.
    b. the letters [which I <u>came across</u>]
    c. *the letters [<u>across</u> which I <u>came</u>]

In the stranded preposition construction, *which* occupies front position in the clause, and the preposition occurs after the verb, separated from its complement, as shown in (5b) and (6b). In the fronted preposition construction, the preposition is fronted along with its complement *which*, as in (5c) and (6c). Both variants are permitted with *ask for*, but only the first is permitted with *come across*: (6c) is not grammatical. The reason is that fossilisation doesn't allow any departure from the fixed order of verb + preposition.

┌─────────────────── B ───────────────────┐
│ (i) a. He accused her of a crime.
│   b. the crime which he accused her of
│   c. the crime of which he accused her
│ (ii) a. I let him off some work.
│   b. the work which I let him off
│   c. the work off which I let him
└──┘

In <B>, identify ONE ungrammatical phrase, and then explain why, ONLY based on the description in <A>.

_____
_____
_____
_____
_____

14 Read the passage and follow the directions. [4 points]

─────────────┤ A ├─────────────

In the light of the syntactic distribution, the prepositional phrases readily modify nouns or function as predicative complement to verbs like *be*; the adverb phrases are used for modifying verbs, adjectives, and other adverbs.

Prepositions take a range of complement types comparable to that of verbs:

(1) a. I was talking [to a friend].   Object NP Complement
    b. I regard her [as a friend].   Predicative Complement
    c. I stayed [until after lunch].   PP Complement
    d. I hadn't met her [till recently].   ADVP Complement
    e. We agreed [on how to proceed].   Clause Complement

As with verbs, we need to make a distinction between objects and predicative complements: *the friend* examples in (1a) and (1b) contrast in the same way as those in (2):

(2) a. I was visiting [a friend].   Object NP Complement
    b. I consider her [a friend].   Predicative Complement

The crucial syntactic difference is that a predicative can have the form of an AdjP (*I regard her as very bright*, where *as* is the preposition) or a bare role NP (*They elected her as treasurer*).

There are a handful of PreP + AdvP combinations, which could be seen as prepositions taking adverb phrases as complements. But there are very few: in addition to the one in (1d), we find *before long, for later, until recently,* and a very few others. They are basically fixed phrases (for example, we get *before long* but not **after long*).

Now consider the following sentence:

(3) She arrived two weeks ago.

What is the categorial status of *ago*? Is it an adverb or a preposition? The order here reflects the historical origin of *ago*: it derives from the form *agone*, containing the past participle of *go*. Originally *two weeks ago* meant something like "two weeks gone", i.e., located at a point in time that is now two weeks gone by into the past.

―――――| B |―――――

(i) a. I took him for dead.

b. It won't last for long.

(ii) a. That was two weeks ago.

b. I recall his behaviour two weeks ago.

In <B>, first, in (i) identify each underlined part with specifying a range of complement types as shown in (1). Second, in (ii) identify whether the phrase *two weeks ago* is the prepositional phrase or the adverb phrase, and explain why, discussing the characteristic of the syntactic distribution, ONLY based on the description in <A>.

15 Read the passage <A> and the sentences in <B>, and follow the directions. [4 points]

| A |

Adverbials can be divided into several types. Where adjuncts are seen as on a par with such sentence elements as Subject and Object, while subjuncts are seen as having a lesser role, disjuncts have by contrast a superior role to sentence elements, being somewhat detached from and superordinate to the rest of the sentence.

There are two types of *Disjuncts*. The first type is *Style Disjuncts*, conveying the speaker's comment on the style and form of what is being said and defining in some way the conditions under which 'authority' is being assumed for the statement, as shown in (1).

(1) *From my personal observation*, Mr. Forster neglects his children.

The second type is *Content Disjuncts*, making an observation on the actual content of an utterance and on its truth conditions, as in (2).

(2) *To the disgust of his neighbours*, Mr. Forster neglects his children.

Subjuncts have a subordinate and parenthetic role in comparison with adjuncts. *Viewpoint Subjuncts,* expressing a viewpoint, are largely concerned with the semantic concept of respect, as in (3).

(3) *From a personal viewpoint*, he is likely to do well in this post.

Item Subjuncts express volition of the subject of a clause, as in (4).

(4) *With great reluctance*, he rose to speak.

The commonest item to be associated with these subjuncts is the subject of a clause; therefore, the sentences with item subjuncts can be paraphrased as follows:

(5) He *deliberately* misled us.
  → He was being deliberate when he misled us.
(6) *With great unease,* they elected him as their leader.
  → They were very uneasy when they elected him as their leader.

───────────────── B ─────────────────

(a) Strictly, she should have conceded the point to her opponent.

(b) Architecturally, the plans represent a magnificent conception.

(c) With great pride, he accepted the award.

(d) To my regret, she did not seek nomination.

(e) Bitterly, he buried his child.

(f) Looked at politically, the proposal seems dangerous.

Based on the description in <A>, first, identify TWO sentences with *Item Subjuncts* in <B>, and paraphrase them in the same way shown in (6) in <A>, using the word *when*.

16 Read the passage <A> and the sentences in <B>, and follow the directions. [4 points]

A

Phrasal verbs are made up of a verb and a following particle. Examples of phrasal verbs are presented in (1).

(1) a. Tom *set up* all the chairs before the class began.
　　b. Daniel *handed in* her homework early.

Phrasal verbs allow the particle to move over the object, as in (2) below:

(2) a. They *called off* the meeting.
　　b. They *called* the meeting *off*.

Even though the following verb is a phrasal verb, it does not allow for the particle movement. Consider the following sentences:

(3) a. John always *picks on* my brother.
　　b. *John always *picks* my brother *on*.

So the phrasal verbs like *set up* or *hand in* in (1) are called separable phrasal verbs while the phrasal verbs like *pick on* in (3) are called inseparable phrasal verbs.

　Prepositional verbs consist of a verb and a following prepositional phrase, and the separation of the verb and preposition will produce an ungrammatical sentence, as in (4).

(4) a. He *applied for* the job.
　　b. *He *applied* the job *for*.

Wh-question test distinguishes phrasal verbs from prepositional verbs. Phrasal verbs do not allow for the movement of the particle with a *wh*-word while prepositional verbs can have two forms, shown in (5) and (6).

(5) a. What are you *looking up*?

　　b. **Up* what are you *looking*?

(6) a. Who(m) were you *shouting at*?

　　b. *At* whom were you *shouting*?

| B |

(a) He stood my old brother by.

(b) He commented the proposal on.

(c) Who(m) did he stand by?

(d) What did he comment on?

(e) On what did he comment?

Identify TWO ungrammatical sentences in <B>, and then explain why, specifying the types of verb, based on the description in <A>.

17 Read the passage <A> and the sentences in <B>, and follow the directions. [4 points]

A

Consider the two canonical active and passive counterpart sentences:

(1) a. The executive committee approved the new policy.
   b. The new policy was approved by the executive committee.

The passive sentence promotes the active object into the passive subject while it demotes the active subject into an optional PP (headed by *by*). We can observe that the complement of the main verb is missing, and the subject of the sentence has the main properties of this missing element. For example, in (2b), the active transitive verb *chosen* must have its object, but it doesn't have the object.

(2) a. John has chosen Bill for the position.
   b. *John has chosen ___ for the position.

However, in the passive, the object NP *Bill* must be absent. That is, it must not appear right after the passive verb:

(3) *John has been [chosen *Bill* for the position].

The absence of the object in the passive is due to the fact that the object of the verb is promoted to the subject in the passive.
  The other subcategorization requirement stays unchanged. For example, the active *handed* requires an NP and a PP [to] as its complements, and the passive *handed* still requires the PP as its complement:

(4) a. Pat handed Chris a book.
   b. *Pat handed Chris. / *Pat handed a book.
   c. Chris was handed a book (by Pat).

The two ungrammatical sentences are (c) and (e).

According to <A>, the passive construction promotes the object of the active sentence to the subject position, adds the auxiliary *be*, and changes the main verb into its past participle form. An active transitive verb like *take* requires a direct object.

(c) "John has been taken Bill to the library" is ungrammatical because it has the passive form (*has been taken*: auxiliary *be* + past participle) but still retains the object *Bill*. In a passive construction, the object of the active must appear as the subject, not remain after the verb.

(e) "John has taken to the library" is ungrammatical because it is an active construction with the transitive verb *take*, but the required direct object is missing. If this were intended as passive, it would need the auxiliary *be* plus the past participle (as in (f) "John has been taken to the library").

18 Read the passage and follow the directions. [4 points]

─┤ A ├─

One important issue in the interpretation of negatives concerns the scope of negation: what part of the sentence the negation applies to. A negative item may be said to govern (or determine the occurrence of) a nonassertive item only if the latter is within the scope of the negative, i.e., within the stretch of language over which the negative item has a semantic influence. The scope of the negation normally extends from the negative item itself to the end of the clause. There is thus a contrast between these two sentences:

(1) a. She definitely didn't speak to him.
    [It's definite that she didn't.]
　 b. She didn't definitely speak to him.
    [It's not definite that she did.]

If an assertive form is used, it must lie outside the scope:

(2) a. I didn't listen to some of the speakers.
    [I listened to some.]
　 b. I didn't listen to any of the speakers.
    [I listened to none.]

Now consider the following example:

(3) I didn't go to the party because I wanted to see Kim.

(3) is ambiguous as to scope. If the *because* adjunct is outside the scope of the negation, it gives the reason for my not going to the party: "The reason I didn't go to the party was that I wanted to see Kim (who wasn't going to be there)". If the *because* adjunct is inside the scope of negation, the sentence says that it is not the case that I went to the party because I wanted to see Kim (who was going to be there): here there is an implicature that I went for some other reason.

┌──────────────── B ────────────────┐
│ (4) I wasn't listening all the time. │
└────────────────────────────────────┘

Identify whether sentence (4) in <B> is ambiguous or not, and then explain why, discussing the scope of the negation and each interpretation, based on the description in <A>.

_____
_____
_____
_____
_____

19 Read the passage and follow the directions. [4 points]

―― A ――

With regard to the NP-internal elements between which we may find instances of agreement, there are two main types of NP in English: simple NPs and partitive NPs, shown in (1) and (2) respectively.

(1) a. *most* students
    b. *all* students
(2) a. *most* of the students
    b. *all* of the students

As in (2), the partitive phrases have a quantifier followed by an *of*-phrase, designating a set with respect to which certain individuals are quantified. In terms of semantics, these partitive NPs are different from simple NPs in several respects.

First, the lower NP in partitive phrases must be definite; and in the *of*-phrase, no quantificational NP is allowed, as shown in (3):

(3) each student vs. *each of students

Second, not all determiners with quantificational force can appear in partitive constructions. As shown in (4), determiners such as *the, every* and *no* cannot occupy the first position:

(4) a. *the of the students vs. the students
    b. *every of his ideas vs. every idea

Finally, simple NPs and partitive NPs have different restrictions relative to the semantic head. Observe the contrast between (5) and (6):

(5) a. She doesn't believe *much of that story*.
    b. I read *some of the book*.

(6) a. *She doesn't believe *much story*.

   b. *I read *some book*.

The partitive constructions in (5) allow a mass (non-count) quantifier such as *much, some, etc.* to cooccur with a lower *of*-NP containing a singular count noun. But as we can see in (6), the same elements serving as determiners cannot directly precede such nouns.

B

(a) neither cars
(b) neither of the cars
(c) some of many problems
(d) One of the people was dying of thirst.
(e) Many of the people were dying of thirst.
(f) We listened to as little speech as possible.

Identify TWO ungrammatical phrase(s) or sentence(s) in <B>, and then explain why, ONLY based on the description in <A>.

20 Read the passage <A> and the sentences in <B>, and follow the directions. [4 points]

| A |

Restrictive relative clauses can be classified in terms of the grammatical function of their relative pronouns. Based on this classification, relative clause types are the following: subject, direct object, and possessive.

There are grounds for recognizing other structures as restrictive relative clauses. In (1), (2), and (3), the preposition + *which* combinations can be replaced by *where, when,* and *why*. Since these three words have an adverbial function, grammarians often refer to the clauses they introduce as *adverbial relative clauses*.

(1) That is the gas station *at which* I am working now.
(2) How well I remember the day _____ *which* he was born.
(3) I have forgotten the reason *for which* the trust fund was established.

Free relative clauses also belong to restrictive relative clauses. The definite free relative is illustrated in (4).

(4) a. Karen ate [what Fred offered to her].
    b. [what Fred offered to her]

If we look just at the bracketed sequence in isolation as in (4b), we find no grounds for viewing them as anything other than indirect questions. The rules for indirect questions definitely allow the creation of the sequence. Thus, we will not be able to differentiate the bracketed sequence in (4) from indirect questions on the basis of their internal structure.

When we turn our attention to the external behavior of the sequence, one striking fact becomes immediately apparent: the sequence can be found in positions that definitely do not allow a broad range of indirect questions. This fact becomes clear when we try to substitute other indirect questions for the bracketed sequence.

(5) a. *Karen *ate* [which dish Norton served to her].

　b. Karen *knew* [which dish Norton served to her].

The simplest account of this substantial difference in acceptability can be summarized as follows: the verb *know* allows indirect questions as complements, whereas the verb *eat* does not.

─┤ B ├─

Now consider the following examples:

(6) Which dish Norton served to her was clear.

(7) Which dish Norton served to her went into the trash.

First, fill in the blank with the ONE most appropriate preposition. Second, identify the grammaticality AND ungrammaticality of each sentence in <B>, and explain why, ONLY based on the description in <A>.

21 Read the passage <A> and the sentences in <B>, and follow the directions. [4 points]

―――――――――――――― A ――――――――――――――

Consider the examples in (1):

(1) a. [Fifteen dollars] in a week is/*are not much.
  b. [Two miles] is/*are as far as they can walk.

In all of these examples with measure nouns, the plural subject combines with a singular verb.

A similar mismatch is also found in cases with terms for social organizations or collections, as in (2):

(2) a. [This/*These England team] have/*has put themselves in a good position to win the championship.
  b. [This/*These England team] *have/has put itself in a good position to win the championship.

The head noun has to be singular so that it can combine with a singular determiner. But the conflicting fact is that the singular noun phrase can combine even with a plural verb as well as a singular verb. Since the only possible number value of the determiner is singular for the head noun, the head noun cannot be anchored to plural entities unless we allow the mode of individuation to be changeable even within the same sentence domain. Thus, in (2) *this* and *team* agree each other in terms of the morphosyntactic agreement number value whereas the index value of *team* is what matters for subject-verb agreement.

What this indicates is that subject-verb agreement and noun-specifier agreement are different. In fact, English determiner-noun agreement is only a reflection of morpho-syntactic agreement features between determiner and noun, whereas both subject-verb agreement and pronoun-antecedent agreement are index-based agreement.

(3) [Four pounds] was quite a bit of money in 1950 and it was not easy to come by.

Consider the example in (1). The nouns *dollars* and *miles* here are morphologically plural and thus must select a plural determiner. But when these nouns are anchored to the group as a whole—that is, conceptualized as referring to a single measure, the index value has to be singular. In (3), the morpho-syntactic number value of *pounds* is plural whereas the index value is singular.

─┤ B ├─

(a) Two drops deodorizes anything in your house.
(b) Fifteen years represents a long period of his life.
(c) This government dislikes change.
(d) This government dislike change.
(e) These government dislikes change.
(f) These government dislike change.

Identify TWO ungrammatical sentences in <B>, and then explain why, discussing the morpho-syntactic number value and the index value, ONLY based on the description in <A>.

22 Read the passage <A> and the sentences in <B>, and follow the directions. [4 points]

─────────────── ┤ A ├ ───────────────

Any is one of a set of words that can appear in negative statements but normally do not appear in affirmative statements. This restriction on the use of *any* can be seen if we remove *not* from a negative sentence such as (1a). The resulting positive statement in (1b) is ungrammatical.

(1) a. She doesn't have *any* money.
    b. *She has *any* money.

Words such as *any*, which normally occur only in negative statements but themselves not negative, are called negative polarity items. Words such as *some*, on the other hand, normally occur in positive statements and are therefore referred to as positive polarity items. Examples are shown in (2).

(2) a. There are *some* crows roosting in that tree.
    b. *There aren't *some* crows roosting in that tree.
    c. There was *somebody* else in the car.
    d. *There wasn't *somebody* else in the car.

The negative polarity items *anymore* and *any longer* have a corresponding positive polarity item, *still*. Notice that negating the verb in (3a) with *doesn't* produces (3b), which is ungrammatical. A corresponding negative version of (3a) can be formed by negating the verb and using the negative polarity items *anymore* or *any longer*, as shown in (3c).

(3) a. She *still* lives in that old house.
    b. *She doesn't *still* live in that old house.
    c. She doesn't live in that old house *anymore/any longer*.

In addition, verbs, adjectives, and prepositions with negative meaning may be followed by negative polarity items, as in (4).

(4) He denies I *ever* told him.

B

(a) They won't finish it somehow.

(b) I'm against going out anywhere tonight.

(c) I like her a great deal.

(d) Her mother is not coming, too.

(e) He doesn't ever visit us.

(f) We were unaware of any hostility.

Based on the description in <A>, identify TWO ungrammatical sentences in <B>, and correct the ungrammatical sentences by replacing with an appropriate polarity item. Do not change the type of statement.

23 Read the passage <A> and the sentences in <B>, and follow the directions. [4 points]

---────── A ───────

In addition to the active and passive voices, in English there exists another voice, often called 'middle'. Consider the following:

(1) a. John opened the door.
    b. John cooked the casserole in the oven.
(2) a. The door was opened by John.
    b. The casserole was cooked in the oven by John.
(3) a. The door opened.
    b. The casserole cooked in the oven.

The sentences in (2) are passive forms of those in (1). Then what about (3)? The subject here is identical with that of the passive, but the verb is not in the passive but in the active form. As such, an intransitive verb that appears to be active but expresses a passive action characterizes the English middle voice. That is, we can say that English middle voices are syntactically active but semantically passive:

(4) a. John broke the window. → The window broke.
    b. John smashed the vase. → The vase smashed.
    c. John melted the ice. → The ice melted.

However, not all transitive verbs have middle voices. Verbs like *kick, buy*, etc. cannot be used in the form of middle voice:

(5) a. John kicked the bell. → *The bell kicked.
    b. John bought the vase. → *The vase bought.

Such middle voices in general describe permanent properties of the subject. This general semantic condition makes middle voice incompatible with duration adverbs:

(6) *This car drove smoothly last night.

In addition, these middle verbs do not allow the *by*-phrase:

(7) a. *The window broke by the child.
    b. *The vase smashed by the baby.

| B |

(a) The window hit.
(b) The bell rang.
(c) The cake is baking.
(d) This clothes washed well yesterday morning.
(e) The bank closes at 5p.m.
(f) Prices increased due to a variety of factors.

Identify TWO ungrammatical sentences in <B>, and explain why, ONLY based on the description in <A>.

_____
_____
_____
_____
_____

24 Read the passage <A> and the sentences in <B>, and follow the directions. [4 points]

┤ A ├

There are various constructions in English where we need to refer to the values of verb form, such as:

(1) a. The monkeys kept [forgetting/*forgot/*forgotten their lines]. (prp)
    b. We caught them [eating/*ate/*eat/*eaten the bananas]. (prp)
    c. John made Mary [cook/*to cook/*cooking Korean food]. (base)

In (1) each main verb here requires a VP as its complement (the part in brackets). For example, the finite verb *kept* selects as its complement a VP whose verb form is *prp* (present participle).

There are at least two types of adjectives in English in terms of complement selection: those selecting no complements at all, and those taking complements. As shown in the following examples, adjectives like *despondent* optionally take a complement, while *intelligent* does not take any complements:

(2) a. The monkey seems despondent (that it is in a cage).
    b. He seems intelligent (*to study medicine).

Adjectives such as *eager, fond* and *compatible* each select a complement, possibly of different categories (for example, VP or PP).

(3) a. Monkeys are eager [to leave/*leaving the compound].
    b. The chickens seem fond [of/*with the farmer].
    c. The foxes seem compatible [with/*for the chickens].
    d. The teacher is proud [of/*with his students].

These adjectives need the appropriate form of complement. For example, in (3b), the adjective *fond* requires the PP complement, and the head of PP needs *of*.

B

(a) The contract is subject to approval by my committee.
(b) It was a time fraught of difficulties and frustration.
(c) I am really terrible at sports.
(d) We were amazed with his reaction to our suggestion.
(e) His memory was tinged with sorrow.
(f) Some men are obsessed with physical exercises to develop their muscles.

Identify TWO ungrammatical sentences in <B>, and then explain why, stating the appropriate preposition, based on the description in <A>.

25 Read the passage <A> and the sentences in <B>, and follow the directions. [4 points]

A

Predicatives may be either obligatory or optional:

(1)   **OBLIGATORY**   **OPTIONAL**
     INTRANSITIVE   Kim became <u>ill</u>.   They departed <u>content</u>.
     TRANSITIVE   He made Kim <u>angry</u>.   He washed it <u>clean</u>.

Obligatory *ill* and *angry* here cannot be omitted without loss of grammaticality (*Kim became*) or an unsystematic change of meaning (the sense of *make* in *He made them angry* is not the same as in *He made them*). Optional *content* and *clean*, by contrast, can be omitted without any change to the rest: *They departed content* entails *They departed*, and *He washed it clean* entails *He washed it*.

Little further need be added here concerning complex-intransitives, where we have the four combinations shown in:

(2)   **OBLIGATORY**   **OPTIONAL**
     DEPICTIVE   They look <u>fantastic</u>.   He died <u>young</u>.
     RESULTATIVE   The boss got <u>angry</u>.   The pond froze <u>solid</u>.

Note that although *die* in *He died young* entails a change of state, the change does not involve his age, so that *young* has a (optional) depictive, not a (optional) resultative, interpretation—this is why we use the terms depictive and resultative for the predicative, rather than static vs dynamic, which apply to the situation as a whole.

Two of the most important kinds of copular clause are illustrated in:

(3) a. His daughter is very bright / a highly intelligent woman. [ascriptive]
    b. The chief culprit was Kim. [specifying]

In the ascriptive use, predicative complement (PC) denotes a property and characteristically has the form of an AdjP or a non-referential NP; the subject is most often referential and the clause ascribes the property to the subject-referent. Thus (3a), for example, ascribes to his daughter the property of being very bright or being a highly intelligent woman. The specifying use defines a variable and specifies its value. We might represent (3b), therefore, it serves to specify, or identify, who the chief culprit was.

┌─────────────────── B ───────────────────┐
(a) The parcel came open.
(b) It arrived open.
└──┘

Identify ONE ambiguous sentence in <B> and provide the two possible interpretations, stating their specific usage such as an (obligatory/optional) depictive, resultative, ascriptive, specifying interpretation, based on the description in <A>. (Do not write the meaning of each sentence.)

26 Read the passage <A> and the sentences in <B>, and follow the directions. [4 points]

---- A ----

The English negator *not* leads a double life: one as a nonfinite VP modifier when it is Constituent Negation and the other as a complement of a finite auxiliary verb when it is Sentential Negation.

For Constituent Negation, the properties of *not* as a nonfinite VP modifier can be supported from its similarities with adverbs such as *never* in nonfinite clauses as given in (1):

(1) a. Kim regrets [never/not [having seen the movie]].
　　b. We asked him [never/not [to try to call us again]].

The adverb *not* modifies any nonfinite VP. For example, in all the good examples in (2), *not* simply modifies a nonfinite VP.

(2) a. [Not [speaking English]] is a disadvantage.
　　b.*[Speaking not English] is a disadvantage.
　　c.*Lee likes not Kim.
　　d. Lee is believed [not [to like Kim]].

For Sentential Negation, *not* can modify a nonfinite VP, but not a finite VP:

(3) a. John could [not [leave the town]].
　　b. *John not could leave the town.

One possible piece of evidence to differentiate two types of *not* may come from scope possibilities in an example like (4). The negation in (4) could have the two different scope readings as given in (5).

(4) The president could not approve the bill.
(5) a. It would not be possible for the president to approve the bill. (Sentential Negation)
　　b. It would be possible for the president not to approve the bill. (Constituent Negation)

─┤ B ├─

(i) a. Duty made them not miss the weekly meeting.
   b. Lee is believed to not like Kim.
   c. John not left the town.
(ii) a. The president could not approve the bill, could he?
    b. The president could not approve the bill, couldn't he?

First, identify ONE ungrammatical sentence in (i) in <B>, and then explain why, specifying the VP. Second, in (ii) identify whether EACH sentence is Constituent Negation or Sentential Negation, ONLY based on the description in <A>.

27 Read the passage <A> and the sentences in <B>, and follow the directions. [4 points]

A

We classify partitive NPs into two types based on the agreement facts, and call them Type I and Type II. In Type I, the number value of the partitive phrase is always singular; the main verb must be singular.

(1) Type I: *Each* of the suggestions *is* acceptable.

In Type II, the number value depends on the head noun inside the *of*-NP phrase.

(2) Type II: a. *Most* of the fruit *is* rotten.
             b. *Most* of the children *are* here.

As shown in (2), when the NP following the preposition *of* is singular or uncountable, the main verb is singular. When the NP is plural, the verb is also plural. From a semantic perspective, we see that the class of quantificational indefinite pronouns including *most, half,* etc. may combine either singular or plural verbs, depending upon the reference of the *of*-NP phrase. If the meaning of these phrases is about how much of something is meant, the verb is singular; but if the meaning is about how many of something is meant, the verb is plural. The expressions in (3) also exhibit similar behavior in terms of agreement.

(3) half of, part of, the majority of, the rest of,
    two-thirds of, a number of (but not *the number of*)

Quantifiers like *each* affect the number value as well as the countability of the *of*-NP phrase. One difference between Type I and Type II is that Type I selects a plural *of*-NP phrase whereas Type II has no such restriction. This is illustrated in (4) and (5).

(4) Type I: each of the suggestions/*the suggestion/*his advice
(5) Type II: most of his advice/students

┌─────────────────────── B ───────────────────────┐
(a) None of these men want to be president.
(b) Some of the soup needs more salt.
(c) Some of the diners need menus.
(d) All of the land belongs to the government.
(e) One of the story has appeared in your newspaper.
(f) Much of that theory is unfounded.
└───┘

Identify TWO ungrammatical sentences in <B>, and then explain why, specifying the Types of partitive phrase (i.e., Type I or Type II), based on the description in <A>.

28 Read the passage <A> and the sentences in <B>, and follow the directions. [4 points]

─────────── A ───────────

Verbs like *resemble* do not have passive forms even if they are transitive verbs. There seems to exist other verbs with no passive counterparts:

(1) a. They have a nice house.
　　b. The coat does not fit you.
(2) a. *A nice house was had by them.
　　b. *You are not fit by the coat.

One can claim that these verbs lexically do not allow passive since they are inherently stative. However, observe the following contrast:

(3) a.*Oil is held by the jar.
　　b. The thief was held by the police.

Why do we have such a contrast? It appears that the semantic role assigned to the object seems to play a key role. Observe the further examples:

(4) a. *Jill was married by Jack.
　　b. They were married by the priest.

Though *married* generally does not allow passive, it can be passivized when the passive subject is influenced or affected by the action denoted by the main verb. This affected condition can be further found in the following contrast:

(5) a. *Six inches were grown by the boy.
　　b. The beans were grown by the gardener.

The main difference between possible and impossible examples here is that the passive subject is acted upon by an agent. That is, the passive subject is physically or psychologically affected by the action performed by the agent. This kind of 'affectedness condition' can account for the contrast in (5a) and (5b). *Six inches* cannot be affected by the action performed by the agent. But *beans* are under the direct influence from the action denoted by *the gardener*.

┌──────────────────────── B ────────────────────────┐
│ (a) The city was soon possessed by the enemy.   │
│ (b) A pound was weighed by the book.   │
│ (c) The plums were weighed by the greengrocer.   │
│ (d) Four is equalled by two and two.   │
│ (e) The gas station was run by a Korean-American. │
└───┘

Identify TWO ungrammatical sentences in <B>, and explain why, based on the description in <A>.

29. Read the passage <A> and the sentences in <B>, and follow the directions. [4 points]

― A ―

The passive verbs in general have verbal properties. However, there are cases with adjectival properties.

(1) a. Her actions embarrassed him.
   b. His success elated him.
(2) a. He was embarrassed by her actions.
   b. He was elated by his success.

These passives, though having corresponding actives, exhibit adjectival features as can be seen from the following contrast:

(3) a. His actions much/*very embarrassed her.
   b. His success much/*very elated him.
(4) a. He was *much/very embarrassed by her actions.
   b. He was *much/very elated by his success.

Though the active verbs in (3) can occur with the verb-modifying adverb *much*, the passive verbs in (4) cannot. They can occur only with the adjective-modifying adverb *very*.

One additional constraint on these verbs is that many of these semi-passives have prepositions other than *by*:

(5) a. They are satisfied with his actions.
   b. John is interested in linguistics.

In certain environments, passives allow *get* instead of *be*:

(6) a. I got phoned by a girl friend.
   b. When I start reading, I get motivated.

Get passives usually convey the speaker's personal involvement or reflect the speaker's opinion as to whether the event described is perceived as having favorable or unfavorable consequences. This is why it is rather unacceptable to use the *get* passive when the subject-referent has no control over the process in question, as in (7a); especially, *get* passives cannot occur with verbs that describe cognition in (7b). This means that the verb *get* selects a VP with an additional semantic or pragmatic condition.

(7) a. *Mary got heard to insult her parents.
  b. *His solution to the problem got known by everyone.

B

(a) John was very startled to move.
(b) She was much concerned by her failure.
(c) They got very frightened.
(d) John deliberately got fired from his job.
(e) Sally got arrested on purpose.
(f) Tom got understood to have asked for a refund.

Identify TWO ungrammatical sentences in <B>, and then explain why, based on the description in <A>.

멘토영어학
문제은행

Part 03
Phonetics & Phonology

PART 03 Phonetics & Phonology

• Answer Key p.49

01 Read the passage and fill in the blank ① with ONE word from the passage and the blank ② with the appropriate feature from the passage. Write your answers in the correct order. [2 points]

> Stops, fricatives, nasals, and liquids are all [+ consonantal]; in their articulation the lower lip or some part of the tongue impedes the flow of air in some way, in some part of the mouth. The four classes together are called consonants. Vowels and glides are articulated without such impedance; they are [− consonantal]. For vowels and glides it is the shape of the oral cavity in which air is flowing freely that determines the quality of the sound produced. Glides are like certain vowels in their production, but they are like _____①_____ in the positions they occupy in syllables and larger units.
>
> The four classes of consonants differ from one another in their manner of articulation, specifically in whether or not the articulation is characterized by periodic vibration of air particles and in whether or not the air stream is escaping from the mouth during the articulation. We can express these differences with the features [sonorant] and [continuant] below.
>
> | liquids | nasals | fricatives | stops |
> |---|---|---|---|
> | + sonorant | + sonorant | − sonorant | − sonorant |
> | + continuant | ② | + continuant | − continuant |

Liquids and nasals are 'musical' like vowels. Although the air stream is obstructed in some way, the vocal tract still acts as a resonance chamber in which air particles flow in periodic waves. Obstruent consonants—fricatives and plosives—are articulated with total or near-total obstruction of the air stream so that resonance is minimal or absent. For liquids and fricatives air flows out from the mouth during articulation; thus any of these consonants can be held—continued—as long as the lungs provide air. Nasals can also be prolonged since air escapes during their articulation, but through the nasal cavity alone. A stop, since it involves complete obstruction of the breath stream, is essentially an instant of silence.

02 Read the passage and follow the directions. [4 points]

The normally accepted definition of the foot is that each phonological foot starts with a stressed syllable, and continues up to, but not including, the next stressed syllable. Feet can be classified into types, three of which are shown in (1).

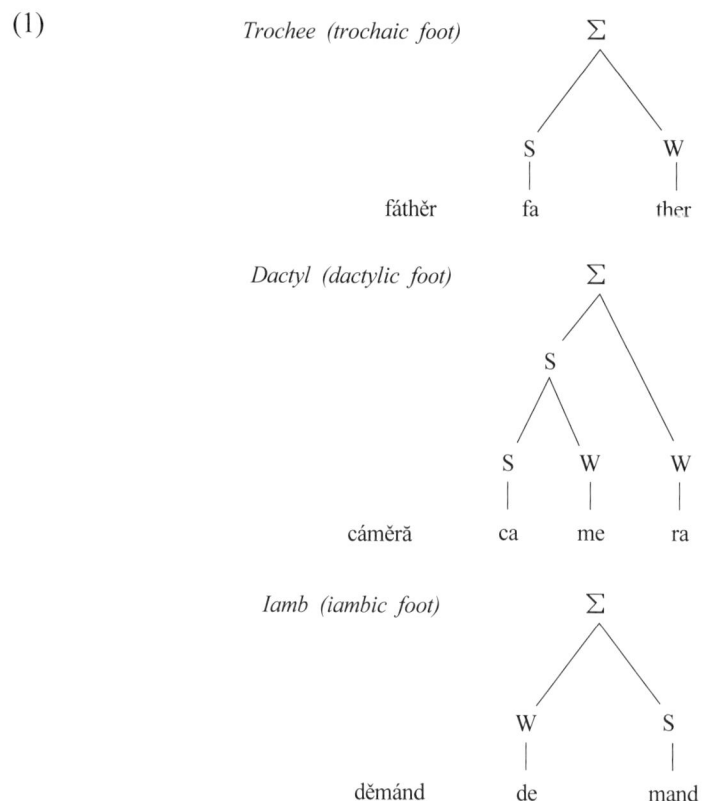

The English process of Iambic Reversal seems designed precisely to avoid either lapses, where too many unstressed syllables intervene between stresses, or clashes, where stresses are adjacent, with no unstressed syllables in between at all. It affects combinations of words which would, in isolation, have final stress on the first word, and initial stress on the second. For instance, (2) shows that the citation form of *thirteen* has final stress.

(2) A: How many people turned up?
   B: ˌThir'teen

However, take a look at the following case when final-stressed words like *thirteen* form phrases with initial-stressed ones like *players*, as illustrated in (3).

(3) W S   S W   S W   S W
    thirteen   players → thirteen players

If these words retained their normal stress pattern, we would find clashing sequences of WSSW, as shown on the left of (3); consequently, the prominence pattern of the first word is reversed. The result is a sequence of two trochaic feet, SWSW.

Now, consider the example in (4).

(4) champagne cocktails

Based on the passage, first, identify whether Iambic Reversal occurs in the phrase 'champagne cocktails' in (4). Second, if so, state the reason why it occurs and the process of stress alternation.

03 Read the passage and follow the directions. [4 points]

Although the word *stem* has multiple meanings in linguistics, it is the minimal constituent within a word that can stand as an independent word. Thus, in *jumping* [[dʒʌmp]ᵥ ɪŋ]ₙ, the stem is [dʒʌmp]ᵥ. In *identifier* [[[aɪdɛnt] ɪfaɪ]ᵥ ɚ]ₙ, the stem is [aɪdɛntɪfaɪ]ᵥ. Although we can recognize a smaller root morpheme [aɪdɛnt] within this word (compare *identity, identical*), we will not consider it to be the stem, since it cannot occur as an independent word.

Consider now an example of a stem-bounded rule. The following rule occurs in some version in a number of English dialects:

(1) Pre-/l/ Monophthongization
    oʊ → o / ___ l

(2) /oʊ/ before /l/: [o]   /oʊ/ in other environments: [oʊ]
    hole [hol]   Poe [poʊ]
    poultry [poltʃɹi]   moat [moʊt]
    mole [mol]   propane [pɹoʊpeɪn]
    mold [mold]   toad [toʊd]

The above are all simple, monomorphemic forms. The more subtle effects occur when we add suffixes to stems that end in /oʊ/ or in /oʊ/ plus /l/.

(3) slow-ly [sloʊli]   toe-less [toʊləs]   low-land-s [loʊləndz]
(4) goal-ie [goli]   hole-y [holi]   roll-ing [ɹolɪŋ]

It can be seen that underlying /oʊ/ gets monophthongized only if it is in the same stem as the immediately following /l/.

Now consider the following examples of Vowel Nasalization:

(5) Venus [vĩnəs]   freeness [fɹinəs]
    bonus [bõʊ̃nəs]   slowness [sloʊnəs]
    Uranus [jʊɹẽɪ̃nəs]   greyness [gɹeɪnəs]
    Linus [lãɪ̃nəs]   dryness [dɹaɪnəs]

Based on the passage, state the environment where the Vowel Nasalization occurs in (5), ONLY using the terms in the passage.

04 Read the passage and fill in the blank ① with ONE word from the passage and the blank ② with the ONE most appropriate word. Write your answers in the correct order. [2 points]

We can classify the suffixes as:

(a) stress-bearing suffixes;
(b) stress-shifting suffixes;
(c) stress-neutral suffixes.

The common element between groups (a) and (b), when added to a root, is that they change the location of the stress from its original position. Stress-bearing suffixes attract the stress to themselves, while stress-shifting suffixes move the stress to some other syllable. Groups (b) and (c) have the common element of not carrying stress.

Below are some common derivational suffixes:

(1) -ade   lemon — lemonade
     -aire   million — millionaire
     -ation   realize — realization
     -ee   absent — absentee
     -eer   mountain — mountaineer
     -ese   Japan — Japanese
     -esque   picture — picturesque
     -ette   kitchen — kitchenette
     -itis   larynx — laryngitis
     -ific   honor — honorific

Expectedly, these stress- _____①_____ suffixes always constitute _____②_____ syllables considering syllable weight. The items above with suffixes should not be confused with the same/similar-looking monomorphemic forms such as *brigade, jamboree, grotesque, brunette, bursitis*, etc.

05 Read the passages and follow the directions. [4 points]

┤ A ├

A morpheme is said to alternate when it appears in different forms in different contexts. The analysis of alternations is one of the central areas of phonology. Alternation often arises because of the way that phonology interacts with morphology.

We will be observing the relationship of three phonological rules with two rules of derivational morphology, given below in (1).

(1) a. *-able* Affixation: Verb + əbəl → Adjective
"able to be Verbed"
b. *-ation* Affixation: Verb + ˈeʃən → Noun
"the process or product of Verbing"

The reason morphological rules are of phonological interest is that they can rearrange the phonological environments of the phonemes. The segments of prefixes and suffixes can themselves be part of the environment of a phonological process. Consider the following data in (2):

(2) note   notable   notation

Let us consider the particular allophone of /t/ that emerges in these forms. In *note* occurring by themselves, the /t/ phoneme is at the end of a word. It is thus eligible for Preglottalization, and emerges as the allophone [ʔt].

Once the morphology has arranged the appropriate suffixes, the phonological form of words is accommodated to the new environments that are created. The selection of the proper allophone of /t/ is not established for the stem /not/ once and for all, but rather is determined on the basis of the environment in which the stem-final /t/ appears.

Referring to the definition of alternation, we see that the morpheme *note* does indeed alternate: depending on the context (which the morphology creates for them), they take on different forms. For example, the phonological form of the word *note* is [ˈnoʔt].

B

Here are some phonological rules of English, all of which apply to the phoneme /t/ and give rise to alternation:

(1) Preglottalization: A voiceless stop is preglottalized [ˀp, ˀt, ˀk] when in final position.
(2) Glottal stop replacement: The glottal stop replacement [ʔ] requires the target /t/ to be in a syllable-final position.
(3) Tapping: The /t/ phoneme is realized as a tap [ɾ] just in case it occurs between two vowels of which the second is stressless.
(4) Aspiration: Voiceless stops are aspirated [pʰ, tʰ, kʰ] when they precede a stressed vowel and are not preceded by /s/.

Based on the passages, first, state the phonological forms of the words 'notable' and 'notation' with the proper allophone of /t/ and the primary stress mark, ONLY using phonetic symbols shown in the passages. Second, state which phonological rule in <B> is applied in each word.

06 Read the passage and follow the directions. [4 points]

--- A ---

The prominence patterns of compounds systematically have nonphrasal stress patterns as shown in (1):

(1) a. ['AB]
   greenhouse
   filing cabinet
 b. [['AB] C]
   blackboard eraser
   house-warming party
 c. [A ['BC]]
   government working party
   university works department
 d. [[ˌAB] ['CD]]
   engine oil filler cap
   car maintenance training course
 e. [[A ['BC]] D]
   parish coffee-morning committee
   university car-park inspector

The prominence patterns displayed in (1) fall into groups, clearly determined by internal syntactic structure, suggests the possibility of a generalisation. Let us simplify matters by merely looking at (1a-c) in the first instance.

The form of metrical trees for compounds is determined by the internal structure. Note that in each case the metrical tree is a copy of the internal syntactic structure of the compound, and that the prominence relations in the metrical tree express the stress patterns indicated in (1).

(2) a.   b.   c.
        /\   /S\   / \
       / \   /   \   /   \
      S   W   /\   W   W   (S)
   green house S W   eraser government /\
               blackboard   S   W
                                    working party

This more restricted set of data reveals the generalisation. Looking again particularly at the behaviour of the right-hand node in each pair, we notice that this node is not invariably strong but only under certain conditions:

(3) Compound Prominence Rule
   In a pair of sister nodes $[N_1\ N_2]_L$, where L is a lexical category, N_2 is strong if it branches above the word level.

   In (2b), for example, N_1 is *blackboard* and N_2 is *eraser*. Since N_2 does not branch above the word level, N_2 is not strong. In contrast, in (2c) N_1 is *government* and N_2 is *working party*. Since N_2 branches above the word level, N_2 becomes strong.

─────────────── B ───────────────

(a) home word-processing equipment
(b) schools liaison committee meeting
(c) Labour party finance committee
(d) arts faculty entrance test
(e) schools liaison committee
(f) word-processing equipment

Based on the passage, first, divide the examples in <B> into two groups of the same internal structure. Second, identify the internal structure of each group, using the numbers (1a)—(1e) in <A>.

07 Read the passage and fill in each blank with the appropriate feature. Write your answers in the correct order. [2 points]

> Liquids, the consonants which begin the words *led* and *red*, for instance, were shown to be
>
> [± syllabic]
> [+ consonantal]
> [+ continuant]
> [+ sonorant]
>
> We can now add two other features which the liquids share: they are [+ voice] and [− sibilant].
>
> How do /l/ and /r/ differ from each other? Phonologists who use the features [anterior] and [coronal] say that /l/ is [+ anterior] and /r/ is _____①_____ since /l/ is sometimes articulated with the tip of the tongue on the alveolar ridge and /r/ is never articulated so far forward. However, both consonants are articulated in different parts of the mouth; neither the articulator nor the place of articulation is truly distinctive for these two consonants. What distinguishes them from each other is the shape of the tongue. One of them, /l/, is articulated with the sides of the tongue curled in and air escaping over the sides. We say that /l/ is [+ lateral].
>
> For /r/ the tongue is also curled but in a different way; the whole body of the tongue is pulled back and bunched up, with a slight groove in the very tip— not a groove along the center line of the surface, which would make it a sibilant. Typically, there is also some rounding of the lips. Instead of pulling the tongue back and humping it up, some speakers turn the tongue-tip backward; hence the term 'retroflex' has been used by some phoneticians, but this name is not appropriate for the most usual articulation. Various appropriate names might be used to describe the physical facts of articulation. To place /r/ in a system of distinctive features it is enough to say that it is _____②_____.

08 Read the passage and follow the directions. [4 points]

English has rules of phonological neutralization. The one to be discussed here takes the form of a deletion: the contrast that is wiped out is that of /t/ with zero. Consider first some minimal pairs demonstrating this contrast. We are particularly interested in cases where the /t/ follows an /n/:

(1) plant [plænt]   vs.   plan [plæn]
    stunt [stʌnt]   vs.   stun [stʌn]
    bent [bɛnt]   vs.   Ben [bɛn]

There are also a fair number of near-minimal pairs:

(2) Bentley ['bɛntli]   vs.   Henley ['hɛnli]
    until [ən'tɪl]   vs.   anneal [ə'nil]

Since all of the examples on the left-hand side are selected to have /t/ preceded by /n/, we can also describe the contrast by saying that /nt/ contrasts with /n/.
  Now, let us consider a number of groups of words that share the same morphological stem. The pronunciations given are not common to all dialects of English, but are common in North America.

(3) plant ['plænt]   planter ['plænɚ]
    plan ['plæn]   planner ['plænɚ]
    stunt ['stʌnt]   stunting ['stʌnɪŋ]
    stun ['stʌn]   stunning ['stʌnɪŋ]
    punt ['pʌnt]   punting ['pʌnɪŋ]
    pun ['pʌn]   punning ['pʌnɪŋ]

Our assertion is that, at least for some speakers and in some speech styles, *planter* is pronounced identically to *planner*, and similarly for the other pairs. The rule involved, to which we will now turn, is evidently a neutralizing one.

From the data, we know that the /t/ is maintained after /n/ when the /t/ is at the end of a word (['stʌnt]); moreover, in the relatively few cases where an /nt/ sequence is followed by a consonant (others include *entry* ['ɛntɹi], *antler* ['æntlɚ] and *Antwerp* ['æntwɚp]), the /t/ survives. Additional data given below indicate that stress also plays a role:

(4) mental ['mɛnəl]   mentality [mɛn'tælɪɾi]
    scientist ['saɪənəst]   scientific [ˌsaɪən'tɪfɪk]

Thus we can state the rule as follows:

(5) /t/ is deleted when _____.

Neutralization creates ambiguous utterances; thus on hearing [ðeɪɹ'plænɪŋəˈgɑɹdən] from a native speaker of this dialect, only context or further queries can determine the speaker's intent.

Based on the passage, first, complete the rule by filling in the blank in (5). Second, state the TWO possible interpretations of [ðeɪɹ'plænɪŋəˈgɑɹdən] (i.e., write the two sentences for the given utterance).

09
Read the passage and fill in the blank ① with the ONE most appropriate word and the blank ② with ONE word from the passage. Write your answers in the correct order. [2 points]

> Complementary distribution is a fundamental concept of phonology, and interestingly enough, it shows up in everyday life. Table 1 shows that aspirated and unaspirated voiceless stop consonants are in complementary distribution. In general, then, the allophones of a phoneme are in complementary distribution—never occurring in identical environments.
>
> | Syllable-Initial before a Stressed Vowel | | | After a Syllable-Initial /s/ | | | Nonword* | | |
> |---|---|---|---|---|---|---|---|---|
> | [pʰ] | [tʰ] | [kʰ] | [p] | [t] | [k] | | | |
> | *pill* | *till* | *kill* | *spill* | *still* | *skill* | [pɪl]* | [tɪl]* | [kɪl]* |
> | [pʰɪl] | [tʰɪl] | [kʰɪl] | [spɪl] | [stɪl] | [skɪl] | [spʰɪl]* | [stʰɪl]* | [skʰɪl]* |
> | *par* | *tar* | *car* | *spar* | *star* | *scar* | [paɹ]* | [taɹ]* | [kaɹ]* |
> | [pʰaɹ] | [tʰaɹ] | [kʰaɹ] | [spaɹ] | [staɹ] | [skaɹ] | [spʰaɹ]* | [stʰaɹ]* | [skʰaɹ]* |
>
> <Table 1. Distribution of Aspirated Voiceless Stops>
>
> Two sounds are in complementary distribution if /X/ never appears in any of the phonetic environments in which /Y/ occurs.
>
> Complementary distribution alone is insufficient for determining the allophones when there is more than one allophone in the set. The phones must also be phonetically similar, that is, share most phonetic features.
>
> In English, the velar nasal [ŋ] and the glottal fricative [h] are in complementary distribution; [ŋ] does not occur word-initially and [h] does not occur word-finally. But they share very few phonetic features: [ŋ] is a voiced velar nasal stop; [h] is a voiceless glottal fricative. Therefore, they are not allophones of the same phoneme; [ŋ] and [h] are allophones of ____①____ phonemes.
>
> Two or more sounds are allophones (positional variants) of the ____②____ phoneme, if (a) they are in complementary distribution, and (b) they are phonetically similar.

10 Read the passage and follow the directions. [4 points]

Languages are permeated with variation: we frequently say the same thing in different ways. The variation in phonology takes two forms. One is the phenomenon of *phonological doublets*, in which one word happens to have two different phonemic forms. For instance, in many people's speech, the word in (1) can be pronounced either way.

(1) economics [ˌikəˈnamɪks], [ˌɛkəˈnamɪks]

This does not refer to instances in which different people say certain words differently; rather, a doublet is a case where one and the same person uses both variants. The usual treatment of phonological doublets posits that in the lexicon (the mental store of words in the mind/brain), they have just one listing for their syntactic properties and meaning, but more than one phonemic representation.

The other kind of variation in phonology is when a single phonemic representation gives rise to more than one phonetic form; this is called *free variation*. Here is one example found in the speech of many Americans. In the dialect in question, the vowel phoneme /æ/ has a diphthongal allophone I will transcribe as [ɛə͡]. Some data on the distribution of [ɛə͡] vs. [æ] are given below:

(2) [æ]   [ɛə͡]
   lap /læp/ [læp]   man /mæn/ [mɛə͡n], [mæn]
   pal /pæl/ [pæl]   Spanish /spænɪʃ/ [spɛə͡nɪʃ], [spænɪʃ]
   pack /pæk/ [pæk]   dance /dæns/ [dɛə͡ns], [dæns]
   lab /læb/ [læb]   flannel /ˈflænəl/ [ˈflɛə͡nəl], [ˈflænəl]

> To summarize the pattern: if an /n/ follows /æ/, then there are two outputs, one with [ɛ̃ə̃] and one with [æ̃]. Otherwise, the observed allophone is [æ]. This [ɛ̃ə̃]~[æ̃] pattern is systematic; it holds not just for these four words, but for any word in this dialect in which /æ/ precedes /n/.
>
> In analyzing the data, we should first dispose of the distribution of nasality. The nasalization seen on both [ɛ̃ə̃] and [æ̃] is plainly the consequence of Vowel Nasalization. More crucial is the free variation between the monophthongal and diphthongal allophones. These cannot be phonological doublets because they are part of a systematic pattern rather than being idiosyncratic. We need to express the variation with a rule.
>
> An appropriate analysis, then, would be as follows. We set up /æ/ as the basic form of the phoneme, and include the following rule.
>
> (3) /æ/ Diphthongization
>   æ → ɛə / _____ n
>   The phoneme /æ/ can be realized as [ɛə] when it precedes /n/.

Based on the passage, first, identify the variation form of the words 'envelope' and 'ban', respectively (i.e., either phonological doublets or free variation). Second, explain why, ONLY based on the description in the passage.

_____
_____
_____
_____
_____

11 Read the passage and follow the directions. [4 points]

─┤ A ├─

Each set of data in (1) exemplifies an alternation of two phonemes, which takes place when an affix is added to the end of the word.

(1) a. medic — medicine
      toxic — toxicity
      classic — classicist
      critic — criticism
  c. suffice — sufficient
      race — racial
      depress — depression
      sense — sensual

b. democrat — democracy
   subvert — subversive
   pirate — piracy
   complacent — complacency
d. revise — revision
   enclose — enclosure
   confuse — confusion
   erase — erasure

The alternations exemplified in this data are quite regular, and can be expressed in the form of a rule; for example, in (1a), /k/ becomes /s/ when the affix begins with the vowel /ɪ/. Similarly, in (1b), /t/ becomes /s/ under the same condition. We can combine these two rules as in (2):

(2) Rule 1 $\left\{\begin{matrix} k \\ t \end{matrix}\right\} \rightarrow s\ /\ \_\_\_ + \text{ɪ}$

(1c) and (1d) illustrate a different rule; /s/ changes to /ʃ/, and /z/ changes to /ʒ/. It seems that this change takes place when the affix begins with /ɪ/ or /j/, followed immediately by a vowel. But when the preceding consonant is /s/, the sequences /sɪ/ or /sj/ coalesce into /ʃ/. Similarly, the sequences /zɪ/ or /zj/ coalesce into /ʒ/. This happens only when another vowel follows immediately. The rule can be formulated as in (3):

(3) Rule 2 $\left\{\begin{matrix} s \\ z \end{matrix}\right\} + \left\{\begin{matrix} \text{ɪ} \\ j \end{matrix}\right\} + \left\{\begin{matrix} ʃ \\ ʒ \end{matrix}\right\}\ /\ \_\_\_ V$

Now look at the following data in (4). From the data given, work out which two phonemes are in alternation:

(4) a. relate — relation
    confident — confidential
    convert — conversion
    infect — infectious

b. magic — magician
   music — musician
   silica — siliceous

Set (4a) illustrates a relationship between /t/ and /ʃ/; set (4b) a relationship between /k/ and /ʃ/. The environment requires an affix which begins with /ɪ/ or /j/, followed immediately by a vowel, as in sets (1c) and (1d) above. The rule for (4a) and (4b) combined is therefore as follows:

(5) Rule 3 $\begin{Bmatrix} k \\ t \end{Bmatrix} + \begin{Bmatrix} \text{ɪ} \\ j \end{Bmatrix} \rightarrow \text{ʃ} /$ __ V

⊣ B ⊢

| logician | fanaticism | incision |
| malicious | permissive | presidential |

Based on the passage, first, identify TWO words in <B> that Rule 3 is applied. Second, state how the rule is applied to each word, just as described in the passage.

12 Read the passage and fill in each blank with the ONE most appropriate word. Write your answers in the correct order. [2 points]

> Assimilation rules in languages reflect coarticulation—the spreading of phonetic features either in the anticipation or in the perseveration of articulatory processes. The auditory effect is that words sound smoother.
>
> There are many assimilation rules in English and other languages. The voiced /z/ of the English regular plural suffix is changed to [s] after a voiceless sound, and that similarly the voiced /d/ of the English regular past-tense suffix is changed to [t] after a voiceless sound. These are instances of voicing assimilation. In these cases the value of the voicing feature goes from [+ voice] to [− voice] because of assimilation to the [− voice] feature of the final consonant of the stem, as in the derivation of *cats*:
>
> (1) /kæt + z/ → [kæts]
>
> We saw a different kind of assimilation rule. Regressive assimilation helps explain the various allomorphic forms of the English negative prefix: *in-, im-, ir-, il-*. Note that the unmarked prefix *in-* occurs in all cases except when the following sound is a bilabial or a liquid: *indecent, inept, invalid*. However, when the following sound is a bilabial, the organs of speech approach a position closer to that of the conditioning sound to produce [ɪm-], as in *impossible* or *immobile* and to produce [ɪŋ-], as in *incongruous* or *incorrect*. In these cases, the negative morpheme prefix spelled *in-* or *im-* agrees in ____①____ of articulation with the word to which it is prefixed. Similarly, when followed by the liquids /l/ and /r/, the negative prefix is conditioned or changed to *il-* and *ir-* respectively, as in *illogical* and *irrational*. In these data, the negative morpheme prefix agrees in ____②____ of articulation.

13 Read the passage and follow the directions. [4 points]

The core of the Scottish Vowel-Length Rule (SVLR) has been stated as follows: while lax vowels are invariably short, tense vowels are either long or short, depending on their contexts. Long realisation of tense-vowel phonemes is somehow related to their position: either word or morphological boundary. Consider the following examples:

(1) a. Long vowel   Short vowel
    /i/ breathe leave ease ear see   Leith leaf leash leap feel keen
    /e/ wave maze bear day   pace waif fake fade fail name
    /a/ halve vase par spa   half pass path mad cap calm
    /u/ smooth groove sure shoe   youth hoof use loot fool tune
    /o/ loathe grove pose shore go   loaf close loath coat foal foam
    /ɔ/ pause paw   cough loss bought cot call done

   b. Short vowel
    /ɪ/ give fizz pith dish fill lip fin
    /ɛ/ rev Des her mess pet tell ten
    /ʌ/ love does duff lush pull cup pun

Example (1a) shows the distribution of long and short realisations of the tense-vowel phonemes: they are realised as long before a/an ____①____ boundary, a non-lateral /r/ and the other environment, but they are short elsewhere. The lax vowel phonemes are realised as short in all contexts, including those where tense vowels would be long *(love, live, rev* etc.).

Of the three diphthongs of Scottish Standard English (SSE), /aɪ aʊ ɔɪ/, the first one somewhat surprisingly is subject to SVLR. Here are some examples:

(2) 'long' [aˑɪ]   'short' [ʌɪ]
    drive rise writhe shy   life rice light file fine

SVLR has presented a problem for the analysis: /aɪ/ is the only diphthong that undergoes SVLR.

Now consider the following data in (3). SVLR occurs in a/an ____②____ boundary rather than the position before a pause or at the end of an utterance:

(3) a. Long vowel
    kneed brewed stayed
    towed gnawed baad sighed
    freely slowness

b. Short vowel
    need brood staid
    toad nod bad side
    Healey bonus

Based on the passage, first, fill in each blank with ONE word from the passage. Write your answers in the correct order. Second, state one more environment where tense-vowel phonemes are realised as long in (1).

14 Read the passage and follow the directions. [4 points]

---- A ----

The words listed in (1) below have final stress (as marked) for many speakers.

(1) a. ca'det   b. ˌmar'quee   c. ba'lloon   d. e'llipse
    ca'nal   de'gree   ˌar'cade   la'ment
    ga'zette   ca'noe   ra'vine   ri'poste
    ˌmarzi'pan   ˌbou'quet   ˌcham'pagne   ˌcomman'dant
    ˌcatama'ran   ˌlam'poon
                                   maga'zine

The syllable-weight requirement for stressed syllables makes the prediction that there are no final-stressed words in English that end in a light syllable—just as there are no monosyllabic words consisting of a light syllable. This prediction is correct: no English word with final stress ends in a lax vowel. All the examples in (1) end in heavy syllables: (1a) ends in VC, (1b) in V:, (1c) in V:C and (1d) in V(:)CC. This fact confirms the correlation between syllable weight and stress. Another observation regarding this correlation can be made among the bisyllabic words in (1).

What the list in (1) does not reveal is the fact that nouns with final stress are comparatively rare in English; indeed, the length of this list is somewhat misleading. Many of the examples given there are rather uncommon loan words, and it would be difficult to compile such a collection if one were to exclude such rare words, just as it would be to double the list.

The reader may well have disagreed with some of the stress patterns given in (1): for example, in some dialects (or for certain speakers, or in colloquial speech) we find 'commanˌdant, 'marziˌpan, 'arcade, 'bouquet etc. Notice also the variable stress patterns in the following words, not listed in (1):

(2) finance: [fɪ'næns] or [ˌfaɪ'næns] or ['faɪˌnæns]
    romance: [rə'mæns] or [ˌro'mæns] or ['roˌmæns]

As a result of these stress shifts (speaker-, dialect-, style- or contextspecific), then, the class of end-stressed nouns is unstable. Now consider common class of nouns that constantly have a primary-secondary stress pattern, as in (3):

(3) ˈrabˌbi   ˈsynˌtax   ˈchromoˌsome
    ˈkumˌquat   ˈtexˌtile   ˈnightinˌgale

─┤ B ├─

Consider the following nouns in (4):

(4) artiste   hotel   camomile
    brigade   bamboo   convoy

Based on the passage, first, identify TWO words in <B> which show the same stress pattern as in (3). Second, state the requirement where secondary stress occurs on the first syllable among the bisyllabic examples in (1).

15 Read the passage and fill in each blank with ONE word from the passage. Write your answers in the correct order. [2 points]

> One of the most important factors in locating stress within the word is syllable structure. Consider the stress placement in the nouns listed below, where syllable boundaries are indicated by dots.
>
> (1) e.le.phant
> wa.lla.by
> al.ge.bra
> oc.to.pus
>
> (2) hy.e.na
> com.pu.ter
> po.ta.to
> ko.a.la
>
> (3) ve.ran.da
> u.ten.sil
> con.vic.tion
> pen.tath.lon
>
> In (1), the words have _____①_____ stress, whereas those in (2) and (3) have stress on the penultimate syllable. For the majority of nouns in English, stress is determined by the nature of the penultimate syllable, or more specifically the nature of the rhyme of the penultimate syllable, since what (if anything) is in the onset is irrelevant to stress placement. In (1) the penultimate rhyme is just a short vowel nucleus, whereas in (2) the penultimate rhyme has a long vowel or a diphthong in the nucleus and in (3) the penultimate rhyme is a short vowel nucleus followed by a consonant in the coda. So there is more 'phonological material' in the rhymes of the penultimate syllables in the words in (2) and (3).

Syllables (or rhymes) consisting of long vowels, diphthongs or those with codas, such as those exemplified by the penults in (2) and (3) are known as heavy; syllables with rhymes consisting only of a short vowel are known as light. For the majority of English nouns of more than two syllables, if the penultimate syllable is heavy, it takes stress; if the penultimate syllable is light, stress is placed one syllable to the left, on the antepenultimate (even if this is also light). In two syllable words, the words typically have stress on the ____②____ syllable irrespective of its weight, as shown in (4).

(4) muskrat   turnip   parrot   cobra

16 Read the passage and follow the directions. [4 points]

> Nasal consonants are particularly susceptible to assimilation. In morpheme-final clusters, the nasal is always homorganic with the following plosive, that is, they share the same place of articulation.
>
> However, the process is even more extensive than this. We can see from this data that the nasal's locus of articulation varies quite precisely according to the following obstruent. Look at the following data:
>
> (1) lamp   [-mp]   (bilabial)
>   lymph   [-ɱf]   (labio-dental)
>   tenth   [-n̪θ]   (dental)
>   hint   [-nt]   (alveolar)
>   inch   [-ɲtʃ]   (palato-alveolar)
>   wink   [-ŋk]   (velar)
>
> Nasal assimilation is sensitive not only to the locus of the following obstruent, but also to the (wider) environments in which it occurs. The examples in (1) above illustrate its operation within the morpheme.
>
> Nasal assimilation operates across syllable boundaries, as in *amphora* ([-ɱf-]); and it also operates in the following environment as in (2).
>
> (2) [ʌmprədʌktiv]   unproductive
>   [ʌmbitn̩]   unbeaten
>   [ɪŋkəplit]   incomplete
>   [ʌŋgreʃəs]   ungracious
>
> In this case the assimilation is optional: pronunciations with [ɪn-, ʌn-] are also possible. There is also optional assimilation as shown in (3):
>
> (3) [ɪm fækt]   in fact
>   [ɪŋ kes]   in case
>   [tʃeŋ gæŋ]   chain gang

Yet, despite the fact that nasal assimilation occurs across some boundaries, it does not occur before a/an _____ suffix and a past tense suffix even though the nasal precedes the obstruent, as shown in (4):

(4) [rɪnz]   rings
     [sɪnz]   sings
     [sʌmz]   sums
     [rɪnd]   ringed
     [rɑnd]   wronged

Based on the passage, first, fill in the blank with the ONE most appropriate word. Second, state each environment where nasal assimilation optionally occurs in (2) and (3).

17 Read the passages and follow the directions. [4 points]

A

A stop is a sound that involves complete closure of the oral cavity. The articulators come so close together that no air can escape between them.

In continuants, on the other hand, the air stream is not totally blocked in the oral cavity—it can escape continuously through the mouth. The consonants in *sue, zoo, lie, you, thigh,* etc. are continuants.

Note that definitions of stops and continuants are mutually exclusive: any sound that is not a stop is a continuant, and vice versa. We may therefore distinguish speech sounds in terms of the binary feature [+ continuant] vs [− continuant]. Example (1) below gives some examples of this phonetic distinction:

(1) [+ continuant]   [− continuant]
    rye, lie, you, woo   pea, tea, key
    thigh, thy, sue, zoo, etc.   buy, die, guy
    all vowels   my, nigh, etc.

Obviously, this distinction alone does not suffice to characterise manners of articulation in precise phonetic terms. A sonorant is a sound whose phonetic content is predominantly made up by the sound waves produced by its voicing. In other words, sonorants are characterised by 'periodic acoustic energy'. There are no voiceless sonorants because, simply speaking, the removal of voicing from a sonorant makes it nondistinct from other members of this set and practically inaudible.

In contrast, obstruent articulation involves an obstruction of the air stream that produces a phonetic effect independent of voicing. Obstruents can typically occur in voiced and voiceless variants. Sonorants are always voiced.

Again, the two categories, sonorant and obstruent, have been defined in a mutually exclusive way: any nonsonorant is automatically an obstruent and vice versa. We may simplify our terminology and characterise speech sounds as either [+ sonorant] or [− sonorant]. The list in (2) below gives some English examples of both.

(2) [+ sonorant]　　[− sonorant]
　　my, nigh　　　pea, tea, key
　　lie, rye　　　　buy, die, guy
　　you, woo　　　thigh, sue, etc.
　　all vowels　　　thy, zoo, etc.

Together, the two features make up manners of articulation or, to put it the other way around, what we refer to as manners of articulation are combinations of the basic properties that the two features describe.

─┤ B ├─

Two features, each of them binary, can be combined with each other in four different ways. In the case of the features [Sonorant] and [Continuant], the four combinations given in (3) below are possible; any given sound will fit into one of these four categories:

(3) a. $\begin{bmatrix} -\text{continuant} \\ +\text{sonorant} \end{bmatrix}$　b. $\begin{bmatrix} -\text{continuant} \\ -\text{sonorant} \end{bmatrix}$　c. $\begin{bmatrix} +\text{continuant} \\ -\text{sonorant} \end{bmatrix}$　d. $\begin{bmatrix} +\text{continuant} \\ +\text{sonorant} \end{bmatrix}$

Based on the passages, first, identify the feature combinations of all stop sounds, using the number (3a—3d) in <B>. Second, state ONE natural class of consonant sounds that the feature combination (3d) refers to.

18 Read the passage and follow the directions. [4 points]

The rhyme of a syllable is a unit that consists of the peak and the coda. But one question arises here: why do we need to recognise the rhyme as a phonological unit? Why do we not simply analyse a syllable (such as *clamp*) as in (1a) and propose instead the rather more complex analysis (1b)?

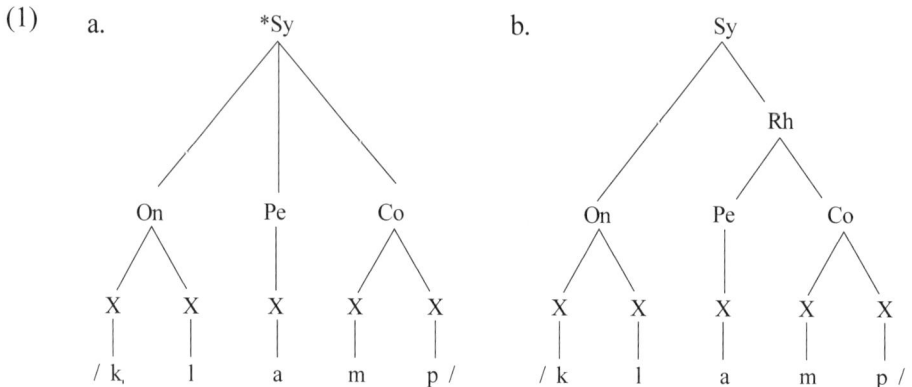

Note: Sy = Syllable, On = Onset, Pe = Peak, Co = Coda, Rh = Rhyme

The reason for having the rhyme as a unit is that peak and coda 'function together' rather than separately in a number of ways. In the case of monosyllabic words, it can be shown that it is the number of X-positions in the rhyme that determines whether or not a syllable is well-formed. Consider the following examples:

(2) a. eye   b. sit   c. seal   d. clamp   e. */klaɪmp/   f. finds

Ignoring the example in (2f), we find that (2a-d) are well-formed syllables while (2e) is not. Here are their full analyses in terms of the notation developed above:

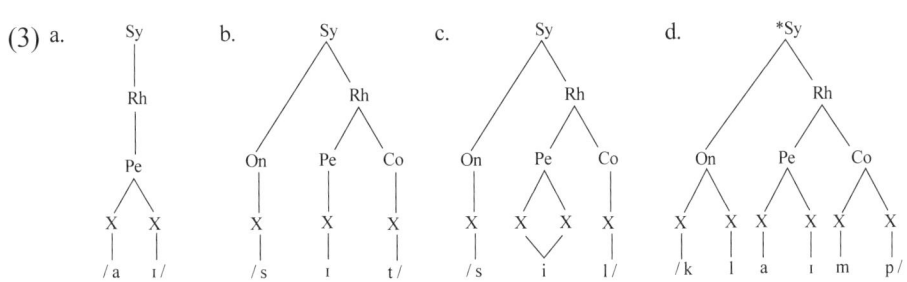

Provided we can account for *finds* and *seals* by different means, we can make the generalisation that well-formed syllables contain no more than three X-positions in the rhyme. Notice how peak and coda interact in this calculation of maximal syllables: it makes no difference to the well-formedness of a syllable whether the peak contains two X-positions and the coda one, or vice versa. It is the sum of X-positions in peak plus coda that counts, not the way in which these X-positions are distributed. This is the reason for introducing the rhyme into our model of syllable structure: without the rhyme, it would be rather difficult to make generalisations about maximal syllables.

Based on the passage, identify whether /ɛlm/ and /silm/ are well-formed or not, and then explain why, including the sum of X-positions of each word in the rhyme.

19 Read the passage and fill in the blank with the TWO most appropriate words. Write your answer with the natural class. [2 points]

> Coalescent assimilation is a type of reciprocal assimilation. Figure 1 illustrates how the first and second sounds in a sequence come together and mutually condition the creation of a third sound with features from both original sounds.
>
>
>
> *Figure 1. The process of coalescent assimilation*
>
> The consonants /s, z/ may undergo palatalization and turn into [ʃ, ʒ] respectively, when they occur before the palatal glide /j/. Consider the following examples:
>
> (1) I miss you　　　　　　　[ʃ]
> 　　this year　　　　　　　　[ʃ]
> 　　I please you　　　　　　 [ʒ]
> 　　Who's your boss?　　　　[ʒ]
>
> Also noteworthy is the fact that /t, d/ may turn into palato-alveolar affricates when they are followed by the palatal glide /j/ in the following word.
>
> (2) Would you mind moving?　[dʒ]
> 　　procedure　　　　　　　　[dʒ]
> 　　ate your dinner　　　　　[tʃ]
> 　　stature　　　　　　　　　[tʃ]
>
> Thus, we can put together the data in (1) and (2), and state the rule as in (3):
>
> (3) _____ become palatoalveolars when followed by a word that starts with the palatal glide /j/.

20 Read the passage and follow the directions. [4 points]

─┤ A ├─

It has been apparent that monosyllabic words can violate the core-syllable pattern: for example, the problems are posed by the initial /s/ in *spring* and by the final /s/ in *clamps*. As regards the rhyme, both of the two constraints on the form of this phonological unit can be violated: there may be more than three X-positions in the rhyme, and there may be violations of our generalisation that sonority decreases from left to right. Both these pattern violations are exemplified by the final consonant in *clamps*.

Consider the examples of *Three-X exceeded* and *Sonority violated* pattern violations in (1).

(1)

Three-X exceeded	Sonority violated	Both	Offending segment
mind	begged	lobed	/d/
paint	dropped	text	/t/
Glides	adze	minds	/z/
bounce	fox	drinks	/s/
	width	length	/θ/
lounge			/dʒ/

Note that it is common for segments at the end of the rhyme to violate both constraints: they may exceed the limit of three X-positions and violate the sonority generalisation. Note also that in some cases, offending segments are inflexional endings (for plural or past tense) while in others they are not. The examples in (1) show clearly that we have to allow for certain consonants to occur after the final consonant of an otherwise well-formed core syllable.

All the examples listed in (1) contain one or more consonants that cannot be part of the core syllable. Here are two examples that contain more than one such consonant: *minds* and *texts*.

(2)

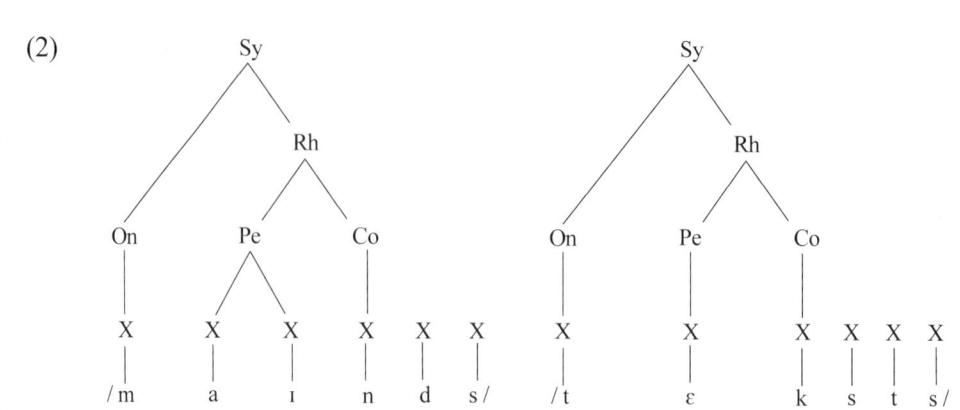

In *minds*, the /n/ must be the final segment of the core syllable because it is the third X in the rhyme, while in *texts*, the /k/ is the final segment of the core syllable because the following /s/ fails to conform with the sonority generalisation.

It would seem at first sight, then, that the constraints on the structure of the rhyme are invalid. However, what makes our previous generalisations still valid is the fact that the segments that can be appended to the core syllable fall into a very clearly defined class. To accommodate the cases listed in (1), we allow a rhyme to contain a core rhyme plus further X-positions, which must contain certain natural class, and which we shall refer to as the appendix.

─┤ B ├─

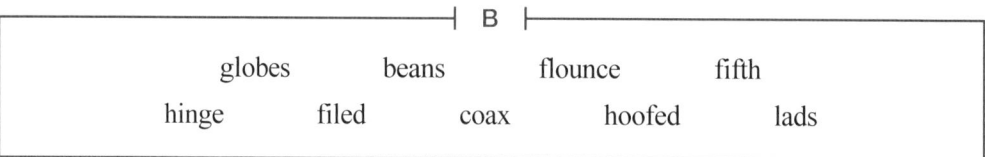

Based on the passage, first, identify ALL and ONLY words in <B> which violate both of the two constraints, *Three-X exceeded* AND *Sonority violated*. Second, state the natural class that can be appended to the core syllable, considering the data in (1).

21 Read the passage and fill in each blank with the appropriate feature. Write your answers in the correct order. [2 points]

> Fricatives are segments like the [f v s z] of *feel, veal, seal, zeal,* respectively. They are articulated by squeezing the outgoing air stream between an articulator (the lower lip or some part of the tongue) and a point of articulation (the upper lip or some part of the roof of the mouth) so that turbulence or friction—rubbing—results. Fricatives are like stops in three features but differ in one. Like stops, they are the result of aperiodic vibration, therefore [− sonorant]; they require some interruption of the air stream, so they are [+ consonantal]; they are not typically the peaks of syllables and so are designated [− syllabic]. Finally, unlike stops, fricatives are [+ continuant] since air is flowing continuously out of the mouth. Say *cup* and see if you can prolong the final sound; say *cuff* and hold the last sound as long as you can.
>
> Nasals are segments like the [m] of *mitt* and the [n] of *knit*, sounds made by stopping the flow of air somewhere in the mouth but letting it exit through the nose. Nasals are musical—[+ sonorant]—as every singer and teacher of singing knows. Since the air stream is interrupted in the mouth, they are [①]. Since air does not escape through the mouth, they are [②]. This is a matter of definition; [+ continuant] is defined to mean 'with air flowing out the mouth'; actually a nasal can be prolonged because air is flowing continuously through another exit. Say *come* and make the last sound continue as long as you have breath. Last, we classify nasals as both plus and minus syllabic—[± syllabic]. They are usually not the peak of a syllable, but they can be, as in the word *kitten*.
>
> Liquids include the [l] of *lead* and the [r] of *read*. In their articulation the tongue is raised, partly impeding the flow of air, but the tongue is shaped in such a way that air flows around it, creating particular patterns of vibration. Because of the impedance liquids are classed as [+ consonantal]; because of the periodic vibration they are [+ sonorant]; because air flows freely they are [+ continuant]. Finally, like nasals, they are [± syllabic]—usually not the peak of a syllable but sometimes the peak, as in *metal* and *manner*.

22. Read the passage and follow the directions. [4 points]

┤ A ├

Take a look at some words that are morphologically complex in that they consist of roots and suffixes. We shall distinguish between two types of suffixes: inflexional and derivational. Inflexional suffixes produce different forms of the same word: for example, the plural form (*cameras*) of *camera*, the present participle form (*developing*) of the verb *develop*, the past tense of verbs (*commented*) and so on. Derivational suffixes, in contrast, produce new words; along with compounding (as in *fireplace, snowball*), the derivational morphology forms part of the word-formation devices in the grammar. Thus the suffix *-less* attaches to a noun base and forms adjectives (*penniless, driverless, luckless*); *-ly* attaches to adjectives and forms adverbs (*nicely, carefully*); *-ee* attaches to verbal bases and forms nouns (*employee, payee*) and so forth.

(1)
	Inflexional	Derivational	Derivational
a.	tallies	b. penniless	c. atomic
	developing	nationhood	solemnity
	commented	solemnly	substantial
	furnishes	interpretable	Newtonian
	cameras	openness	humidity

On the phonological side, such suffixes may be divided into two classes—stress-shifting and stess-neutral; and, as is shown in (1), this division is not congruent with the division, on the morphological side, into inflexional and derivational suffixes.

Let us deal with stress-neutral suffixes first. Such suffixes have two properties that set them apart from the other, stress-shifting class, Firstly, they never make any difference to the stress pattern of their base, that is, of the word to which they are attached. When, for example, the third person singular -s is added to the verb *tally*, the final syllable becomes heavy (*tallies*); nevertheless, the stress remains on the initial syllable. The second property of stress-neutral suffixes is that such suffixes are always unstressed—even where they constitute heavy syllables, and even where several such suffixes are stacked together. Stress-neutral suffixes, then, are simply appended as unstressed material to an entirely unmodified base.

The behaviour of stress-shifting suffixes is different in both respects. Firstly, the stress pattern of the word may radically differ from that of the base to which stress-shifting suffixes are attached. Secondly, stress-shifting suffixes differ from stress-neutral ones in that they themselves can bear the main stress of the word.

─┤ B ├─

Consider the following data in (2):

(2) *-ant*   ascendant, exhalant, reactant
　-ette   usherette, maisonette, launderette
　-ese   Japanese, Cantonese, Chinese
　-esque   picturesque, picaresque, arabesque
　-some   burdensome, toilsome, heartsome

Based on the passage <A>, first, state the class of derivational suffixes in (1b) and (1c), using the terms, *stress-shifting* and *stress-neutral*. Second, identify ALL stress-shifting suffixes in (2).

23 Read the passages and follow the directions. [4 points]

─┤ A ├─

The basic generalisation concerning the stress contours of phrases is exemplified by ₂black ¹bird: the second (phrase-final) one (bird) bears the main stress and the first one (black) a lesser stress. Here are some more examples:

(1) a. Noun phrases
    good work
    heavy metal
    scientific investigations
    b. Adjective phrases
    very good
    incredibly heavy
    allegedly scientific
  c. Verb phrases
    drinks heavily
    knows everything
    rested after lunch
    d. Adverb phrases
    rather enthusiastically
    quite clearly
    very well
  e. Sentences
    Roger disapproved
    Cigars stink
    Jennifer smokes

Let us now express these stress patterns in terms of metrical trees. In the construction of such trees, two questions arise: what is the form of the tree, and what are the prominence relations among its branches? The answer to the former question is here trivial: the metrical tree is here automatically a copy of the syntactic structure as the examples shown in (2).

(2)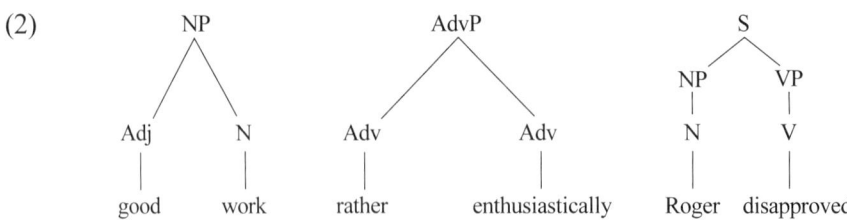

The metrical trees, expressing both structure and prominence relations, then look like in (3):

(3)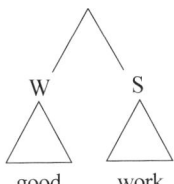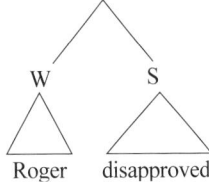

The rule that governs such prominence relations among word trees within phrases has the following form:

(4) Phrasal Prominence Rule

In a pair of sister nodes $[N_1\ N_2]_P$, where P is a phrasal category, N_2 is strong.

─┤ B ├─

In more complex constructions, the form of the metrical tree is determined by that of the syntactic tree structure. Now consider the construction in (5):

(5) Many students attend lectures regularly.

Bearing in mind the metrical tree of the construction in (5), first, identify the strongest stress in the noun phrase (i.e., Subject) and the higher verb phrase of the construction in (5), respectively. Second, state which word should be the strongest stress of the WHOLE construction in (5).

24 Read the passage and fill in each blank with ONE word from the passage. Write your answers in the correct order. [2 points]

> Vowel articulations are not as easy to feel at first as consonant articulations because the vocal tract is not narrowed as much. To become acquainted with vowel articulation, alternately pronounce the vowels of *he* and *awe*. You will feel the tongue move from a high front to a low back position. Once you feel this tongue movement, alternate between the vowels of *awe* and *at*. You will feel the tongue moving from the low back to low front position. Finally, alternate between the vowels of *he* and *who*. You will notice that in addition to a tongue movement between the high front and high back positions, you are also rounding your lips for the [u].
>
> Vowels for which the tongue is neither raised nor lowered are called mid vowels. The front vowel of English *made* and *fame* is mid, front, and unrounded. The vowel of *code* and *soak* is mid, back, and rounded. The vowels are summed up in table 1. Note that in describing the vowels, the articulatory parameters are presented in the order *height, backness, rounding*.
>
> | TABLE 1. Basic phonetic parameters for describing Canadian English vowels | | |
> |---|---|---|
> | h<u>ea</u>t | [i] | high front unrounded |
> | f<u>a</u>te | [eɪ] | mid front unrounded |
> | m<u>a</u>d | [æ] | low front unrounded |
> | S<u>ue</u> | [u] | high back rounded |
> | b<u>oa</u>t | [ow] | mid back rounded |
> | s<u>u</u>n | [ʌ] | mid central unrounded |
> | c<u>o</u>t, c<u>au</u>ght | [ɑ] | low back ①_____ |

As shown in table 1, in standard Canadian English, there is no difference between the vowels of a pair of words like *cot* and *caught*, both of which contain the vowel [ɑ]. In some dialects of North American English, as well as in many other dialects of English worldwide, the vowel of *caught* (and certain other words such as *law*) is the mid back ____②____ lax vowel [ɔ].

Note that non-front vowels are traditionally divided into central and back vowels; often the term *back* alone is used for all non-front vowels.

25 Read the passage and follow the directions. [4 points]

The IPA represents speech in the form of segments—individual phones like [p], [s], or [m]. Segments are produced by coordinating a number of individual articulatory gestures including jaw movement, lip shape, and tongue placement. Many of these individual activities are represented as smaller subunits called features, of which segments are composed.

Some articulatory features are distinctive and others are redundant. There are four features for distinguishing classes of speech sounds: [sonorant], [syllabic], [continuant] and [consonantal]. We need to recognize that even features which are distinctive in some areas may be used redundantly in other areas.

The feature [+ syllabic] is sufficient to designate the class of vowels; no other class has this feature. So the other features, [+ sonorant, + continuant, − consonantal], while they describe true facts about the pronunciation of vowels, have no role in telling how vowels are different from other classes of segments. For classification, one feature is distinctive, the other features are redundant. We can express this fact in a redundancy statement as in (1):

(1) Whatever is [+ syllabic] is redundantly [+ sonorant, + continuant, − consonantal].

Or more briefly like this:

(2) If [+ syllabic], then [+ sonorant, + continuant, − consonantal].

For glides we need two features together, [− consonantal] and [− syllabic], for a distinctive label. The feature [− consonantal] distinguishes vowels and glides together from other classes, and the feature [− syllabic] distinguishes glides from vowels. So the features [+ sonorant] and [+ continuant] are redundant. The redundancy statement for glides is shown in (3):

(3) If [− consonantal, − syllabic], then [+ sonorant, + continuant].

What is the redundancy statement for nasals?

(4) If [+ sonorant, ___①___], then [___②___ , − syllabic].

First, fill in each blank with ONE feature from the passage. Write your answers in the correct order. Second, state the redundancy statement for *Liquids*, starting with the feature *sonorant*, as shown in the passage.

26 Read the passage and follow the directions. [4 points]

The context in which aspiration occurs is the syllable-initial position. The general rule of aspiration is as follows:

(1) Rule 1: Aspiration is strongest in the initial position of stressed syllables.

Let us consider the following examples in (2):

(2) a. pit [pʰɪt]   b. spit [spɪt]   c. bit [bɪt]
    tie [tʰaɪ]   sty [staɪ]   die [daɪ]
    come [kʰʌm]   scum [skʌm]   gum [gʌm]

Aspiration does not occur in the examples in (2b), where voiceless stops are preceded in syllable onsets by /s/. Hence, the /p/ is aspirated in *pit* but not in *spit*, in *tie* but not in *sty*, etc. There is also no aspiration of the voiced stops in (2c)—aspiration is clearly restricted to voiced stops.

Consider the further examples in (3) where aspiration also occurs:

(3) polite [pʰəlaɪt]   vacuum [vakʰjuəm]   pickle [pʰɪkʰəl]

These data imply the following rule:

(4) Rule 2: Aspiration also occurs in _____.

The production of the sonorant falls partly or completely within the aspiration period of the stop, and devoicing of the sonorant occurs:

(5) Rule 3: A sonorant is devoiced when it follows a voiceless aspirated stop in syllable onset position.

Now consider the data in (6):

(6) a. pray /pre/ b. spring /sprɪŋ/ c. apron /eprən/
    play /ple/   split /splɪt/   applaud /əplɔd/
    crew /kru/   screw /skru/   across /əkrɒs/
    clue /klu/   proclaim /prəklem/
    try /traɪ/   attract /ətrakt/
    twig /twɪg/   matron /metrən/
    tune /tjun/
 d. atlas /atləs/ e. brew [bru]
    butler /bʌtlə/   drew [dru]
    Watney /wɒtnɪ/   glue [glu]

Based on the passage, first, complete the rule in (4) by filling in the blank with **TWO** words. Second, identify **TWO** data sets in (6) where devoicing of the sonorant occurs, using the number (6a)—(6e).

27 Read the passage and follow the directions. [4 points]

In a *dynamic neutralization*, there is alternation: morphemes are actively changed in order to respect the pattern of contextually limited contrast. In English words, it is impossible for two final obstruents to disagree in their value for voicing.

The past tense suffix, which is analyzed as underlying /-d/, is actively devoiced (surfacing as [-t]) whenever this is necessary to avoid a disagreement in voicing between two _____ in the syllable final position as shown in (1).

(1) a. paid [peɪ-d]
filled [fɪl-d]
barred [bɑɹ-d]
slammed [slæm-d]

b. rubbed [ɹʌb-d]
eased [iz-d]
dragged [dɹæg-d]
lived [lɪv-d]

c. picked [pɪk-t]
tapped [tæp-t]
missed [mɪs-t]
laughed [læf-t]

The usual analysis given for this pattern is to assume that a phonological rule of Voicing Assimilation changes the voicing of the /d/ where necessary to avoid a voicing conflict.

Consider now a case of *static neutralization* in (2), also from English. English words can end in two stops, but only under certain condition.

(2) a. concept [ˈkɑnsɛpt]   b. *[ˈkɑnsɛtp]
    contact [ˈkɑntækt]   *[ˈkɑntætk]
    milked [mɪlkt]   *[mɪltk]
    rubbed [ɹʌbd]   *[ɹʌdb]
    bagged [bægd]   *[bædg]

Speakers of English immediately recognize such hypothetical words in (2b) as ill-formed, and often regard them as hard to pronounce. Unlike Voicing Assimilation, however, there are no cases of repair in (2).

Based on the passage, first, fill in the blank with ONE word from the passage. Second, state the natural class of the second consonant where English words can end in two stops in (2).

28 Read the passage and fill in each blank with the ONE most appropriate word. Write your answers in the correct order. [2 points]

> Deletion is a process that removes a segment from certain phonetic contexts. Deletion occurs in everyday rapid speech in many languages. In English, a schwa [ə] is often deleted when the next vowel in the word is ____①____, as shown in (1). (Notice that in the first two words, the deletion of the schwa creates the environment for the [r] to become devoiced.)
>
> (1) *Slow speech*   *Rapid speech*
>   [pʰəred]   [pred̥]   parade
>   [kʰərowd]   [krowd̥]   corrode
>   [səpʰowz]   [spowz]   suppose
>
> Deletion also occurs as an alternative to dissimilation in words such as *fifths*. Many speakers delete the [θ] of the final consonant cluster and say [fɪfs]. In very rapid speech, both the second [f] and the [θ] are sometimes deleted, resulting in [fɪs].
>   Epenthesis is a process that inserts a syllabic or a non-syllabic segment within an existing string of segments. For example, in careful speech, the words *warmth* and *something* are pronounced [wɔrmθ] and [sʌ̃mθɪ̃ŋ]. It is common in casual speech for speakers to insert a [p] between the [m] and the [θ] and pronounce the words [wɔrmpθ] and [sʌ̃mpθɪ̃ŋ]. Consonant epenthesis of this type is another example of a coarticulation phenomenon. In English, the articulatory transition from a sonorant consonant to a non-sonorant appears to be eased by the insertion of a consonant that shares properties of both segments. Notice that the epenthesized consonants are all non-sonorant, have the same ____②____ of articulation as the sonorant consonant to their left, and have the same voicing as the non-sonorant consonant to their right as shown in table 1.

TABLE 1. Some examples of English consonant epenthesis		
Word	Non-epenthesized pronunciation	Epenthesized pronunciation
something	[sʌ̃mθɪ̃ŋ]	[sʌ̃mpθɪ̃ŋ]
warmth	[wɔrmθ]	[wɔrmpθ]
length	[lɛ̃ŋθ]	[lɛ̃ŋkθ]
prince	[prĩns]	[prĩnts]
tenth	[tɛ̃nθ]	[tɛ̃ntθ]

29. Read the passage and follow the directions. [4 points]

Some of the alternation rules in English can be illustrated as follows:

(1) Velar softening: $\left\{ \begin{matrix} k \\ t \end{matrix} \right\} \to s \atop d \to z \right\} / \_\_ +\mathrm{I}$

(2) Palatalization: $\left\{ \begin{matrix} s \\ z \end{matrix} \right\} + \left\{ \begin{matrix} \mathrm{I} \\ j \end{matrix} \right\} \to \left\{ \begin{matrix} \int \\ 3 \end{matrix} \right\} / \_\_ V$

(3) Z-devoicing: $z \to s / \_\_ + \mathrm{IV}$

(4) Vowel lengthening: $V \to \left\{ \begin{matrix} [V] / \_\_ [-\text{voice}] \\ [V'] \text{ elsewhere} \end{matrix} \right\}$

(5) Past tense: $+d \to \left\{ \begin{matrix} \text{əd} / \left\{ \begin{matrix} t \\ d \end{matrix} \right\} \_\_ \\ T / [-\text{son.}] \_\_ \\ d / [+\text{son.}] \_\_ \end{matrix} \right\}$

(6) Flapping: $\left\{ \begin{matrix} t \\ d \end{matrix} \right\} \to [\mathrm{r}] / \text{'V} \_\_ V$

We shall illustrate the rules, and the ordering sequence, with some sample 'derivations' which proceed, step by step, from the underlying representation to an approximate pronunciation.

(7)   corrosion   corroded
    Input   /kə'roʊd+ɪən/   /kə'roʊd+d/
    Output   [kə'roʊ·ʒən]   [kə'roʊ·rəd]

Note: · *indicates lengthened vowel*

(8)   delighted   corrosive
    Input   /dɪ'laɪt+d/   /kə'roʊd+ɪv/
    Output   [dɪ'laɪrəd]   [kə'roʊsɪv]

The derivations show that the ordering of these rules is quite important. The flapping rule (6) has to follow the past-tense rule (5), because the latter provides the unstressed vowel which is needed as (part of) the environment for the rule (6) (as in *delighted* in (8)). In the sequence, the flapping rule (6) has been put after the vowel length rule (4). The result is that a word with a 'voiceless' origin (*delighted*) is pronounced with a short vowel (/aɪ/ in terms of length) before the flap. If the rules had been put in the opposite order, we would have the output [dɪˈlaɪ·ɾəd].

Based on the passage, in (7) state THREE rules applied to the words 'corrosion' AND 'corroded', respectively.

30 Read the passage and follow the directions. [4 points]

In casual speech, assimilation frequently causes the breakdown of phonemic distinctions that are operative in citation forms.

(1) of   /ɒv/   Head of [əf] Spanish
                   Head of [əv] English
    at   /æt/   stay at [ət] home
    as   /æz/   good as [əz] gold
    us   /ʌs/   give us [əz] a break

In (1), assimilation occurs in *of* [ɒf] *Spanish* vs. [ɒv] *English*. Similarly, compare the citation form us /ʌs/ with the weak form *give us* [ʌz] *a break*.

Here are some further examples in (2):

(2) ten pounds   /tɛnpaʊndz/
                 [tɛmpaʊndz]
    in Crewe   /ɪnkru/
                 [ɪŋkru]

Assimilations such as these are extremely common in casual speech, illustrating once again the simplification—even the breakdown—of the phonological structure found in citation forms, [m] is not an allophone of [n]; but here we have [tɛm] as a realisation of *ten*.

To gain a final impression of just how much phonological information present in citation forms may be lost in casual speech, consider the examples given below. These are more complex than earlier ones in that they display reduction, elision as well as assimilation at the same time:

(3) grand piano   /grændpɪæno/
                   [græmpɪænə]
    hand Colin   /hændkɒlɪn/
                   [hæŋkɒlɪn]

In *grand piano*, /o/ is reduced to [ə], *grand* loses its final /d/, and then the /n/ assimilates to the following /p/.

Based on the passage, in (3) in *hand Colin*, explain how *hand* /hænd/ turns into [hæŋ] in order, as described in the passage.

31 Read the passage and fill in the blank ① with the ONE most appropriate word and the blank ② with the TWO most appropriate words. Write your answers in the correct order. [2 points]

> A number of different processes, collectively known as assimilation, result from the influence of one segment on another. Assimilation always results in a sound becoming more like another nearby sound in terms of one or more of its phonetic characteristics.
>
> Nasalization of a vowel before a nasal consonant (nasal assimilation) is caused by speakers expecting the lowering of the velum in advance of a nasal segment. The result is that the preceding segment takes on the nasality of the following consonant, as in [kʰæ̃nt] *can't*. (Nasality is marked with a tilde [~].) This type of assimilation is known as _____①_____ assimilation in terms of direction, since the nasalization is, in effect, moving backwards to a preceding segment.
>
> Flapping is a process in which a dental or alveolar stop articulation changes to a flap [ɾ] articulation. In English, this process applies to [t] and [d] when they occur between vowels, the first of which is generally stressed. Flaps are heard in the casual speech pronunciation of words such as *butter, writer, fodder,* and *wading*, and even in phrases such as *I bought it* [ajbáɾɪt]. The alveolar flap is always voiced. Flapping is considered a type of assimilation because it involves a stop consonant being weakened and becoming less stop-like when it occurs between vowels, which involve no closure at all in the vocal tract.
>
> Voicing assimilation is also widespread. For many speakers of English, voiceless liquids and glides occur after _____②_____ in words such as *please* [pl̥iz], *try* [tr̥aj], and *cure* [kj̥ur]. These sounds are said to be devoiced in this environment. Devoicing is a kind of assimilation since the vocal folds are not set in motion immediately after the release of the voiceless consonant closure.
>
> Dissimilation, the opposite of assimilation, results in two sounds becoming less alike in articulatory or acoustic terms. The resulting sequence of sounds is easier to articulate and distinguish. It is a much rarer process than assimilation. One commonly heard example of dissimilation in English occurs in words ending with three consecutive fricatives, such as *fifths*. Many speakers dissimilate the final [fθs] sequence to [fts], apparently to break up the sequence of three fricatives with a stop.

32. Read the passage and follow the directions. [4 points]

In connected speech, schwa can occur in positions in which corresponding citation forms have full vowels. Consider the following examples:

(1) veto /ˈvi̩to/   veto the proposal [ˌvitəðəprəˈpozəɫ]
    potato /pəˈte̩to/   potato peeler [pəˈtetəˌpilə]
    uneven /ˌʌnˈivən/   rather uneven [ˌrɑðərənˈivən]

Similar variation between stressed and unstressed forms of the same word can be observed in function words. Below are some examples:

(2) and /ænd/   the king and [ənd] I   come and [ən] see
                    Fred and [n̩d]~[n̩] I   bread and [n̩] butter
    but /bʌt/   smart but [bət] casual
    them /ðɛm/   show them [ðəm]   give them [əm] a drink

Elision of schwa is common especially before sonorant consonants. Consider the following:

(3) | | a. | b. | c. |
|---|---|---|---|
| police | /pəˈlis/ | [pl̩is] | [plis] |
| canoe | /kəˈnu/ | [kn̩u] | [knu] |
| balloon | /bəˈlun/ | [bl̩un] | [blun] |
| solicitor | /səˈlɪsɪtə/ | [sl̩ɪsɪtə] | [slɪstə] |
| catalyst | /ˈkatəlɪst/ | [katl̩ɪst] | [katlɪst] |
| botany | /ˈbɒtəni/ | [bɒtn̩i] | [bɒtni] |

In (3b) schwa is elided before sonorants; the syllable is maintained through syllabicity of the sonorant. In (3c) sonorant consonants are no longer syllabic; hence, the words in (3c) have monosyllabic pronunciations in fast speech.

Again, this kind of consonant elision and cluster simplification is not restricted to weak forms of words. Here are some more examples where the second consonant is elided in consonant clusters:

(4) We<u>st G</u>ermany   /ˌwɛstˈdʒɜmənɪ/   [wɛsdʒɜmənɪ]
    thousa<u>nd t</u>imes   /ˈθaʊzəndˈtaɪmz/   [θaʊzn̩taɪmz]
    ho<u>ld s</u>till   /holdˈstɪl/   [holstɪl]

In addition, certain consonants at word or morpheme boundaries are usually simplified in connected speech:

(5) keenness /kinnəs/ [kinəs]   bus stop /bʌsstɒp/ [bʌstɒp]
    call Linda /kɔllɪndə/ [kɔlɪndə]   red dress /rɛddrɛs/ [rɛdrɛs]
    big glass /bɪgglæs/ [bɪglæs]   both things /boθθɪŋz/ [boθɪŋz]

Based on the passage, first, in (3c) identify ONE word that violates phonotactic constraints. Second, state the condition where consonant cluster simplification occurs in (5).

33 Read the passage and follow the directions. [4 points]

The sonority-based phonetic theory identifies peaks, slopes, and troughs in the sonority profiles of words, thereby predicting the analysis of these syllables into onsets, peaks and codas. It also predicts that syllable boundaries occur in the close vicinity of sonority troughs.

But this is all that our phonetic syllable theory is able to predict. It does not tell us where, precisely, a syllable boundary is located. We have to amend our theory by a rule for the placement of syllable boundaries.

(2) a. ma.ri.na   b. al.ti.tude   c. a.pri.cot
    a.ro.ma   nigh.tin.gale   re.flect
    pho.ne.   mica.gen.da   de.crease
    co.di.fy   stan.dard   ma.tron

Let us attempt to establish a general rule for the placement of syllable boundaries in polysyllabic words. In (2a), we have simple consonant-vowel sequences: (C)VCV(C), where each C constitutes a trough in sonority and each V a peak. The generalisation is a simple one: a single consonant between vowels is a syllable onset rather than the coda of the preceding syllable. In (2b) and (2c), we have examples of ...VCCV... sequences. In (2b), the first C is more sonorous than the second: in *altitude*, /l/ is more sonorous than /t/, and the second C /t/ constitutes the sonority trough. In (2c), however, the first C in a consonant cluster does not show the same pattern.

Drawing together our findings regarding (2), we can conclude that syllable boundaries occur immediately before the consonant that constitutes a sonority trough. And this trough is always part of the _____ rather than being the coda of the preceding syllable. But before we state this rule in its final form, let us consider a few more examples:

(3) e.nig.ma   /gm/   at.las   /tl/
    Ag.nes   /gn/   hem.lock   /ml/
    Ed.na   /dn/   de.cath.lon   /θl/

Just like those in (2c), the examples in (3) contain consonant clusters in which the leftmost consonant is less sonorous than the right one. The /tr/ in *matron* and the /gm/ in *enigma* have in common. While in (2c) the syllable boundary regularly precedes the cluster, the clusters in (3) are divided by the syllable boundary. None of the clusters listed in (3) are possible English syllable onsets. Accounting for all the facts discussed so far, the rule for the placement of syllable boundaries can be formulated like this:

(4) Syllable-Boundary Rule
    Within words, syllable boundaries are placed in such a way that onsets are maximal (in accordance with the phonotactic constraints of the language).

Based on the passage, first, fill in the blank with the ONE word from the passage. Second, identify the first C in a CC cluster in (2c) with the sonority profiles of words (i.e., a peak, a slope, or a trough).

34 Read the passage and fill in each blank with the ONE most appropriate word. Write your answers in the correct order. [2 points]

Tense vowels are produced with greater vocal tract constriction than non-tense vowels and are longer in duration than non-tense vowels. Some vowels of English are made with roughly the same tongue position as the tense vowels but with a less constricted articulation; they are called *lax*.

TABLE 1. Tense and lax vowels in Canadian English

Tense		Lax	
h<u>ea</u>t	[i]	h<u>i</u>t	[ɪ]
m<u>a</u>te	[ej]	m<u>e</u>t	[ɛ]
—	—	m<u>a</u>t	[æ]
sh<u>oo</u>t	[u]	sh<u>ou</u>ld	[ʊ]
c<u>oa</u>t	[ow]	c<u>u</u>t	[ʌ]
—	—	Can<u>a</u>da	[ə]
—	—	—	—
l<u>o</u>ck	[ɑ]		
l<u>ie</u>s	[aj]		
l<u>ou</u>d	[aw]		
b<u>oy</u>	[oj]		

Table 1 provides examples from English comparing tense and lax vowels. Note that not all the vowels come in tense/lax pairs. The difference between two of the vowels illustrated in table 1 is often not easy to hear at first. Both the vowel [ʌ] in *cut, dud, pluck,* and *Hun,* and the vowel [ə] of *Canada, about, tomahawk,* and *sofa* are mid, central(back), _____①_____, and lax. The vowel of the second set of examples, called *schwa,* is referred to as a reduced vowel. In addition to being lax, its duration is briefer than that of any of the other vowels.

A simple test can help determine whether vowels are tense or lax. In English, ____②____ words spoken in isolation do not end in lax vowels. We find *see* [si], *say* [sej], *Sue* [su], *so* [sow], and *saw* [sɑ] in English, but not *s[ɪ], *s[ɛ], *s[æ], *s[ʊ], or *s[ʌ]. Schwa, however, frequently appears in unstressed syllables in polysyllabic words like *sof[ə]* and *Can[ə]d[ə]*. It should be pointed out—especially for those who think their ears are deceiving them—that many speakers produce the final vowel in the last two examples as [ʌ], not as [ə].

35. Read the passages and follow the directions. [4 points]

─┤ A ├─

An interesting aspect of phonological systems is that some rules evidently apply in environments that are defined phonemically, rather than phonetically. The crucial mechanism for analyzing such cases is to apply the phonological rules in a particular order.

Our discussion of this phenomenon will be based on one phonological rule of North American English. It is found in a large number of dialects, especially in the northeastern US and throughout Canada. /aɪ/ is realized as [ʌɪ] when it precedes a/an _____ consonant.

(1) tripe /tɹaɪp/ [tɹʌɪp]   tribe /tɹaɪb/ [tɹaɪb]
   right /ɹaɪt/ [ɹʌɪt]   ride /ɹaɪd/ [ɹaɪd]
   hiker /haɪkɚ/ [hʌɪkɚ]   tiger /taɪgɚ/ [taɪgɚ]
   life /laɪf/ [lʌɪf]   live /laɪv/ [laɪv]
   rifle /ɹaɪfəl/ [ɹʌɪfəl]   rival /ɹaɪvəl/ [ɹaɪvəl]
   rice /ɹaɪs/ [ɹʌɪs]   rise /ɹaɪz/ [ɹaɪz]
     rye /ɹaɪ/ [ɹaɪ]
     ion /aɪɑn/ [aɪɑn]

The other rule we will need is the rule of Tapping, where the /t/ phoneme is realized as a tap [ɾ]. Tapping also affects /d/, converting it as well into a tap. The generalized version of Tapping can be stated as follows: an alveolar stop is realized as [ɾ] when it is preceded by a vowel or /ɹ/, and followed by a stressless vowel.

(2) wet   wetting   wed   wedding
   /ˈwɛt/   /ˈwɛt-ɪŋ/   /ˈwɛd/   /ˈwɛd-ɪŋ/
   [ˈwɛt]   [ˈwɛɾɪŋ]   [ˈwɛd]   [ˈwɛɾɪŋ]
   butt   butted   bud   budded
   /ˈbʌt/   /ˈbʌt-əd/   /ˈbʌd/   /ˈbʌd-əd/
   [ˈbʌt]   [ˈbʌɾəd]   [ˈbʌd]   [ˈbʌɾəd]

┌──────────────────────────── B ────────────────────────────┐

  With the two rules of /aɪ/ Raising and Tapping in hand, we can now see how they might interact. Crucial words that would bear on the question are the following, which for the moment we give in spelled and phonemic form only:

  (3) cite   cited   side   sided
      /ˈsaɪt/   /ˈsaɪt-əd/   /ˈsaɪd/   /ˈsaɪd-əd/
      white   whiter   wide   wider
      /ˈwaɪt/   /ˈwaɪt-ɚ/   /ˈwaɪd/   /ˈwaɪd-ɚ/

  A widely employed method of analyzing differences such as the one just shown is to suppose that phonological rules must be ordered. Under such a theory, the difference between the two dialects just described is a difference of rule ordering. While /aɪ/ Raising is ordered before Tapping in one dialect, Tapping is ordered before /aɪ/ Raising in the other dialect.

└──┘

Based on the passages, first, in <A>, fill in the blank with the ONE most appropriate word. Second, state the order of the two rules of /aɪ/ Raising and Tapping in the dialect in which *writing* and *riding* are pronounced the same.

36 Read the passages and follow the directions. [4 points]

─┤ A ├─

A fully explicit phonological analysis of a language would use no phonetic symbols. Only the feature matrices have theoretical status, and the phonetic symbols are meant only as convenient abbreviations for particular feature matrices. Here are ways in which rules benefit by writing them with features.

We capture an assimilation by showing that the assimilating segment adopts a feature value already possessed by one of its neighbors. For example, in English, /k, g, ŋ/ become fronted [k̟, g̟, ŋ̟] as in *keel* [ˈk̟il], *gale* [ˈgeɪl], or *dinghy* [ˈdɪŋi]:

(1) Velar Fronting

　　Velars become fronted _____.

(2) $\begin{bmatrix} +\text{dorsal} \\ +\text{consonantal} \end{bmatrix} \rightarrow \begin{bmatrix} +\text{front} \\ -\text{back} \end{bmatrix} / \underline{\quad} \begin{bmatrix} +\text{syllabic} \\ +\text{front} \end{bmatrix}$

Only one or two feature values show that a change is minor. For example, if a rule changes /p/ to [b], one would write p → [+ voice] rather than p → b, to show that nothing other than [voice] is changing.

There are good reasons to include only just as many features in a rule as are needed. Here is an example. In English, all voiced fricatives can be realized as voiceless when they precede a pause; that is to say, they are at the end of an utterance.

(3) save /seɪv/ [seɪf], [seɪv]　　bathe /beɪð/ [beɪθ], [beɪð]
　　maze /meɪz/ [meɪs], [meɪz]　rouge /ɹuʒ/ [ɹuʃ], [ɹuʒ]

Since there are four voiced fricatives in English, we could, in principle, write four rules. But phonological rules make reference to natural classes; certainly a more elegant approach would be to adopt a single rule:

(4) Final Fricative Devoicing
Voiced fricatives are realized as voiceless at the end of an utterance.

(5) $\begin{bmatrix} \quad \end{bmatrix} \rightarrow [- \text{voice} / \underline{\quad}]_{\text{Utterance}}$ (optional)

< B >

A restrictive set of distinctive features keep sound distinct. Some distinctive features simply translate the phonetic parameters in a self-explanatory manner: [± sonorant], [± voice], [± nasal], [± lateral] and [± continuant].

Based on the passage, first, considering the feature values in (2), complete Velar Fronting rule in (1) by filling in the blank with THREE words. Second, in (5), fill in the square bracket with THREE feature values to translate Final Fricative Devoicing rule in (4), using the distinctive features described in <B>.

37 Read the passage and follow the directions. [4 points]

A

One case of the interaction of morphology and phonology occurs in zero derivation, sometimes called conversion. This refers to a kind of derivational morphology in which there is no overt affix, but there is a change in category accompanied by a corresponding change in meaning. In English, the major cases involve a noun and a verb of identical phonological form and closely related meanings. Among disyllabic cases, there are some where stress remains the same for the noun and the verb in (1a), whereas, in (1b), the stress patterns are distinct.

(1) a. pattern, comfort, picture, focus
　　b. torment, conflict, increase

Besides the stress, there are certain other differences between the pairs in groups (1a) and (1b). Semantically, verbs of the form (1a) mean 'to do something with N.' On the other hand, nouns of (1b) mean 'that which Vs' or 'that which is Ved,' as an *increase* is 'something which increases.'

We can explain this pattern by saying that the noun is basic in (1a), while the verb is basic in (1b). If we assign stress to the basic form, before the morphological conversion, we obtain exactly the right results. In (1a), stress is assigned to the noun, which is the basic form. When the zero derivation takes place, the noun's stress carries over to the verb, since no restressing occurs. In (1b), the noun has a remnant of the verb's stress in the form of a secondary stress on the second syllable.

As a further demonstration of the correctness of this approach, the model predicts zero derivations of the form V→N→V, but makes zero derivations N→V→N impossible. Some example words are given in (2).

(2) a. [protést]ᵥ → [prótèst]ɴ → [prótèst]ᵥ
    'stage a protest'
  b. [discóunt]ᵥ → [dískòunt]ɴ → [dískòunt]ᵥ
    'sell at a discount'
  c. [compóund]ᵥ → [cómpòund]ɴ → [cómpòund]ᵥ
    'join or become joined in a compound'
  d. [digést]ᵥ → [dígèst]ɴ → [dígèst]ᵥ
    'make a digest'

In each case the verb derived from the noun has a meaning distinct from the verb that the noun was originally derived from.

B

(a) import   (b) permit   (c) poison
(d) ransom   (e) export

Based on the passage, in <B>, identify TWO words that show the same stress pattern as the words in (1a), and then, state the basic form of each word (i.e., a verb or noun).

38 Read the passage and fill in each blank with ONE word from the passage. Write your answers in the correct order. [2 points]

In languages that allow more than one consonant to appear in onsets and codas, two general principles apply; syllables that follow these principles are called *basic syllables*. The first principle, the Sonority Requirement, makes reference to sonority (roughly, a sound's degree of resonance).

(1) *The Sonority Requirement*

In basic syllables, sonority rises before the nucleus and declines after the nucleus.

A sonority scale is provided in figure 1 below, with the numbers from 0 to 4 indicating relative sonority levels. (Remember that an obstruent is an oral stop, a fricative, or an affricate.)

FIGURE 1. The sonority scale

0	1	2	3	4
Obstruent	Nasal	Liquid	Glide	Vowel

The sonority profile of basic syllables can be seen in a monosyllabic word like *grant* /grænt/. There is rising sonority within the onset, peak sonority at the nucleus, and falling sonority within the coda. The nucleus represents the peak of sonority in the syllable.

FIGURE 2. The sonority profile of *grant*

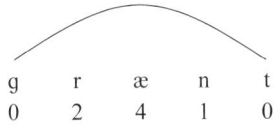

```
g   r   æ   n   t
0   2   4   1   0
```

In contrast, there are no words such as */rgænt/, with ____①____ sonority in the onset. And there are no words such as *gratn*, with ____②____ sonority in the coda.

The second major principle with which basic syllables must comply is the Binarity Requirement, which can be stated as follows:

(2) *The Binarity Requirement*
   Within basic syllables, each constituent can be at most binary (i.e., branching into two).

This means that an onset or coda can't contain more than two consonants.

39 Read the passage and follow the directions. [4 points]

Vowels are affected by the surrounding consonants, and this effect is much more noticeable with certain consonants. The words *bead* and *bean* form a minimal pair, and any native speaker of English can tell that the final consonants in these words are responsible for the contrast. Besides this obvious fact, however, there lies another difference between these two words and that has to do with the vowel sounds. While both vowels belong to the phoneme /i/, the phonetic manifestation of the vowel of the second word, *bean*, is nasalized and, phonetically, an [ĩ]. This predictable allophonic rule of English is valid for all vowels; that is, English vowels are nasalized when they occur before a nasal consonant.

In addition, length of vowels varies predictably according to the context they appear in. For example, vowels are longer before voiced consonants than before their voiceless counterparts. Thus, the phonetic realization of the vowel /æ/ in *bag* [bæg] is longer than its realization in *back* [bæk].

Now consider another phonological phenomenon. All vowels of English except the schwa can occur in monosyllabic words ending in [t], and so for each vowel we can find a monosyllabic word containing that vowel followed directly by [t], and give both the spelling and the phonetic transcription as shown in (1).

(1)

Vowel	Sample	Word	Vowel	Sample	Word
[i]	meet	[mit]	[o]	moat	[mot]
[ɪ]	bit	[bɪt]	[ɔ]	bought	[bɔt]
[u]	moot	[mut]	[æ]	mat	[mæt]
[ʌ]	hut	[hʌt]	[a]	pot	[pat]
[ʊ]	foot	[fʊt]	[aɪ]	fight	[faɪt]
[e]	mate	[met]	[aʊ]	grout	[graʊt]
[ɛ]	met	[mɛt]	[ɔɪ]	Hoyt	[hɔɪt]

However, in monosyllabic words we cannot find all vowels with velar nasal [ŋ], but only some vowels can appear in that position as in (2).

(2) | **Vowel** | **Sample** | **Word** | **Vowel** | **Sample** | **Word** |
| --- | --- | --- | --- | --- | --- |
| [ɪ] | sing | [sɪŋ] | [ɛ] | length | [lɛŋkθ] |
| [ʌ] | rung | [rʌŋ] | [æ] | sang | [sæŋ] |

Based on the passage, state the environment where velar nasal [ŋ] can occur in (2).

40 Read the passages and follow the directions. [4 points]

─┤ A ├─

If the basic rules of stress looked rather untidy and replete with exceptions, the rules accompanying affixes can easily be said to overshadow the monomorphemic roots. While the addition of prefixes does not change word stress, there are the varying effects of suffixes on word stress. The suffixes can be classified as follows: stress-bearing suffixes, stress-shifting suffixes and stress-neutral suffixes.

Stress-bearing suffixes change the location of the stress from its original position. Stress-bearing suffixes attract the stress to themselves as shown in (1):

(1) -ade   lemonade   -aire   millionaire
    -ation   realization   -ee   absentee
    -ette   kitchenette   -itis   laryngitis
    -ific   honorific

Stress-neutral suffixes never make any difference to the stress pattern of the resulting word. Stress-neutral suffixes do not carry stress themselves as in (2).

(2) -ant   ascendant   -cy   celibacy
    -dom   freedom   -ful   graceful
    -hood   nationhood   -ism   alcoholism
    -ize   specialize   -th   growth

Stress-shifting suffixes, when added to a root, shift the stress from its original position to the syllable immediately preceding the suffix as the data shown in (3).

(3) -ial   substantial   -ical   geometrical
    -icide   insecticide   -ify   personify
    -ious   laborious   -ual   contextual

┤ B ├

There are some suffixes that put the stress on the syllable immediately before them. Now consider the following data:

(5) a. refusal, recital, accidental
    b. seasonal, practical, temporal
(6) a. emergency, consistency, contingency
    b. presidency, competency, impotency

Based on the passage, first, in <B>, identify TWO sets of data in which the stress falls on the syllable immediately before the suffix. Second, considering all the data in (5) and (6), state the condition where the stress falls on the syllable immediately before the suffix in terms of the syllable weight.

41 Read the passage and fill in each blank with the TWO most appropriate words. Use the SAME answer for both blanks. [2 points]

> How do we go about identifying allophones of the same phoneme—such as [n] and [n̪] or [i] and [i:] in English? Non-contrastive differences like these typically arise when a segment's articulation is affected by its neighbours: that is, it has one pronunciation in one position or environment and another pronunciation in other environments. When two sounds occur in non-overlapping, (i.e., mutually exclusive) environments, they are said to be in complementary distribution.
>
> As we have seen, English [n̪] and [n] work this way: we find dental [n̪] in front of other dental sounds (like [θ] and [ð]), and we find [n] elsewhere.
>
> (1) An example of complementary distribution:
>   a. [n̪] occurs in front of dental consonants such as [θ] and [ð]:
>   *one thing, on them, in there*
>   b. [n] occurs elsewhere:
>   *one ship, one egg, one cent, one dollar*
>
> And of course English [i:] and [i] are in complementary distribution too: [i:] occurs in front of _____, and [i] occurs elsewhere—in front of some sounds like [t] in *heat* and [s] in *cease*, in front of the nasal consonant in *lean*, and so on.
>
> (2) Another example of complementary distribution:
>   a. [i:] occurs in front of _____:
>   *heed, seize, leave*
>   b. [i] occurs elsewhere:
>   *heat, cease, leaf, lean, sea*
>
> In sum, phonetic distinctions may or may not create contrasts that distinguish between words. When they do, the sounds in question belong to separate phonemes; when they don't, the sounds in question are allophones of the same phoneme.

42 Read the passages and follow the directions. [4 points]

─┤ A ├─

There are particular languages may impose restrictions on the types of sequence permitted. Often, certain types of consonant may follow, or precede, only certain types of vowel, and vice versa. Sometimes the restrictions can be stated in quite general terms; for example, in English, the consonants /j, w, h/ (and /r/ in 'non-rhotic' accents) can only occur prevocalically (they must be followed by a vowel). At other times the restrictions are more particular. For example, in English, long vowels (including diphthongs) are never followed by clusters, unless the second consonant of the cluster is _____. English has no words like /aɪlk/, /emp/, /aʊŋk/, despite the existence of the clusters themselves, as in *silk, bump, wink*, etc. The possible (i.e. existing) combinations are as follows:

(1) short vowel plus cluster
   a. help, bulb, sump, shelf, shelve
   b. bulk, sink

(2) long vowel (including diphthong) plus single consonant
   a. ape, strike, tube, rogue, pouch, leaf

(3) long vowel (including diphthong) plus _____ cluster
   a. paint, count, field, sound, spoilt
   b. aches, ached, plagues, plagued, robes, robed

The reason for the restriction appears to be largely historical; at a certain stage during the Middle English period (eleventh to fifteenth centuries) long vowels became short when a cluster followed. But there were certain exceptions to this change, all of them involving _____ clusters. In Modern English we therefore find a number of words like *paint, sound*, etc. which constitute exceptions to the general rule.

Note that the restriction extends to /-ŋ/, i.e. there are no words in which /-ŋ/ follows a long vowel, though /-ŋ/ may follow short vowels, as in *bring, hang, song,* etc. The reason is again historical; /-ŋ/ was originally /-ŋg/, as the spelling suggests (and indeed as it still is in many Midlands dialects). The restriction prohibiting non-alveolar clusters after long vowels thus included /-ŋg/, so it now applies likewise to /-ŋ/.

---- B ----

None of the following are actual English words. However, some are more likely, as possible words, than others.

(4) a. [zɪlp] [trɛlk] [prʌsk] [jɛsp]
    b. [zilp] [trelk] [prusk] [jaɪsp]

Based on the passage, first, fill in each blank with ONE word (i.e., a natural class). Use the SAME answer for all the blanks. Second, in <B>, identify which set of data is much less acceptable, and state the restriction it violates.

43 Read the passages and follow the directions. [4 points]

─┤ A ├─

Consider the stress patterns demonstrated in (1):

(1) a. ˌchamˈpagne   b. ˈchamˌpagne ˈbreakfast
    ˌDunˈdee   ˈDunˌdee ˈmarmalade
    ˌHeaˈthrow   ˈHeaˌthrow ˈAirport
    ˌPiccaˈdilly   ˈPiccaˌdilly ˈCircus

The words in (1a) all share the same metrical structure in that they consist of two feet, of which the second one is stronger than the first. In (1b) the same words are first members of phrase-level constituents; they are followed in each case by a stronger stress. In such a context, considering foot level, the weak-strong pattern of the word uttered in isolation (as well as in contexts other than those in (1b)) is reversed to strong-weak.

(2)

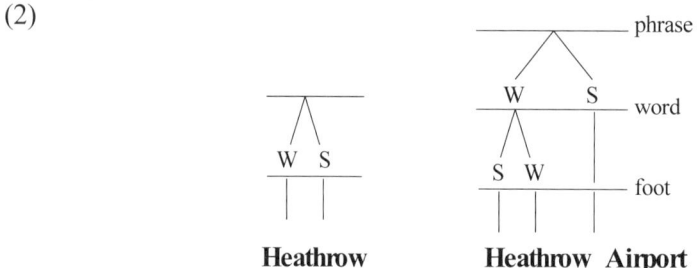

In general terms, we may state this regularity of stress reversal in terms of the following rule:

(3)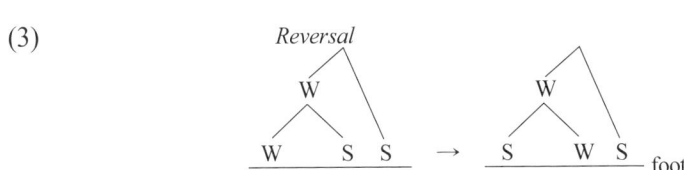

Reversal only happens among nodes in a metrical tree that dominate entire feet; in other words, a word-initial syllable whose stress is strengthened through (3) must have some stress to start with. There is no reversal in cases like *deferred 'entry* where the initial syllables are unstressed: unstressed initial syllables are not part of the word's structure but extensions of the preceding foot.

─┤ B ├─

Now consider the following data in (4):

(4) a. twenty-five lectures
   b. divine will
   c. thirteen men
   d. anticommunist views
   e. aroma therapy

Based on the passage, identify TWO examples in (4) where stress reversal does not occur, and then explain why, ONLY based on the passage <A>.

44 Read the passage and fill in each blank with ONE word from the passage. Write your answers in the correct order. [2 points]

> The vocal cords vibrate during some articulations and not during other articulations. Articulations with such vibration are voiced, or, in the notation of a binary system, [+ voice]. Consonants without vocal cord vibration are voiceless, or [− voice]. English stops and fricatives exist in pairs like /t, d/ or /s, z/ such that the two members of the pair are alike in all respects except that one is [− voice] and the other is [+ voice]. Therefore the feature [voice] is _____①_____ for stops and fricatives. On the other hand, all liquids and nasals are [+ voice], and voicing is not _____①_____ in these classes—it is not relevant for telling how one liquid differs from the other or one nasal from the other nasals.
>
> Although we use the feature [voice], with plus and minus values, for both stops like /t, d/ and fricatives like /s, z/, it must also be noted that the feature is not identical in phonetic terms. In the articulation of /s/ as in *sue* and *loose* the vocal cords do not vibrate, whereas for the articulation of /z/ in *zoo* and *lose* they do vibrate. For the articulation of /t/ and /d/, as in *two* and *do*, the difference is not in vocal cord vibration during the articulation of these stops but rather in voice onset time. In the articulation of stops the air stream is held back, so that no vibration occurs. When the air stream is released at the beginning of *do*, for instance, vocal cord vibration begins almost immediately. When the release is made at the beginning of *two*, vibration does not come immediately. Instead, there is first an instant of aspiration—air is released between the closely positioned, but non-vibrating, vocal cords. Then vibration begins. So the 'voicedness' of a voiced stop and the 'voicelessness' of a voiceless stop are not so much in the actual articulation of the stops as in their environment.
>
> The front part of the tongue, the blade, may be flat or it may be shaped so that it has a groove along the center line of the top surface, or it may be drawn in at the sides, or drawn back at the tip. To deal with these differences we recognize two features, [sibilant] and [lateral]. The feature [+ sibilant] indicates the presence of a groove, or slight trough, along the center line, and [− sibilant] means that there is no such groove. The feature [+ lateral] means that the tongue sides are

curled inward, and [− lateral] indicates the absence of such curl. The feature [sibilant] is distinctive among fricatives and stops, the feature [lateral] indicates differences in the class of _____②_____. All nasal consonants are articulated with a flat tongue, so that these features are not distinctive for nasals.

45 Read the passages and follow the directions. [4 points]

┤ A ├

Like consonant phonemes, vowel phonemes may have allophones. For instance, speakers of many accents of English have two realizations of the vowel phoneme /i:/: [i:] and [i:ə], as the following data show:

(1) Allophones of /i:/

    feet [fi:t]   feel [fi:əɫ]   deep [di:p]   deal [di:əɫ]

    peak [pʰi:k]   peel [pʰi:əɫ]   seem [si:m]   seal [si:əɫ]

We postulate /i:/ rather than /i:ə/ as the form of the phoneme, since we assume that the realization of the phoneme when it precedes a dark l is influenced by the dark l.

We are also assuming that the phoneme /l/ has two allophones, [l] and [ɫ]. There is an /l/ realization rule: /l/ is realized as [l] immediately before vowels, and as [ɫ] immediately after vowels.

These two claims appear to commit us to the idea that the rule governing the occurrence of [ɫ] must, in some sense, 'precede' the rule governing the phoneme /i:/, since we are claiming that [ɫ] only ever arises as a result of the application of the /l/ rule, and that [i:ə] only ever arises when an [ɫ] follows. We may depict this claim about the interaction of the two rules as follows:

(2) /fi:l/   /l/ rule   [fi:ɫ]

                /i:/ rule   [fi:əɫ]

Another example of vowel allophones in English concerns vowel length. In many languages, vowel length is phonemic. But in other languages, vowel length is allophonic. In Scottish Standard English (SSE), for instance, some (not all) of the vowel phonemes have long and short allophones:

(3) Long and short vowels in Scottish Standard English

heave [hi:v]	breathe [bɹi:ð]	breeze [bɹi:z]
beer [bi:ɹ]	bee [bi:]	
beef [bif]	heath [hiθ]	fleece [flis]
deal [diɫ]	beat [bit]	
move [mʉ:v]	smooth [smʉ:ð]	lose [ɫʉ:z]
boor [bʉ:ɹ]	blue [blʉ:]	
hoof [hʉf]	tooth [thʉθ]	loose [ɫʉs]

The long allophones of the phonemes /i/, /u/ occur in the following contexts: at the end of a word, before /ɹ/ and before the other environment. Vowel length is therefore allophonic, rather than phonemic, in SSE.

─┤ B ├─

(a) Assimilation: An aspect of connected speech, where one sound, usually a consonant becomes more like, or identical with, a neighbouring sound regarding one or more of the distinctive features.
(b) Coalescence: A sound change where two or more phonetic segments merge into one segment.
(c) Dissimilation: The process whereby one sound becomes less like a neighbouring sound or a sound in close proximity.
(d) Elision: The omission of one or more sounds in connected speech.

Based on the passages, first, in <B>, identify the phonetic process which the schwa articulation in (1) is related to. Second, state one more environment where vowel lengthening occurs in (3), using the natural class.

46 Read the passage and follow the directions. [4 points]

Certain nouns have stress on their final syllable. It is, of course, a condition on final stressed syllables that they are heavy. But not all such heavy syllables are stressed.

(1) a. balloon
    rabbi
    textile
    colonnade
   b. moped
    ellipse
    syntax
    commandant
   c. comic
    parent
    August
    discipline

Under what conditions do nouns have penultimate stress? Example (2) below shows a range of stress patterns, on which our discussion will be based.

(2) a. a'roma
    ho'rizon
    de'cathlon
   b. 'nightin‚gale
    ‚caval'cade
    ‚chimpan'zee
   c. ‚bam'boo
    ‚cham'pagne
    ‚fi'nance

Penultimate syllables in nouns are stressed if they are heavy, as those in (2a) are, and unstressed if they are light. This rule, which is widely attested in polysyllabic English nouns, has few exceptions; but there are further conditions attached to it. Consider first the examples in (2b), which have unstressed heavy penultimate syllables, contrary to the rule as it stands. Heavy penults are evidently not stressed if the _____ syllable has stress; in other words: a foot aligned with the penultimate syllable has to be bisyllabic, also including the final syllable. It cannot do that if the final syllable is itself a foot. However, in (2c), monosyllabic feet do occur on heavy penultimate syllables after all, but only where that syllable also happens to be the first one of the word.

Based on the passage, first, fill in the blank with ONE word from the passage. Second, identify one group in (1a)—(1c) which the word 'cadet' should belong to. Then, explain why, stating whether the group you choose has final stressed syllables and the rhyme structure of the final syllables.

47 Read the passage and fill in each blank with ONE word from the passage. Write your answers in the correct order. [2 points]

> Many rules change features from one value to its opposite or even add features not present in the phonemic representation. It is understandable that so many languages have assimilation rules; they permit greater ease of articulation. It might seem strange, then, to learn that languages also have feature-changing rules called dissimilation rules, in which certain segments become less similar to other segments. Ironically, such rules have the same explanation: it is sometimes easier to articulate dissimilar sounds.
>
> An example of easing pronunciation is found in some varieties of English, in which there is a fricative ____①____ rule. This rule applies to sequences /fθ/ and /sθ/, changing them to [ft] and [st]. For example, the words *fifth* and *sixth* come to be pronounced as if they were spelled *fift* and *sikst*.
>
> Another example of easing pronunciation is found in nasalization of vowels. Nasalization of vowels in English is nonphonemic because it is predictable by rule. The vowel nasalization rule is an assimilation rule that makes neighboring segments more similar by adding the feature [+nasal] to the vowel. There is a tendency when we speak to increase the ease of articulation. It is easier to lower the velum while a vowel is being pronounced before a nasal stop than to wait for the completion of the vowel and then require the velum to move suddenly.
>
> Some feature-changing rules are neither assimilation nor dissimilation rules. The rule in English that aspirates voiceless stops at the beginning of a syllable simply adds a nondistinctive feature. Generally, aspiration occurs only if the following vowel is stressed. The /p/ in *pit* and *repeat* is an aspirated [pʰ], but the /p/ in *inspect* or *compass* is an unaspirated [p]. In the word *compass*, the /p/ is not aspirated because the /p/ is not in the ____②____ syllable. Aspiration is not specified in any phonemic feature matrices of English. The aspiration rule adds this feature for reasons having to do with the timing of the closure release rather than in an attempt to make segments more alike or not alike, as with assimilation and dissimilation rules.

48 Read the passages and follow the directions. [4 points]

Consider the sentence *Jennifer must have been in the refectory*. The only lexical words in this sentence are *Jennifer* and *refectory*; the words in between are function words, to which no metrical structures are assigned—they are adjoined to the preceding foot. It is quite clear that a foot, containing no fewer than eight unstressed syllables, constitutes a serious disruption of stress timing in any utterance. Speakers are more likely to adopt one of the following scansions in (1):

(1) a. 'Jennifer ˌmust have been in the re'fectory
    b. 'Jennifer must have ˌbeen in the re'fectory
    c. 'Jennifer ˌmust have ˌbeen in the re'fectory

Note that none of these three versions of the sentence places any particular emphasis on any of the words that have now received additional beats in performance.

What function words are capable of receiving such rhythmically motivated stresses? Consider the following examples:

(2) a. 'Jennifer must ˌbe in the re'fectory
    b. 'Jennifer ˌmust be in the re'fectory
    c. *'Jennifer ˌmust ˌbe in the re'fectory
    d. 'John must ˌbe in the re'fectory
    e. *'John ˌmust be in the re'fectory

Note that the starred sentences (2c, e) are only acceptable if they carry some emphasis on the stressed function words; the others have once again no particular emphasis on any of the stressed syllables. In (2c), *ˌmust ˌbe* cannot both receive a nonemphatic stress while ˌmust have ˌbeen (1c) can; and similarly *'John ˌmust be* in (2e) is possible only under emphasis while 'Jennifer ˌmust be is again unmarked for emphasis.

Another device of creating rhythmic beats in an utterance is that of inserting *silent stresses*—beats that are not filled by syllables but by brief pauses. Consider again the statement of Jennifer's whereabouts, this time uttered like this: *Jennifer ∧ must have ˌbeen in the reˈfectory* (where the '∧' indicates a silent stress).

Unlike the distribution of (hesitation) pauses in speech, that of silent stresses in a sentence is not random. Silent stresses seem to occur principally at major syntactic boundaries—indeed, it is one of the functions of silent stresses to mark such boundaries in speech, and thereby possibly to resolve ambiguities. Now consider the ambiguous phrase *old ˈmen and ˈwomen*. In speech the ambiguity may be resolved by silent stresses.

Based on the passage, first, considering the data in (1) and (2), state the environment where a function word receives a Nonemphatic Stress in an utterance. Second, resolve the ambiguity of the phrase "old ˈmen and ˈwomen" by using silent stresses, including each interpretation, respectively.

49 Read the passage and follow the directions. [4 points]

─┤ A ├─

Take a look at a subclass of stress patterns where the final syllable of a word bears no stress (primary or secondary). Here are some examples:

(1) a. a'roma   b. u'tensil   c. A'merica
    to'mato   Be'linda   'camera
    sa'lami   a'malgam   'cinema
    po'tato   e'nigma   'capital
    ho'rizon   de'cathlon   'anagram

The words in (1a, b) have stress on the penultimate syllable and those in (1c) on the antepenultimate syllable. This distribution of stress illustrates the central regularity within this subclass; and this regularity is governed by syllable weight. The penultimate syllable is stressed if it is heavy; otherwise, stress falls on the antepenultimate syllable.

Let us look at the penultimate syllables of the words in (1) in more detail. Those in (1a) all contain long vowels (diphthongs or tense monophthongs), those in (1b) contain vowel-plus-consonant sequences, while the examples in (1c) have penultimate syllables whose rhymes merely contain lax vowels.

We are now in a position where we can be more specific about ambisyllabicity. Regular stress (in nouns) falls on the penultimate syllable if it is heavy, otherwise on the antepenultimate syllable. The antepenultimate syllable in a word like *America*, and the penult in *apple*, is the 'last resort' for the stress to go to. In such a case, where a light syllable must take the stress, this syllable becomes heavy, under stress, through ambisyllabicity. Typically, ambisyllabicity occurs in words. such as those listed in (1c) as well as in bisyllabic words. For this subclass, we have found a rule whereby the penultimate syllable takes stress if it is heavy and the antepenult does if the penult is light. But it would be wrong to assume that any noun that falls within this subclass has entirely predictable stress:

(2) a. 'badminton   b. va'nilla
    'calendar   ma'donna

The words in (2a) have heavy penultimate syllables; nevertheless, the stress falls on the antepenult. And the words in (2b) ought to have antepenultimate stress because they have light penultimate syllables; instead, they stress the penult and resort to ambisyllabicity to make that syllable heavy. It is perhaps worth noting that words of this type commonly have double consonant spellings, indicating perhaps the ambisyllabicity of the doubled consonant, and thereby the irregular stress behaviour of the word.

B

| discipline | cylinder | marina | vertebra |
| confetti | angina | synopsis | agenda |

Based on the passage, in <B>, identify TWO words that show the same stress pattern as in (2), and then explain the stress patterns of each word, just as described in the passage.

50 Read the passage and fill in the blank ① with the ONE most appropriate word, and the blank ② with ONE word from the passage. Write your answers in the correct order. [2 points]

Sometimes it is possible to predict not only the choice of allophones in the phonetic representation, but also the appearance of entirely new segments. One example of this concerns the mid tense vowels [e] and [o], which are diphthongized in most dialects of English: [e] occurs with [j], as in [dej] *day*, and [o] occurs with [w], as in [dow] *dough*. The choice of glide is not arbitrary: [w] is back and _____①_____, just like [o], and [j] is non-back and unrounded, like [e].

(1) [dej] *day*   [dow] *dough*
    [e] + [j]   [o] + [w]

The following generalization states the distribution of the two glides.

(2) A mid tense vowel in English is predictably followed by a glide that has the same backness and roundness.

Thus, although the phonetic representations of English mid tense vowels include the glides, the corresponding phonemic representations do not (see table 1 below).

TABLE 1. Phonemic and phonetic representations for English mid tense vowels			
Word	Phonemic representation	Phonetic representation	Extra segment in the phonetic representation
day	/de/	[dej]	the glide [j]
dough	/do/	[dow]	the glide [w]

Once again, we see that the _____②_____ representation contains only information that is not predictable. Phonetic details—whether they are about vowel nasalization or which glide follows a mid vowel—are added later.

51 Read the passage and follow the directions. [4 points]

In the speech of many English speakers there is an allophonic rule whereby the phoneme /æ/ is diphthongized to [æɪ̯]. The effects of the rule can be seen in pairs such as the following:

(1) pan   /pæn/   [pæn]
    fan   /fæn/   [fæn]
    gander   /ˈgændɚ/   [ˈgændɚ]
    pang   /pæŋ/   [pæɪ̯ŋ]
    fang   /fæŋ/   [fæɪ̯ŋ]
    anger   /ˈæŋgɚ/   [ˈæɪ̯ŋgɚ]

In the same dialect there is an optional rule of /n/ Assimilation. Consider the following data:

(2) input   [ˈɪnˌpʊt] or [ˈɪmˌpʊt]
    unprepared   [ˌʌnpɹəˈpeɪd] or [ˌʌmpɹəˈpeɪd]
    unbelievable   [ˌʌnbəˈlivəbəl] or [ˌʌmbəˈlivəbəl]
    I live in Minnesota   [aɪ ˈlɪv ɪn ˌmɪnəˈsoʊɾə] or [aɪ ˈlɪv ɪm ˌmɪnəˈsoʊɾə]
    phone call   [ˈfoʊn ˌkɔl] or [ˈfoʊŋ ˌkɔl]
    concourse   [ˈkɑnˌkɔɹs] or [ˈkɑŋˌkɔɹs]
    con game   [ˈkɑnˌgeɪm] or [ˈkɑŋˌgeɪm]
    in college   [ɪn ˈkɑlɪdʒ] or [ɪŋ ˈkɑlɪdʒ]

These data in (2) are the effects of /n/ Assimilation rule as given below:

(3) /n/ Assimilation Rule:
    Assimilate /n/ in _____ of articulation to a following consonant.

Now assess the implications of the following forms for the relative ordering of /æ/ Diphthongization and /n/ Assimilation:

(4) pancake   /ˈpænˌkeɪk/   [ˈpæŋˌkeɪk]
    Vancouver   /vænˈkuvɚ/   [væŋˈkuvɚ]
    Dan Gurney   /ˈdæn ˈgɚni/   [ˈdæŋ ˈgɚni]
    sank   /ˈsæŋk/   [ˈsæɪ̃ŋk]
    anchor   /ˈæŋkɚ/   [ˈæɪ̃ŋkɚ]
    Rangoon   /ɹæŋˈgun/   [ɹæɪ̃ŋˈgun]
    pang cake   /ˈpæŋˌkeɪk/   [ˈpæɪ̃ŋˌkeɪk]

Based on the passage, first, fill in the blank in (3) with the ONE most appropriate word. Second, state the relative ordering of /æ/ Diphthongization and /n/ Assimilation in (4).

52 Read the passage and follow the directions. [4 points]

Nonrhotic accents such as Received Pronunciation (RP) have a phonotactic constraint whereby /r/ can occur in syllable onsets but not in rhymes. Such accents have retained some residue of historic rhyme—/r/ in the form of the centring diphthong phonemes /ɪə/, /ɛə/ and /ʊə/, but in other vowels no such traces of historic /r/ are left. In such accents, then, /r/ occurs only in a syllable onset: it fails to occur in *hear* /hɪə/ but it is present in *hearing* /hɪərɪŋ/. Consider the following examples:

(1) a. hammer   /hamə/
     bar   /bɑ/
     hear   /hɪə/
     cure   /kjʊə/
     tear   /tɛə/
     fur   /fɜ/

   b. hammering   /hamərɪŋ/
     barring   /bɑrɪŋ/
     hearing   /hɪərɪŋ/
     curing   /kjʊərɪŋ/
     tearing   /tɛərɪŋ/
     fury   /fɜrɪ/

   c. hammer it   /hamərɪt/
     bar it   /bɑrɪt/
     hear it   /hɪərɪt/
     cure it   /kjʊərɪt/
     tear it   /tɛərɪt/
     fur is   /fɜrɪz/

Example (1a) shows the range of vowel phonemes that are found in contexts of historic /r/. Example (1b) demonstrates the occurrence of /r/ in RP in words that are morphologically related to those in (1a). In these cases /r/ is in the syllable-_____ position and is therefore not barred from occurring.

What is of interest here is the list of items in (1c), where /r/, although word-final, does occur in the context of the following word beginning with a vowel. This is the phenomenon of 'linking /r/', common in nonrhotic accents including the most formal variety of RP. Liaison provides us with the means of accounting for such cases. With regard to /r/, liaison has the same effect as the regularities of word-internal syllabification do: just as in *hammering*, the /r/ in *hammer it* occupies the syllable-_____ position in connected speech (due to liaison) and is therefore pronounced in the speech of nonrhotic speakers.

No account of linking /r/ is complete without a discussion of the closely related phenomenon of intrusive /r/, the insertion of /r/ in the same contexts as those in which linking /r/ is found, but in words where there is no historic /r/. Like linking /r/, intrusive /r/ is common in nonrhotic accents, but unlike the former, it is stigmatised in formal RP. Examples of intrusive /r/ are given in (2b). In contrast, no intrusive /r/ is possible after the vowels exemplified in (2c):

(2) a. Brenda   /ə/
    spa   /ɑ/
    skua   /ʊə/
    Eritrea   /ɛə/
    ?   /ɜ/

   b. Brenda and   /brɛndərənd/
      spa is   /spɑrɪz/
      skua is   /skjʊərɪz/
      Eritrea is   /ɛrɪtrɛərɪz/
      ? is   /...ɜrɪz/

   c. see it   */sirɪt/
      do it   */durɪt/
      boy is   */bɔɪrɪz/
      now is   */naʊrɪz/
      why is   */waɪrɪz/

Based on the passage, fill in the blank with ONE word from the passage. (Use the SAME answer for both blanks.) Second, considering the data in (2), state the environment where intrusive /r/ does not occur, using the distinctive feature of the vowels.

53 Read the passage and fill in the blank with the ONE most appropriate word. [2 points]

The simplest and best way to show that two sounds contrast with each other (that is, that they belong to separate phonemes) is to find a minimal pair. Occasionally, though, gaps in a language's vocabulary make it difficult to find minimal pairs for contrasting sounds. Under these circumstances, it is sometimes possible to rely on near-minimal pairs that contain differences other than the one involving the key contrast, as long as the extra differences don't involve sounds right next to the contrast. One such example in English is [mɪʃən] and [vɪʒən], *mission* and *vision*. Although not a perfect minimal pair, these words can help establish that [ʃ] and [ʒ] contrast with each other if actual minimal pairs are not available. (In fact, there are a few minimal pairs for the [ʃ]/[ʒ] distinction, such as *mesher* and *measure*, but they are few and far between, and could easily be missed.)

Sometimes, even near-minimal pairs are not available to establish that two sounds contrast with each other. A notorious example of this involves [h] and [ŋ] in English. Because [h] occurs only at the beginning of syllables and [ŋ] occurs only at the end of syllables, we don't find the usual minimal or near-minimal pairs. There are lots of words like *hope* and *ham*, with [h] in initial position, but no words like *ngope* and *ngam* to contrast with them. And there are lots of words like *long* and *king*, with [ŋ] in final position, but no words like *loh* and *kih*. This does not mean that [h] and [ŋ] are allophones of the _____ phoneme, though. The allophones of a phoneme must be phonetically similar to each other. Because [h] and [ŋ] are so different phonetically, we can be confident in assigning them to separate phonemes even in the absence of minimal and near-minimal pairs.

54 Read the passage and follow the directions. [4 points]

There are also many pairs of sounds that do not contrast. Here is a simple case from English, involving the length of vowels. If you listen to a native speaker say the following pairs of words in (1), you will find that the vowel phoneme /eɪ/ is quite a bit shorter in the second member of each pair.

(1) save [seɪv]   safe [sĕɪf]
    Abe [eɪb]   ape [ĕɪp]
    made [meɪd]   mate [mĕɪt]
    maze [meɪz]   mace [mĕɪs]
    age [eɪdʒ]   H [ĕɪtʃ]
    Haig [heɪg]   ache [ĕɪk]

*Note: ' ̆ ' indicates the IPA shortness marker

Although [eɪ] and [ĕɪ] are audibly different, they are not separate _____ — one could not use them to form a distinction between words. The reason is that their distribution is predictable. [eɪ] occurs when the next sound in the word is voiced, and [ĕɪ] occurs when the next sound in the word is voiceless.

Let us consider some other cases of allophonic variation in English. The following pair illustrates words containing alveolar [n] and dental [n̪].

(2) know ['noʊ]   tenth ['tɛn̪θ]
    annoy [ə'nɔɪ]   month ['mʌn̪θ]
    onion ['ʌnjən]   panther ['pæn̪θɚ]
    nun ['nʌn]   chrysanthemum [kɹə'sæn̪θəməm]

It is not hard to see that the dental [n̪] occurs in a specific context: before [θ]. There is no particular context for alveolar [n]; it occurs pretty much everywhere else.

The next data set illustrates four allophones of the /l/ phoneme as they occur in a number of dialects of English. [ɫ] is a velarized l, articulated with high back tongue body position. [ɫ̪] is the same as [ɫ], only with a dental instead of alveolar place of articulation. [l̥] is an l which starts out voiceless and ends voiced.

(3) Words with [ɫ]   Words with [l̥]   Words with [ɫ]   Words with [l]
    file ['faɪɫ]   slight ['sl̥aɪt]   wealth ['wɛɫθ]   listen ['lɪsən]
    fool ['fuɫ]   flight ['fl̥aɪt]   health ['hɛɫθ]   lose ['luz]
    all ['ɔɫ]   plow ['pl̥aʊ]   filthy ['fɪɫθi]   allow [ə'laʊ]
    ball ['bɔɫ]   cling ['kl̥ɪŋ]   tilth ['tɪɫθ]   aglow [ə'gloʊ]
    fell ['fɛɫ]   discipline ['dɪsəpl̥ən]   stealth ['stɛɫθ]   blend ['blɛnd]
    feel ['fiɫ]

At the level of conscious awareness, people are characteristically attuned only to the distinctions between phonemes; to make people aware of allophones requires that their attention be carefully directed to the distinction.

Based on the passage, first, fill in the blank with ONE word from the passage. Second, state the environment where [l̥] occurs.

55 Read the passage and follow the directions. [4 points]

In many accents of English, for example Received Pronunciation (RP), the lateral phoneme /l/ has two major realisational variants, or allophones: a 'clear' one, transcribed simply as [l], and a 'dark' one—[ɫ]. Both are laterals with alveolar contact; the articulatory difference between the two is that in the former the back of the tongue is lowered while in the latter it is raised towards the velum or retracted towards the uvula. Here are some examples for RP:

(1) a. 'clear' [l]: *l*ull, *l*ip, *l*ow, b*l*ind, sp*l*ice, ye*l*low, foo*l*ish
    b. 'dark' [ɫ]: lu*ll*, hi*ll*, poo*l*, he*l*p, so*l*ve, e*l*bow, litt*l*e

The accent that exemplifies the phonetic difference between the two allophones, as well as their distribution, most clearly is RP; in General American (GA) the distribution is the same but the phonetic difference is not as strong in that the 'clear' [l], too, is somewhat velarised. In many varieties of Scottish Standard English (SSE) all realisations of /l/ are dark; while other accents (for example, Welsh English and Southern Irish English) have clear [l] in all contexts.

What, then, is the distribution of clear and dark /l/ in RP? It is quite clear that there is a rule for this distribution and that this rule derives the quality of the /l/ realisation from the place that it occupies in the syllable. All the cases of clear [l] in (1a) are sited in syllable onsets while the instances of dark [ɫ] in (1b) occur in syllable rhymes. But there are some that deserve a full syllable-structure analysis, if only to confirm the point:

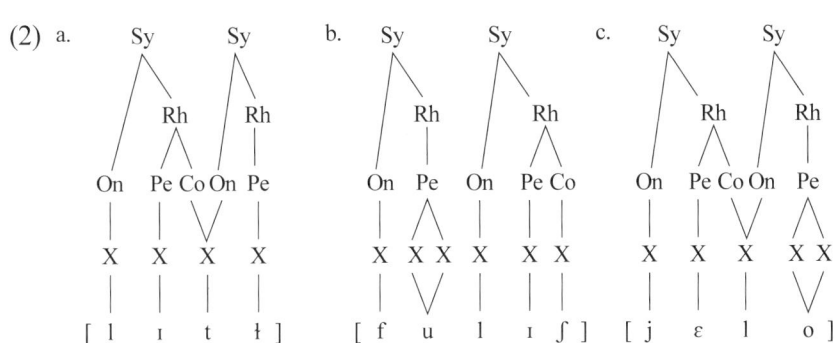

In *little* (2a), the /l/ occupies the syllable peak: it is not only dark but also syllabic. In transcription, this syllabicity is marked by a stroke underneath the syllabic sound: [lɪtɫ̩]. Note that in the alternative pronunciation [lɪtəɫ], the [ɫ] occurs in the coda, as it does in all other examples of (1b). In *foolish* (2b), /l/ occupies a syllable onset and is clear as predicted, while in *yellow* (2c) it is ambisyllabic. In this case the /l/'s association with the onset is decisive in RP: it is clear rather than dark.

From this analysis of the facts, the complementary distribution of [l] and [ɫ] in RP is evident:

(3) Generalisation
/l/ is realised as [ɫ] in rhymes and as [l] elsewhere.

Based on the passage, first, identify ONE counterexample in (1) to the generalisation in (3). Second, considering the counterexample you choose, revise the generalisation in (3).

56 Read the passage and fill in the blank ① with the ONE most appropriate word and the blank ② with ONE word from the passage. Write your answers in the correct order. [2 points]

Let us begin by considering voiceless unaspirated and voiceless aspirated stops in English and Korean.

(1) Aspirated and unaspirated voiceless stops in English

    (a) [ˈpʰuːɫ]   'pool'   (b) [əˈpʰɪə]   'appear'
    (c) [ˈspɜːt]   'spurt'   (d) [dəˈspaɪt]   'despite'
    (e) [ˈtʰɒp]   'top'   (f) [əˈtʰæk]   'attack'
    (g) [ˈstɒp]   'stop'   (h) [dəˈstɹɔɪ]   'destroy'
    (i) [ˈkʰɪlɪŋ]   'killing'   (j) [əˈkʰɹuː]   'accrue'
    (k) [ˈskoʊɫd]   'scold'   (l) [dɪˈskʌvə]   'discover'

From these data, it appears that voiceless stops are aspirated when they are at the beginning of a stressed syllable, but unaspirated when preceded by a voiceless alveolar fricative. Compare the English data with the following data from Korean:

(2) Aspirated and unaspirated voiceless stops in Korean

    (a) [pʰul]   'grass'   (b) [pul]   'fire'
    (c) [tʰal]   'mask'   (d) [tal]   'moon'
    (e) [kʰɛda]   'dig'   (f) [kɛda]   'fold'

In these Korean data, aspirated and unaspirated voiceless stops may occur in the same place (at the beginning of a word). In the English data we have looked at, the distribution of unaspirated and aspirated stops is mutually exclusive: where you get one kind of stop, you never get the other. This is called complementary distribution. Compare the English situation with the Korean one. It is clear that the distribution of aspirated and unaspirated voiceless stops in Korean is _____①_____ distribution.

The distinction between aspirated and unaspirated voiceless stops is ____②____ in Korean but allophonic in English. Both English and Korean speakers habitually utter both aspirated and unaspirated voiceless stops. On the phonetic level, the two languages are therefore equivalent as far as bilabial, alveolar and velar voiceless stops are concerned. But at the phonemic level (the mental level), the two languages are quite distinct: the Korean speaker has six mental categories where the English speaker has only three.

57 Read the passage and follow the directions. [4 points]

The sounds of a language exist in order to make audible the higher-level structural units that do bear meaning: morphemes, words, phrases, sentences. Phonology is closely connected with morphology and syntax, the two components of grammar that create these higher-level units.

A phonological rule normally has a focus, which is the segment that gets changed, and one or two environment strings, on the left and/or on the right. This is shown below for the generic rule A → B / P _____ Q.

/aɪ/ Raising in (1) accounts for the [ʌɪ] allophone of /aɪ/ that appears in many English dialects before voiceless consonants.

(1) life /laɪf/ [lʌɪf]   live /laɪv/ [laɪv]
    wright /ɹaɪt/ [ɹʌɪt]   ride /ɹaɪd/ [ɹaɪd]
    white /waɪt/ [wʌɪt]   wide /waɪd/ [waɪd]
    rifle /ɹaɪfəl/ [ɹʌɪfəl]   rival /ɹaɪvəl/ [ɹaɪvəl]

/aɪ/ Raising rule needs to be formulated a bit more carefully in order to show the focus and environment strings clearly:

(2) /aɪ/ Raising

a → [−low]/ _____ ɪ [−voice]   Bounding domain: word

The focus of this rule is /a/, there is no left environment string, and the right environment string is ɪ [−voice]. Moreover, the rule is now stated with a bounding domain, the word. This means that the rule will apply only if the focus segment /a/ and all the segments matched up with the right environment string fall within the same word.

Here is an example. The underlying representation /[ɹaɪs]_word [eɪlz]_word/ (*rice ales*, 'ales brewed from rice') has an /aɪ/ that precedes a voiceless consonant within the same word. Hence the word-bounded rule of /aɪ/ Raising can apply, yielding [ɹʌɪs eɪlz]. On the other hand, the underlying representation /[ɹaɪ]_word[seɪlz]_word/ (*rye sales*, 'sales of rye') has an /aɪ/ that precedes a voiceless consonant in the next word. Hence the word-bounded rule of /aɪ/ Raising is blocked, and the output is [ɹaɪ seɪlz]. While *rice ales* and *rye sales* contain the same phonemes in the same order, they have different surface representations because of the grouping of the phonemes into words.

(3) utterance   underlying representation   surface representations
   a. rice ales   /[ɹaɪs]_word [eɪlz]_word/   [ɹʌɪseɪlz]
   b. rye sales   /[ɹaɪ]_word [seɪlz]_word/   [ɹaɪseɪlz]

Now take a look at two cases:

(4) a. /baɪpəteɪtoʊz/
    b. /waɪpəteɪbəl/

Based on the passage, state the phonetic (i.e., surface) representation of each underlined phonemic representation (/aɪ/) in (4). And then, explain why, discussing whether the word-bounded rule of /aɪ/ Raising can apply.

58 Read the passage and fill in the blank ① with ONE word from the passage and the blank ② with the ONE most appropriate word. Write your answers in the correct order. [2 points]

There are two general principles related to *Basic Syllables*: the Sonority Requirement and the Binarity Requirement.

(1) The Sonority Requirement: In basic syllables, sonority rises before the nucleus and declines after the nucleus.
(2) The Binarity Requirement: Within basic syllables, each constituent can be at most binary (i.e., branching into two).

Don't be fooled by words such as *button* /bʌtn̩/. It consists of two syllables: /bʌ.tn̩/, with /t/ in the ____①____ of the second syllable and /n̩/ functioning as the nucleus.

Some onsets in English comply with the Sonority Requirement. Consider the following data:

(3) a. /pl/ please   b. /tr/ trade   c. /kl/ clean
    /pr/ proud   /tw/ twin   /kr/ cream
    /pj/ pure   /sr/ Sri Lanka   /kw/ queen
    /br/ bring   /sl/ slow   /kj/ cute
    /bl/ blight   /dr/ dry   /gr/ grow
    /fr/ free   /gl/ glow

In (3a), the two consonants in the onset are ____②____ + sonorants, in (3b) alveolars + sonorants, and in (3c) velars + sonorants. In the onset, sonority rises before the nucleus.

The second major principle with which basic syllables must comply is the Binarity Requirement. This means that an onset or coda can't contain more than two consonants. Thus, a word such as *grant*, with two consonants in its onset and two in its coda, represents the most complex basic syllable permitted in English.

(4)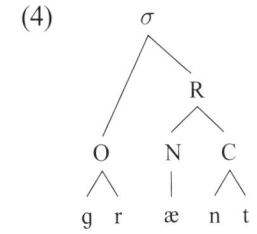

59 Read the passage and follow the directions. [4 points]

The voiceless set of stops is pronounced with aspiration at the beginning of stressed syllables.

(1) pay [pʰe]   take [tʰek]   cab [kʰæb]
   apart [əpʰaɹt]   attack [ətʰæk]   occur [əkʰɝ]

In addition, voiceless stops may be produced with weak aspiration in the following positions:

(2) a. polite [pəlaɪt]   vacuum [vækjum]   certain [sɝtən]
   b. pickle [pɪkl̩]   bottom [batm̩]   couple [kʌpl̩]
   c. sit [sɪt]   sick [sɪk]   stop [stɑp]

In their release stage, syllable-final (especially word-final) single coda stops are often produced with no audible release. The following examples illustrate the point with the appropriate diacritic for unreleased stops:

(3) mop [mɔp̚]   sit [sɪt̚]   sack [sæk̚]
   mob [mab̚]   sad [sæd̚]   bag [bæg̚]

When it is not following a vowel, most speakers release the final /t/ (e.g. *fast*).
  When we have a word with two _____ stops in a row, there is no audible release for the first stop; the closure of the second stop in sequence is made before the release of the first stop.

(4) sipped [sɪp̚t]   cheap date [tʃip̚det]   sobbed [sɑb̚d]

When we have two homorganic stops in a sequence, there is no separate release for the first stop; rather, there is one prolonged closure for the two stops in question. This is valid for cases where there is voicing agreement as well as sequences with different voicing:

(5) big girl   black cat   sad dog   stop please
     top block   white dog   black girl

Based on the passage, first, fill in the blank with the ONE most appropriate word. Second, state the conditions where weak aspiration occurs in (2a) and (2b), respectively.

_____
_____
_____
_____
_____

60. Read the passages and follow the directions. [4 points]

A

Length of vowels (and diphthongs) varies predictably according to the context they appear in. More specifically, vowels are longer before voiced consonants than before their voiceless counterparts. Consider the data in (1):

(1) back — bag   duff — dove   leaf — leave
    ice — rise   pat — pad   rope — robe

In each pair, the phonetic realization of the vowel in the second member is longer than its realization of the one in the first member. For example, the vowel in *robe* is longer before the voiced consonant /b/ than before its voiceless counterpart /p/ in *rope*.

Vowels are longer before sonorant consonants than before obstruents. For example, the phonetic realization of the vowel /o/ in *goal* [gol] is longer than its realization in *goad* [god].

(2) goal — goad   can — cat   well — wet
    team — teeth   beam — beat   more — moss

Vowels are longer in open syllables than in closed syllables. Thus, the phonetic realization of the vowel /e/ in *bay* [be] is longer than its realization in *bait* [bet]. More examples are below:

(3) bay — bait   see — seize   no — nose
    me — meet   you — youth   so — soul

We can combine the three rules above and say that we find a vowel longest in an open syllable (e.g. /i/ in *knee* [ni]); next longest in a syllable closed by a sonorant consonant (e.g. /i/ in *kneel* [nil]); next longest in a syllable closed by a voiced obstruent (e.g. /i/ in *need* [nid]); and shortest in a syllable closed by a voiceless consonant (e.g. /i/ in *neat* [nit]).

Lastly, vowels are longer in stressed syllables than in unstressed syllables. Thus, the phonetic realization of the phoneme /i/ in the stressed (bold-faced) syllable of the word *appreciate* [ə.pɹi.ʃi.et] is longer than its realization in the following unstressed syllable.

> **B**
>
> Now consider the following pairs:
>
> (4) a. mouth (verb) — mouth (noun)
>   b. advice — advise
>   c. house (noun) — house (verb)
>   d. loath — loathe
>   e. use (noun) — use (verb)
>   f. lose — loose

Based on the passage <A>, identify TWO pairs in <B> where the vowel in the first member is longer than the one in the second member. Then, explain why, comparing the exact two phonemes which affect the length of vowels for each pair, as described in the passage.

_____
_____
_____
_____
_____

61 Read the passage and fill in the blank ① with the ONE most appropriate word and the blank ② with ONE word from the passage. Write your answers in the correct order. [2 points]

> Stress-neutral suffixes never make any difference to the stress pattern of the resulting word. Such suffixes include all eight inflectional suffixes (plural; possessive; third person singular present tense -s; progressive -ing; past -ed; past participle -en/-ed; comparative -er; and superlative -est), and several derivational ones:
>
> (1) -al   arríve — arríval   -ize   spécial — spécialize
>   -ant   ascénd — ascéndant   -less   bóttom — bóttomless
>   -cy   célibate — célibacy   -ly   fríend — fríendly
>   -dom   frée — fréedom   -ment   aménd — améndment
>   -er   pláy — pláyer   -ness   fránk — fránkness
>   -ess   líon — líoness   -ship   fríend — fríendship
>   -ful   gráce — gráceful   -some   búrden — búrdensome
>   -hood nátion — nátionhood   -wise   clóck — clóckwise
>   -ish   gréen — gréenish   -th   grów — grówth
>   -ism   álcohol — álcoholism   -ty   cértain — cértainty
>   -ist   húman — húmanist   **-y   sílk — sílky**
>   -ive   submít — submíssive
>
> We should point out that the last item, adjective-forming suffix -y, should not be treated in the same way as the noun-forming -y, which shifts the stress to the antepenultimate, as in *homophone — homophony, photograph — photography,* etc.
> While the above-listed suffixes do not normally change the location of the stress, when several ___①___ syllables are piled up to the right of the stress, we see that the stress moves to the ___②___, as in (2).
>
> (2) móment — mómentary but momentárily

62 Read the passage and follow the directions. [4 points]

A

The rhythm of English is stress-timed. What this means is that the regular recurring beats found in the speech of English speakers (the rhythm of English speech) fall on stressed syllables. That is, stressed syllables in English occur at more or less equal intervals.

One of the consequences of this kind of rhythm is that English feet may consist of a stressed syllable followed by a sequence of unstressed syllables, as in the phrase *heard in the park*, in which the stressed syllable in *heard* is followed by two unstressed syllables, or the phrase *heard it in the park*, where *heard* is followed by three, or the phrase *heard it in the announcement*, where it is followed by four.

Having said that English allows for really quite extensive sequences of unstressed syllables, it has to be said that the ideal or optimal rhythmic structure is one in which strong and weak syllables alternate in an S-W-S-W pattern. It appears to be the case that such sequences of 'alternating opposites' are optimal in a perceptual sense: they seem to make the speech signal more easily decoded. Such optimal rhythmic structures are often referred to as eurhythmic stuctures.

One kind of evidence for eurhythmic constraints comes from co-ordinated constructions ('A and B'). This is one of the rare cases in English where the speaker has some scope for changing the word order in a sentence without changing its meaning: 'B and A' is usually synonymous with 'A and B'. And in such cases, speakers favour the construction that has rhythmic alternation over the alternative one that is less eurhythmic. Consider the following:

(2) slim and slender chances   hot and spicy
    hot and bothered   sweet and sour
    neat and tidy   fruit and fibre
    hale and hearty   rum and raisin

The 'A' elements in these examples have no obvious semantic precedence over the 'B' elements. The reason for the preference is purely rhythmic: one has the optimal rhythmic alternation and the other does not.

---- B ----

(3) a. bleak and lonely
    b. lonely and bleak
(4) a. crunchy and crisp
    b. crisp and crunchy

Based on the passage, first, in <B>, identify TWO constructions that speakers favour. Second, explain the reason for the preference.

63 Read the passage and follow the directions. [4 points]

┤ A ├

An assimilatory situation arises when a non-alveolar stop is preceded by an alveolar stop, while maintaining the original voicing.

(1) night cap [naɪt kæp] → [naɪk:æp]
   red badge [ɹɛd bædʒ] → [ɹɛb:ædʒ]
   white paper [waɪt pepɚ] → [waɪp:epɚ]
   weed killer [wid kɪlɚ] → [wigkɪlɚ]

The stop closure is maintained and nasally released in cases in which the stop is followed by a homorganic nasal. In this process, the air is released through the nasal cavity. This happens in the following environments:

(2) a. button [bʌtn̩]   sudden [sʌdn̩]   taken [tekŋ̍]
   b. submarine [sʌbməɹin] madness [mædnəs]
   c. hard nails [haɹdnelz] sad news [sædnuz]

A comparable release, this time laterally, is provided when the stop is followed by a homorganic lateral. This process can be observed in the following words as well as in sequences of words:

(3) cattle [kætl̩]   middle [mɪdl̩]
   bud light [bʌdlaɪt] at last [ətlæst]

Certain stops have characteristics of their own. Alveolar stops are realized as dental when they occur immediately before interdentals, as illustrated in the following:

(4) bad [bæd] — bad things [bæd̪θɪŋz]
   great [gɹet] — great things [gɹet̪θɪŋz]

The two sets that do NOT have the same pattern as (5) are **(c) detest – detestable** and **(e) retard – retardant**.

In pattern (5), the /t/ in the left-column word is in an unstressed syllable and undergoes flapping, while the /t/ in the right-column word is in a stressed syllable and does not undergo flapping.

In (c), the underlined /t/ in *detest* [dɪtɛ́st] is the onset of the stressed second syllable, so it does not flap. Likewise, in *detestable* [dɪtɛ́stəbl̩], the /t/ remains in the stressed syllable and does not flap. Since neither word undergoes flapping, this set does not match the left-flaps / right-doesn't-flap pattern of (5).

In (e), the underlined /t/ in *retard* [rɪtɑ́rd] is the onset of the stressed syllable, so it does not flap. Similarly, in *retardant* [rɪtɑ́rdənt], the /t/ is still in the stressed syllable and does not flap. Again, neither word undergoes flapping, so this set also fails to match the pattern in (5).

64 Read the passage and fill in the blank ① with ONE word from the passage and the blank ② with the ONE most appropriate word. Write your answers in the correct order. [2 points]

> A phoneme /l/ has only two main allophones in English, depending on its position in the word. If you say *lull*, or *lilt*, you will notice that the first *l* in each case is pronounced with the tip of your tongue up behind your top front teeth, while the second additionally has the tongue raised further back.
>
> In the case of /l/, what matters (roughly speaking) is whether the /l/ precedes or follows the vowel in the word. If /l/ comes first, it is pronounced as 'clear', fronter [l], as also in *clear*; and if the ____①____ comes first, /l/ is realized as 'dark', more back [ɫ], as in *dull*. The two are obviously in ____②____ distribution, and hence can both straightforwardly be assigned to the same phoneme, /l/, in Modern English.
>
> The rule for velarization of /l/ was informally stated as:
>
> (1) The liquid /l/ is velarized when it follows a vowel in a word.
>
> This rule specification gives the correct results for *clear* versus *hill*, for instance. This works well enough when we are only dealing with word-initial versus word-final clusters, but it leaves a grey area in word-medial position, where we find dark [ɫ] in *falter, hilltop*, but clear [l] in *holy, hilly*. This is resolvable if we state the rule in terms of the syllable:
>
> (2) Clear [l] appears in onset position, and dark [ɫ] in coda position.
>
> In fact, this process does not only provide evidence for the contrast between onset and coda position, but for the superordinate rhyme constituent, which consists of the nucleus plus the optional coda. In cases of consonant syllabification, where /l/ (or another sonorant consonant) comes to play the role of a/an ____①____ and therefore occupies the nuclear position, as in *bottle, little,* we find the dark allophone. Therefore, /l/-velarization, then, takes place in syllable rhymes.

65 Read the passage and follow the directions. [4 points]

The basic Germanic pattern of bisyllabic adjectives is trochaic, i.e. with stress on the penult as in (1):

(1) angry   brilliant   central   crazy   dozy   timid
    fragile frigid   happy   honest   lazy   urgent
    modest   narrow   orange   purple   sudden   yellow

However, there are bisyllabic adjectives with final stress. These contain historical prefixes which are Latinate in origin:

(2) complete   immense   intense   precise   select

The basic pattern of polysyllabic is trochaic, with antepenultimate stress:

(3) general   intelligent   juvenile   taciturn

However, there is a set of adjectives with a consonant cluster after the penultimate vowel, and these take penultimate stress, as in (4).

(4) dependent   disastrous   indulgent   clandestine
    momentous   objective   tremendous

The basic trochaic tendency in most varieties of English is much less evident in bisyllabic verbs: there are many with final primary stress:

(5) compact   detract   deny   export   impose   object
    permit   produce   record   subsume   transgress

There are, however, bisyllabic verbs with the basic trochaic stress pattern, such as:

(6) argue   canter   dither   enter   equal   falter   gather   govern
    hurry   manage   market   marry   narrow   rattle   sully   travel

As with bisyllabic verbs, polysyllabic verbs often flout the basic trochaic English word stress pattern: there are many verbs with three or more syllables which have final primary stress, as in *entertain, intervene, intersect*.

It is also worth noting the stress patterns of -*ate* words. Consider the following examples:

(7) a. Polysyllabic adjectives ending in -*ate*
       deliberate   elaborate   fortunate   inadequate   legitimate
    b. Bisyllabic verbs ending in -*ate*
       create   deflate   locate   migrate   placate   sedate
    c. Polysyllabic verbs ending in -*ate*
       co-ordinate   deliberate   elaborate   investigate   originate

Based on the passage, first, identify TWO groups in (7) which show the same stress pattern. Second, explain why, stating the position of primary stress of the two groups.

66 Read the passage and fill in the blank ① with ONE word from the passage and the blank ② with the ONE most appropriate word. Write your answers in the correct order. [2 points]

> The limitations on sequences of segments are called phonotactic constraints. Phonotactic constraints have as their basis the syllable, rather than the word. That is, only the clusters that can begin a syllable can begin a word, and only a cluster that can end a syllable can end a word. In multisyllabic words, clusters that seem illegal may occur, for example the /kspl/ in *explicit* /ɛksplɪsɪt/. However, there is a syllable boundary between the /k/ and /spl/, which we can make *explicit* using $: /ɛk$splɪ$sɪt/. Thus we have a permitted syllable coda /k/ that ends a syllable adjoined to a permitted onset /spl/ that begins a syllable. On the other hand, English speakers know that "condstluct" is not a possible word because one of the syllables of the word would have to have an impermissible ____①____.
>
> Consider the following example *constructs*. Which, if any, of these consonants n-s-t-r are associated with the syllable to the right? In pronouncing the word *constructs*, you may judge that the sequence *str* forms the onset of the second syllable. In other words, *constructs* would be syllabified as *con-structs*. We can adduce evidence that supports this analysis. If the syllabification were *ns-tr*, then the *t* would appear at the beginning of the stressed syllable, and syllable-initial *t* must be ____②____, but the *t* in the sequence *nstr* is not. That means that the putative syllabification of *ns-tr* is ruled out. Other considerations rule out all but the division *n-str*. This syllabification is the one that assigns the maximal number of allowable consonants to the second syllable, that is, it is following Maximal Onset principle: Onset should be maximal consonant sequence.

67. Read the passage and follow the directions. [4 points]

While all vowels of English (except [ə]) can occur in stressed syllables, many of these vowels reveal alternations with an [ə] in unstressed syllables in a morphologically related word.

(1) **Stressed syllable with a full vowel**   **Reduced syllable with [ə]**

/i/ homogeneous [homodʒiniəs]   homogenize [həmadʒənaɪz]
/ɪ/ implicit [ɪmplɪsət]   implication [ɪmpləkeʃən]
/e/ rotate [ɹotet]   rotary [ɹotəɹi]
/ɛ/ perpetuate [pɚpɛtʃuet]   perpetuity [pɚpətʃuəti]
/æ/ enigmatic [ənɪgmætɪk]   enigma [ənɪgmə]
/ɑ/ stigmata [stɪgmatə]   stigma [stɪgmə]
/ɔ/ author [ɔθɚ]   authoritarian [əθɔɹtɛɹiən]
/o/ photograph [fotəgɹæf]   photography [fətɑgɹəfi]
/ʌ/ confront [kənfɹʌnt]   confrontation [kɑnfɹənteʃən]
/u/ compute [kəmpjut]   computation [kɑmpjəteʃən]
/aɪ/ design [dəzaɪn]   designation [dɛzəgneʃən]

We should immediately point out, however, that a vowel's appearance in an unstressed syllable does not necessarily result in a reduced vowel [ə]. It is perfectly possible for the English vowels to appear in full (unreduced) form in unstressed syllables or in syllables with secondary stress, as shown in the following:

(2) /i/ labial   /æ/ sarcasm   /o/ location   /aɪ/ titration
    /ɪ/ implicit   /ɑ/ October   /ʊ/ boyhood   /aʊ/ outside
    /e/ rotate   /ɔ/ causality   /u/ acoustician   /ɔɪ/ exploitation
    /ɛ/ centennial

Thus, the unidirectional generalization to be made is the following:

(3) Generalization

While a reduced vowel is necessarily in an unstressed syllable, a vowel in an unstressed syllable is not necessarily reduced.

Although we have consistently used [ə] in reduced syllables, it is not uncommon to find an [ɪ] in people's speech. That is, for a word such as *implication* we can get [ɪmplɪkeʃən] as well as [ɪmpləkeʃən]. In general, [ɪ] is found before _____ and velars:

(4) selfish [sɛlfɪʃ]   sandwich [sændwɪtʃ]   marriage [mæɹɪdʒ]
    metric [mɛtɹɪk]   running [ɹʌnɪŋ]   topic [tɑpɪk]

It should be noted, however, that the syllable structure is also a factor. For example, we tend to find [ɪ] in *topic* [tɑpɪk], which is likely to change to an [ə] in a related word such as *topical* [tɑpəkəl]. Individuals should check their pronunciation of such syllables and transcribe the vowels accordingly. However, reduced syllables are necessarily unstressed, and [ə] cannot appear in a stressed syllable (but [ɪ] can).

Based on the passage, first, fill in the blank with the ONE most appropriate word. Second, considering the syllable structure, explain why [ɪ] in *topic* is likely to change to an [ə] in *topical*.

68 Read the passage and follow the directions. [4 points]

The constraints in relation to the sequencing of sounds in syllables via sonority have far-reaching implications in many applied situations, such as in normal phonological development, in clinical populations, and in foreign language learning. For example, the process of consonant cluster reduction, which is commonly observed in all three populations mentioned above, is far from being haphazard.

(1) play [ple] → [pe]/*[le]

A target such as *play* [ple] is much more likely to be reduced to [pe] than to the alternative [le]. The reason for this is that the former is the more unmarked (more expected) one because it provides a higher jump in sonority from a single onset to a/an _____ (in [pe] the sonority index of /p/ = 1, the sonority index of /e/ = 9; thus the resulting sequence is a change from 1 to 9; [le], on the other hand, would result in a change from 6 to 9 in sonority indices). Since a CV sequence is more natural when the contrast between the C and the nucleus V is greater, [pe] is the more valuable of the two logical alternatives.

Looking at several examples, the child applied the reduction process to those targets where the sonority difference between C_1 and C_2 was less than 3 (i.e. *stove* 3 to 1 = −2, *snow* 3 to 5 = 2). Targets that had a difference of 3 in sonority from C_1 to C_2 (*sleep* 3 to 6 = 3, *brush* 2 to 7 = 5) were not subject to reduction.

Another subject revealed the following patterns:

(2) a. stop + approximant → stop (*twin* [dɪn], *drum* [dʌm], *play* [pe])
    b. fricative + sonorant → fricative (*few* [fu], *swim* [sɪm], *shrub* [ʃʌb])
    c. fricative + stop → stop (*spoon* [bun], *stove* [dov], *sky* [daɪ])

The child's modification patterns do not allow us to state whether C_1 or C_2 of the cluster is deleted, as C_2 is deleted in (2a) and (2b), but C_1 is the one that is deleted in (2c). If, however, we analyze the results in terms of sonority rises, we see that the behavior of the subject is very regular.

Based on the passage, first, fill in the blank with ONE word from the passage. Second, explain why C_1 is deleted in (3c), considering sonority, just as described in the passage.

69 Read the passage and follow the directions. [4 points]

Restrictions between syllabic elements are, overwhelmingly, either within the onset or within the rhyme. For example, while the restriction that a stop cannot be followed by a nasal is valid in the onset in (1a), we can find these stop + nasal sequences in (1b):

(1) a. play [ple]   *[pne] / [pme]
    brown [bɹaʊn]   *[bnaʊn] / [bmaʊn]
    train [tɹen]   *[tnen] / [tmen]
    drive [dɹaɪv]   *[dnaɪv] / [dmaɪv]
    clean [klin]   *[knin] / [kmin]
    glow [glo]   *[gno] / [gmo]
  b. batman [bætmən]
    admonish [ædmɑnɪʃ]
    mapmaker [mæpmekɚ]
    abnormal [æbnɔɹməl]
    darkness [dɑɹknəs]
    enigmatic [ɛnɪgmætɪk]

Similarly, the statement that English does not allow non-homorganic nasal + stop is valid for coda clusters as in (2a), because while a form such as [lɪmk] is impossible, but we can get such non-homorganic sequences in (2b).

(2) a. link [lɪŋk]   *[lɪnk] / [lɪmk] / [lɪŋb]
    second [sɛkənd]   *[sɛkəmd] / [sɛkəŋd] / [sɛkənp]
    fluent [fluənt]   *[fluəmt] / [fluəŋt] / [fluənp]
    camp [kæmp]   *[kænp] / [kæŋp] / [kæmk]
  b. kumquat [kʌmkwat]
    pumpkin [pʌmkɪn]
    sunbow [sʌnbo]
    filmdom [fɪlmdəm]
    input [ɪnpʊt]

Further attesting the existence of rhyme as a constituent, dependencies between nuclei and codas are commonly found. To give an example from English, we can look at the /aʊ/ nucleus and its relationship with its coda:

(3) brown [bɹaʊn]   *[bɹaʊŋ] / [bɹaʊm]
    spouse [spaʊs]   *[spaʊf]
    trout [tɹaʊt]   *[tɹaʊp] / [tɹaʊk]
    rouse [ɹaʊz]   *[ɹaʊv]
    crowd [kɹaʊd]   *[kɹaʊg] / [kɹaʊb]

What these examples demonstrate is that the coda that follows /aʊ/ has to be alveolar; this nucleus cannot be followed by _____ or velar consonants.

Based on the passage, first, fill in the blank with the ONE most appropriate word. Second, state why stop + nasal sequences are possible in (1b), and non-homorganic nasal + stop sequences are possible in (2b), respectively.

70 Read the passage and fill in each blank with an appropriate FEATURE from the passage. Write your answers in the correct order. [2 points]

> For the articulation of a dental/alveolar or a palatal consonant the tip or front of the tongue is raised, dividing the oral cavity into two areas of different size, one in front and one in back of the body of the tongue. The distinguishing feature is named [coronal] after the bone in the skull which lies above this part of the mouth. Dental/alveolar and palatal consonants are [+ coronal], and labial and velar consonants are [− coronal].
>
> Liquids, the consonants which begin the words *led* and *red*, for instance, were shown to be:
>
> (1) ± syllabic   + consonantal   + continuant   + sonorant
>
> We can now add two other features which the liquids share: they are [+ voice] and [− sibilant].
>
> How do /l/ and /r/ differ from each other? Phonologists who use the feature [anterior] say that /l/ is [+ anterior] and /r/ is _____①_____ since /l/ is sometimes articulated with the tip of the tongue on the alveolar ridge and /r/ is never articulated so far forward. However, both consonants are articulated in different parts of the mouth; neither the articulator nor the place of articulation is truly distinctive for these two consonants. What distinguishes them from each other is the shape of the tongue. One of them, /l/, is articulated with the sides of the tongue curled in and air escaping over the sides. We say that /l/ is _____②_____.
>
> For /r/ the tongue is also curled but in a different way; the whole body of the tongue is pulled back and bunched up, with a slight groove in the very tip—not a groove along the center line of the surface, which would make it a sibilant. Typically, there is also some rounding of the lips. Instead of pulling the tongue back and humping it up, some speakers turn the tongue-tip backward; hence the term 'retroflex' has been used by some phoneticians, but this name is not appropriate for the most usual articulation. Various appropriate names might be used to describe the physical facts of articulation. To place /r/ in a system of distinctive features, it is enough to say that it is [− lateral].

71 Read the passage and follow the directions. [4 points]

It is worthwhile to ask why the distinction is necessary, and what is its significance in a broader context. The question 'why' can be put in the form of a challenge: if phonemes alone distinguish meanings, why should we be even slightly interested in allophonic variation? Of what use is it to point out that, for example, /k/ is pronounced [k̟] before front vowels and [k̠] before a back vowel?

(1) a. key   case   kitten   kedge
    b. cook   cold   couger   coach

And why should we bother to record that the vowels of *mat* and *tan* are partially nasalized, when we know that this is due to the preceding [m] or following [n]?

In almost every area to which phonology makes a significant contribution, the phonemic-phonetic distinction has proved an important one; the learning and teaching of foreign languages; language acquisition; historical linguistics (the study of language change); clinical phonology; dialectology; all these disciplines regard the distinction as fundamental. A child pronounces the following words with the pronunciation given:

(2) [p]   [b]
    soup [su:p]   band [b̥ɛn]
    bump [b̥ʌp]   beetle [b̥i:gu]
    stamp [d̥ɛp]   ball [b̥ɔ:]
    escape [g̥eɪp]   bump [b̥ʌp]

From this data, it looks as though the child has acquired both /p/ (as in *soup, stamp*, etc.) and /b/ (as in *band, ball*, etc.), since both [p] and [b] appear in the transcriptions, and since the child's [p] matches the adult /p/, and his [b] the adult /b/. But we must consider the possibility that [p] and [b] are not ①  for the child.

(3) pudding [b̥ʊdɪn]   apple [ɛbu]
    please [b̥iː]   shopping [wɒbɪn]
    pedal [b̥ɛgu]   crib [g̊ɪp]

The distribution of the sounds, for the child, is now clear: [b] occurs word-initially, and [p] and [b̥] occur in certain environments. It is important to see that, although the child pronounces *p* and *b*, they are not ___①___ in his system, but ___②___ in complementary distribution.

Based on the passage, first, fill in the blank ① with ONE word from the passage and the blank ② with the ONE most appropriate word. Write your answers in the correct order. Second, considering the data in (2) and (3), state the environments where [p] and [b] occur, respectively.

72 Read the passage and follow the directions. [4 points]

> Deletion can affect vowels, but mainly this is confined to the unstressed vowels [ə] and [ɪ]. The grammatical items are the ones most affected. We have the examples like *has* → [həz] → [əz] → [z], and *have* → [v].
> Look at the following series of changes:
>
> (1) /fɪʃ ænd ʧɪps/
>   [fɪʃ ənd ʧɪps]   (vowel reduction)
>   [fɪʃ ən ʧɪps]   (C deletion)
>   [fɪʃ n̩ ʧɪps]   (V deletion)
>
> At the final stage, the sequence: [ə] + nasal becomes syllabic nasal. Similar examples are:
>
> (2) [fr̩ ɪnstəns] 'for instance'   [aɪkŋrid] 'I can read'
>   [sm̩ bʌɾə] 'some butter'   [wɒɾl̩ wɪ du] 'What'll we do'
>   [beɾə ðn̩ ðæt] 'better than that'
>
> An unstressed vowel can be deleted from lexical items too, under certain conditions. One common type of environment is an unstressed initial syllable, as in:
>
> (3) [spoʊz] suppose   [bliv] believe
>   [plis] police   [krekt] correct
>
> In these examples, the resulting consonant cluster is one which occurs quite normally elsewhere, for example /sp-, bl-, kr-/. But we also find deletions of [ə] which result in 'impossible' clusters, as for examples in:
>
> (4) [pteɪtoʊ] 'potato'   [ktoʊniæstə] 'cotoniaster'
>   [vrɒnɪkə] 'Veronica'   [mlɪʃəs] 'malicious'

The unstressed vowel [ə] can undergo deletion not only in word-initial syllables, but also word-medially before certain consonants as in (5a). However, deletion does not occur followed by certain consonants as in (5b):

(5) a. diff<u>e</u>rent   temp<u>o</u>rary   int<u>e</u>rrupt
       ['dɪfrənt]   ['tempreri]   [ɪntr'ʌpt]
       fam<u>i</u>ly   imag<u>i</u>native   test<u>a</u>ment
       [fæmli]   [ɪ'mædʒnətɪv]   ['testmənt]
   b. prohib<u>i</u>tive   not<u>i</u>ceable   man<u>a</u>gerial
       *[prə'hɪbtiv]   *['noʊtsəbl]   *[mændʒeriəl]
       mot<u>i</u>vate   fall<u>a</u>cy   princ<u>i</u>pality
       *[moʊtveɪt]   *['fælsi]   *[prɪnspæləti]

Based on the passage, state each environment where the unstressed [ə] is deleted in (5a) and retained in (5b), using a natural class.

73 Read the passage and fill in the blank ① with ONE word from the passage and the blank ② with an appropriate FEATURE from the passage. Write your answers in the correct order. [2 points]

Five consonants are articulated with the lower lip:

(1) nasal /m/ as in *mat* /mæt/
   stops /p/ as in *pat* /pæt/ and /b/ as in *bat* /bæt/
   fricatives /f/ as in *fat* /fæt/ and /v/ as in *vat* /væt/

The first three, /m p b/, are typically articulated by stopping the flow of air with the two lips pressed together (bilabial articulation). The fricatives /f v/ are made by resting the lower lip lightly against the upper teeth (labiodental articulation) and letting air flow out between lip and teeth. What makes /f/ and /v/ different from the other labial consonants is the fact that they are fricative, [+ continuant]. The small difference between bilabial and labiodental articulation is not contrastive. Labial fricatives are predictably labiodental, and labial stops and nasal are typically bilabial.

As you know, /p/ and /b/ differ in voicing, and the same is true for /f/ and /v/; /p/ and /f/ are [− voice], /b/ and /v/ are [+ voice]. The nasal /m/ is also [+ voice], but that feature is not ___①___ for /m/ or other nasals. If English had both voiced and voiceless nasal consonants, as does the Welsh language, voicing would be distinctive for nasals just as it is for obstruents, but this is not the case.

The consonants /tʃ dʒ/ are called affricates. An affricate is a combination of stop and fricative. To produce the first and last consonants of *church* /tʃərtʃ/ and *judge* /dʒʌdʒ/, for instance, the tongue-front, with a groove along the center line, makes contact with the alveolar ridge or the area just behind it, stopping the flow of air; then the tongue is lowered and air passes along the groove creating friction. If the tongue-front does not make contact but is positioned near the alveolar ridge, only friction or turbulence occurs. This is what happens in the articulation of /ʃ/ and /ʒ/. Compare /tʃ/ and /ʃ/, as in *witch* /wɪtʃ/ and *wish* /wɪʃ/; compare /dʒ/ and /ʒ/, as in *pledger* /plɛdʒər/ and *pleasure* /plɛʒər/.

All four have the same articulator, the front of the tongue. Fricatives /ʃ ʒ/ are produced with air flowing continuously out from the mouth; they are [+continuant]. For /tʃ dʒ/ the air stream is first interrupted, then allowed to exit through a narrow channel. Since air does not escape continuously during the articulation, /tʃ dʒ/ are counted as [②]. Though /tʃ dʒ/ differ from /p b t d k g/ in being affricates rather than plain stops, they are classified as stops.

74 Read the passage and follow the directions. [4 points]

Vowel length in English offers the example of the phonological relevance of syllables. Consider the following examples:

(1) a. *vowel lengthening* b. *no vowel lengthening*
  bad [bæ:d]   bat [bæt]
  Abe [e:jb]   ape [ejp]
  phase [fe:jz]   face [fejs]
  leave [li:v]   leaf [lif]
  tag [tʰæ:g]   tack [tʰæk]
  brogue [bro:wg]   broke [browk]
            say [sej]
            meal [mil]
            soar [sor]
            show [ʃow]

The phonological rule in (1) could be assumed as shown in (2):

(2) English vowels are lengthened when followed by a voiced obstruent.

It turns out, though, that this is not quite right. As the next examples show, if the consonant (voiced obstruent) is in the ____①____ of the ____②____ syllable, the vowel is not lengthened.

(3) obey [owbej]   (compare to lobe [lo:wb])
  redo [ridu]   (compare to read [ri:d])
  crazy [krejzi]   (compare to craze [krej:z])
  ogre [owgɚ]   (compare to brogue [bro:wg])
  Odin [owdɪn]   (compare to ode [o:wd])

Syllable structure is crucial. We need to revise the phonological rule in (2) as follows:

(4) English vowels are lengthened when followed by a voiced obstruent in _____.

First, fill in each blank with the ONE most appropriate word. Write your answers in the correct order. Second, complete the rule in (4), based on the passage.

75 Read the passage and follow the directions. [4 points]

The two sounds, voiced approximant [j] and voiceless fricative [ç], are allophones of one phoneme /j/. Consider the following data:

(1) [j]
  yet [jet]
  yarn [jɑn]
  yeast [jist]
  news [njuz]
  value [vælju]
  music [mjuzɪk]

[ç]
  queue [kçu]
  pure [pçuə]
  tube [tçub]
  accuse [əkçuz]
  attitude [ætɪtçud]
  piano [pçænoʊ]

Since the two sounds [j] and [ç] are allophones of one phoneme, we can expect their distributions to be complementary. [j] occurs initially and is apparently not affected by the kind of vowel which follows, since it precedes both front vowels (*yeast*) and back vowels (*yarn*); it also precedes rounded vowels (*news*) and unrounded vowels (*yet*). Nor is [j] affected by syllable stressing, since it occurs in both stressed (['mjuzɪk]) and unstressed (['vælju]) syllables. In addition to its occurrence word-initially, [j] is also found after _____ consonants.

[ç] is more restricted in its distribution; it is not influenced by the kind of vowel which follows (compare the back, rounded vowel of *pure* with the front, unrounded vowel of *piano*), but it occurs only after a certain natural class. The distributions of [j] and [ç] are, in fact, complementary.

Now consider the following data in (2). The liquids /l, r/ have devoiced (i.e. partly voiceless) allophones, represented as [l̥, ɹ̥], and voiceless fricative allophones, represented as [ɬ, ɹ̥].

(2) [l̥, ɹ̥]
  flat [fl̥æt]
  slow [sl̥oʊ]
  freeze [fɹ̥iz]
  through [θɹ̥u]
  shrink [ʃɹ̥ɪŋk]
  afraid [əfɹ̥eɪd]

[ɬ, ɹ̥]
  clear [kɬɪə(r)]
  plot [pɬɒt]
  trees [tɹ̥iz]
  cry [kɹ̥aɪ]
  proud [pɹ̥aʊd]
  approve [əpɹ̥uv]

Based on the passage, first, fill in the blank with ONE word from the passage. Second, state the environment where voiceless fricatives [ç], [ɬ], and [ɹ̥] occur by using a natural class.

76 Read the passage and follow the directions. [4 points]

One of the major types of assimilation involves the alveolar plosives /t, d/ before another plosive. Look at the following data:

(1) [ðæp pis] that piece   [hɑb pəteɪtoʊz] hard potatoes
    [ðæp bot] that boy   [hɑb bagɪnz] hard bargains
    [ðæt dɪʃ] that dish   [hɑd taɪmz] hard times
    [ðæt tʃɜtʃ] that church   [hɑd tʃiz] hard cheese
    [ðæk kɪd] that kid   [hɑg keɪs] hard case
    [ðæk gɜl] that girl   [hɑg goʊɪŋ] hard going

Assimilations like these are, of course, optional, though they do occur very frequently in informal conversation. What happens is that the alveolar plosive retains its _____ feature but shifts its locus in sympathy with (i.e. assimilates to) the locus of the following plosive or affricate.

One interesting fact is that /t, d/ are the only plosives which are subject to assimilation. /p, b/ and /k, g/ do not assimilate, but keep their own locus whatever the locus of the following plosive:

(2) 'black pan' we do not find [blæp pæn]
    'black box' we do not find [blæp bɒks]
    'black tin' we do not find [blæt tɪn]

A phrase like [raɪp bəˈnɑnəz] can therefore mean either *ripe bananas* or, by an assimilation from /t/, *right bananas*. But [raɪt təˈmɑtoʊz] can only mean *right tomatoes* because the /p/ of *ripe* never assimilates, and [raɪk kɔn] can only mean *right corn* by assimilation of the /t/. The condition [alveolar] on the left-hand side of the assimilation rule is therefore correct.

Assimilation of /t, d/ can combine with nasal assimilation. In a phrase like *can't bear*, the /t/ of *can't* assimilates to [p], and the nasal /n/ then assimilates to this [p], giving as the pronunciation, [kɑmp beə]. These double assimilations are particularly common when the contracted negative (*n't*) follows an auxiliary verb: *can't, don't, isn't, won't*, etc.

Another type of assimilation affects the voicing feature: in particular, voiced sounds become voiceless when followed by another voiceless sound. Look at the following data:

(3) [faɪf pɑst] five past
[hæf tə goʊ] have to go
[lʌf tə goʊ] love to go
[ʃis tɔkɪŋ] she's talking
[əf kɔs] of course
[dʌʃ ʃi] does she

The sounds which assimilate their voicing are usually, as the examples show, fricatives. Grammatical items in particular are affected: the /v/ of *of, have* changes to [f], and the /z/ of *is, has, does* becomes [s].

Based on the passage, first, fill in the blank with ONE word from the passage. Second, state the environment where fricatives become voiceless in (3).

멘토영어학
문제은행

Part 04

Morphology

PART 04 Morphology

• Answer Key p.81

01 Read the passages and follow the directions. [4 points]

--- A ---

A word is not a simple sequence of morphemes. It has an internal structure. For example, the word *unsystematic* is composed of three morphemes: *un-, system,* and *-atic*. The order of derivation is shown in (1) below:

(1) First, the root is *system*, a noun, to which we add the suffix *-atic*, resulting in an adjective, *systematic*. Second, to this adjective, we add the prefix *un-* forming a new adjective, *unsystematic*.

In order to represent the hierarchical organization of words (and sentences), linguists use tree diagrams. The tree diagram for *unsystematic* is as follows:

(2)
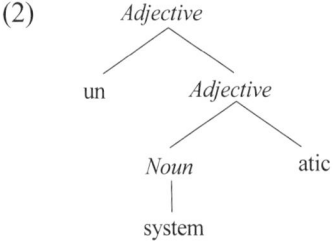

This tree represents the application of two morphological rules:

Rule 1. Noun + *atic* → Adjective
Rule 2. *un* + Adjective → Adjective

Rule 1 attaches the derivational suffix *-atic* to the root noun, forming an adjective. Rule 2 takes the adjective formed by rule 1 and attaches the derivational prefix *un-*. The diagram shows that the entire word—*unsystematic*—is an adjective that is composed of an adjective—*systematic*—plus *un*. The adjective is itself composed of a noun—*system*—plus the suffix *-atic*.

Hierarchical structure is an essential property of human language. Words (and sentences) have component parts, which relate to each other in specific, rule-governed ways. Although at first glance it may seem that, aside from order, the morphemes *un-* and *-atic* each relate to the root *system* in the same way, this is not the case. The root *system* is "closer" to *-atic* than it is to *un-*, and *un-* is actually connected to the adjective *systematic*, and not directly to *system*. Indeed, **unsystem* is not a word.

─┤ B ├─

There is an example of a word with four morphemes in (3) below; try to determine for yourself the order in which the morphemes are put together.

(3) activation

Based on the description in <A>, analyze the word given in (3) in <B>. Provide the order of derivation, identifying the types of affixes and the grammatical form (part of speech) as in (1). Notice that write the exact affixes in your answer.

02 Read the passage and follow the directions. [4 points]

┤ A ├

English orthography is not consistent in representing compounds, which are sometimes written as single words, sometimes with a hyphen, and sometimes as separate words. In terms of pronunciation, however, an important generalization can be made, as shown in (1) and (2): adjective-noun compounds are characterized by more prominent stress on their first component. In non-compounds consisting of an adjective and a noun, in contrast, the second element is generally stressed.

(1) Compound word
    greénhouse   'a glass-enclosed garden'
    bláckboard   'a chalkboard'

(2) Non-compound expressions
    green hoúse   'a house painted green'
    black boárd   'a board that is black'

A second distinguishing feature of compounds in English is that tense and plural markers can typically not be attached to the first element, although they can be added to the compound as a whole. There are some exceptions, however, such as *parks supervisor*.

(3) a. Compound noun with internal plural:
       *The [ducks hunter] didn't have a licence.
    b. Compound noun with external plural:
       The [duck hunter]s didn't have a licence.

┌─────────────── B ───────────────┐

(i) a. The craftsman beat the gold into rings.

  b. The film tells the story of a lonely swordsman.

  c. The player dropped kick the ball through the goal post.

  d. The player drop kicked the ball through the goal post.

(ii) a. wet suit: 'a suit that is wet'

  b. wet suit: 'a diver's costume'

Based on the description in <A>, in <B>, first, identify ONE ungrammatical sentence in (i), and explain why. Second, in (ii), specify each phrase *wet suit* in (iia) and (iib) (i.e., *Compound Word* or *Non-compound Expression*).

03 Read the passage and fill in the blank ① with the ONE most appropriate word and the blank ② with an appropriate natural class. Write your answers in the correct order. [2 points]

> Derivation is often subject to special constraints and restrictions. For instance, the suffix -*ant* can combine with bases of Latin origin, such as *assistant* and *combat*, but not with those of native English origin, such as *help* and *fight*. Thus, we find words such as *assistant* and *combatant* but not **helpant* and **fightant*.
>
> In other cases, derivation may be blocked by the existence of an alternative word. For instance, the word *cooker* (to mean 'one who cooks') is blocked by the existence of the word ____①____, which already has that meaning; *famosity* (from *famous*) is blocked by *fame*; and so on.
>
> Sometimes, a derivational affix is able to attach only to bases with particular phonological properties. A good example of this involves the suffix -*en*, which can combine with some adjectives to create verbs with a causative meaning as shown in table 1 (*whiten* means roughly 'cause to become white').
>
> | TABLE 1. Restrictions on the use of -*en* | |
> |---|---|
> | *Acceptable* | *Unacceptable* |
> | whiten | *abstracten |
> | soften | *bluen |
> | madden | *angryen |
> | quicken | *slowen |
> | liven | *greenen |
>
> The contrasts illustrated here reflect the fact that -*en* can be attached only to a monosyllabic base that ends in a consonant other than /l/, /r/, /m/, /n/, or /ŋ/. Thus, it can be added to *white, quick, mad,* and *live*, which are monosyllabic and end in a consonant of the right type. But it cannot be added to *abstract*, which has more than one syllable; to *slow* or *blue*, which end in a vowel; or to *green*, which ends in the wrong type of consonant. Therefore, the suffix -*en* can only combine with a monosyllabic base that ends in a/an ____②____.

04 Read the passage and follow the directions. [4 points]

Morphemes are not the same as phonemes. Consider the following examples:

(1)   tacking   tagging
    Allophones: [tʰækĩŋ]   [tʰægĩŋ]
    Phonemes: /tækɪŋ/   /tægɪŋ/
    Morphemes: /tæk/ + /ɪŋ/   /tæg/ + /ɪŋ/

Consider some words formed with the English suffix -*able* (*washable, lovable, thinkable, growable, doable*). The rule can be expressed in the following form:

(2) -*able* Affixation
    Verb + əbəl → Adjective
    Verb + əbəl means "able to be Verbed"

The structure of the word *washable* created by the rule can be expressed on just a single line with brackets: [[wɔʃ]$_{Verb}$ əbəl]$_{Adj}$.

Here are some further word formation rules of English. To express the derivation of words in -*ity* (for example, *divinity, obscurity, obesity, insanity, sensitivity*), we could write the rule given below:

(3) -*ity* Affixation
    Adjective + ɪti → Noun
    Adjective + ɪti means "the quality of being Adjective"

This creates structures like [[oʊbis]$_{Adj}$ ɪti]$_N$, for *obesity*.

To handle words formed with the prefix *un*- (*unfair, unkind, unjust, unspoken, unattested, unidentifiable*), we could write this rule:

(4) *un*- Affixation
    ʌn + Adjective → Adjective
    ʌn + Adjective means "not Adjective"

> Words with multiple morphemes can be derived by applying multiple word formation rules, one after the other. For example, we can derive the long word *unidentifiability* by applying the following rules in succession.
>
> (5) identify + able → identifiable (Verb + əbəl → Adjective)
>   un + identifiable → unidentifiable (ʌn + Adjective → Adjective)
>   unidentifiable + ity → unidentifiability (Adjective + ɪti → Noun)

Based on the passage, explain the formation rules of the word 'unmindfulness' in succession, as shown in (5).

MEMO

멘토영어학
문제은행

Part 05
Semantics

PART 05 Semantics

01 Read the passage <A> and the sentences in <B>, and follow the directions. [4 points]

─┤ A ├─

There is an important difference between entailment and presupposition. If we negate an entailing sentence, then the entailment fails. However, negating a presupposing sentence allows the presupposition to survive. Take for example the entailment pair in (1):

(1) a. John killed the bear.
    b. The bear is dead.

If we negate (1a) to form (2a) then it no longer entails (1b), repeated as (2b):

(2) a. John didn't kill the bear.
    b. The bear is dead.

Now (2b) no longer automatically follows from the preceding sentence.
   However, negating the presupposing sentence does not affect the presupposition. Consider the presupposition pair in (3):

(3) a. I do regret leaving New York.
    b. I left New York.

If we negate (3a) to form (4a) the resulting sentence still has the presupposition, shown as (4b):

(4) a. I don't regret leaving New York.
    b. I left New York.

Therefore, negating a presupposing sentence allows the presupposition to survive, whereas negating an entailing sentence destroys the entailment. So it seems that viewing presupposition as a truth relation allows us to capture one interesting difference between the behaviour of presupposition and entailment under negation.

─┤ B ├─

(i) a. I am sorry that the team lost.
   b. The team lost.
(ii) a. The mayor of Liverpool is in town.
   b. There is a mayor of Liverpool.
(iii) a. John has arrived in Edinburgh.
   b. John is in Edinburgh.
(iv) a. Mary's sister has just got back from Boston.
   b. Mary has a sister.

In <B>, identify ONE pair of sentences that shows the semantic relation of entailment, and explain why, based on the description in <A>.

02 Read the passage <A> and the sentences in <B>, and follow the directions. [4 points]

─┤ A ├─

Some types of presupposition are produced by particular words or constructions, which together are sometimes called presupposition triggers. Some of these triggers derive from syntactic structures, for example the cleft construction in (1) and the pseudo-cleft in (2) share the presupposition in (3), and a *wh*-question also serves as a presupposition trigger, but a *yes-no* question doesn't.

(1) It was his behavior with frogs that disgusted me.
(2) What disgusted me was his behavior with frogs.
(3) Something disgusted me.

Other forms of subordinate clauses may produce presuppositions, for example, time adverbial clauses and comparative clauses. In the following sentences, the (a) sentence has the presupposition in (b):

(4) a. I was riding motorcycles before you learned to walk.
    b. You learned to walk.

Many presuppositions are produced by the presence of certain words. Many of these lexical triggers are predicates. For example, some predicates like *realize* are called factive predicates (or verbs) because they presuppose the truth of their complement clause. Compare sentences (5) and (6) below: only the sentence with the factive verb *realize* presupposes (7). There is no such presupposition with the non-factive verb *think* in (6).

(5) Sean realized that Miranda had dandruff.
(6) Sean thought that Miranda had dandruff.
(7) Miranda had dandruff.

> **B**
>
> (a) You didn't explain that your train was late.
> (b) It is true that Jill had lent Ed her key.
> (c) It matters that they lied to us.
> (d) He's even more gullible than you are.
> (e) Will you take out that trash?
> (f) When will you take out that trash?

In <B>, identify TWO sentences which DO NOT produce presupposition, and explain why, specifying the type of presupposition triggers, based on the description in <A>.

_____
_____
_____
_____
_____

03 Read the passage and follow the directions. [4 points]

―| A |―

  Hyponymy is a relation of inclusion. A hyponym includes the meaning of a more general word, for example: *dog* and *cat* are hyponyms of *animal*, and *sister* and *mother* are hyponyms of *woman*. The more general term is called the superordinate or hypernym (alternatively hyperonym). Some taxonomies reflect the natural world, like (1) below:

(1)
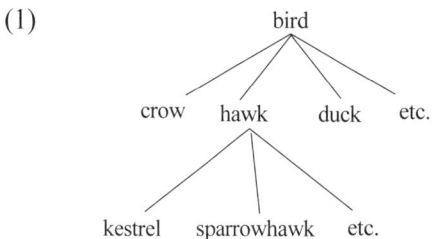

Here *kestrel* is a hyponym of *hawk*, and *hawk* a hyponym of *bird*. We assume the relationship is transitive so that *kestrel* is a hyponym of *bird*.

  Meronymy is a term used to describe a part-whole relationship between lexical items. Thus *cover* and *page* are meronyms of *book*. The whole term, here *book*, is sometimes called the holonym. We can identify this relationship by using sentence frames like *X is part of Y*, or *Y has X*, as in *A page is part of a book*, or *A book has pages*. Meronymy reflects hierarchical classifications in the lexicon somewhat like taxonomies, as shown in (2).

(2)
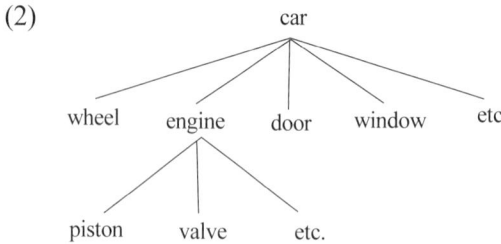

Meronymic hierarchies are less clear cut and regular than taxonomies. Meronyms vary for example in how necessary the part is to the whole. Some are necessary for normal examples, for example *nose* as a meronym of *face*; others are usual but not obligatory, like *collar* as a meronym of *shirt*.

Meronymy also differs from hyponymy in transitivity. ①_____ is always transitive, as we saw, but ②_____ may or may not be. A transitive example is: *nail* as a meronym of *finger*, and *finger* of *hand*. We can see that *nail* is a meronym of *hand*, for we can say *A hand has nails*. A non-transitive example is: *pane* is a meronym of *window* (*A window has a pane*), and *window* of *room* (*A room has a window*); but *pane* is not a meronym of *room*, for we cannot say *A room has a pane*.

─┤ B ├─

(a) *hole* is a meronym of *button*.
(b) *button* is a meronym of *shirt*.
(c) *hole* is not a meronym of *shirt*.
(d) *cellar* is a meronym of *house*.
(e) *house* is a meronym of *building*.
(f) *saw* is a meronym of *tool*.

First, in <A>, fill in each blank with ONE word from the passage. Write your answers in the correct order. Second, identify TWO wrong sentences in <B>, and correct the sentences, replacing ONLY ONE word in the sentence.

04 Read the passage and follow the directions. [4 points]

⊣ A ⊢

Main clause verbs that report speech—for example, *reply, say,* and *tell,* as in (1a)—occur with *that* complements. Also common with *that* complements are verbs that express mental acts—for example, *believe, comprehend, feel, find, guess, know, see, think,* and *understand,* as shown in (1b). Certain of these verbs that take *that* clauses have been called "factive predicates" because their complement is assumed to be a fact. For some native speakers, sentences with factive predicates are unacceptable when the complementizer is omitted, as in (1c).

(1) a. She replied that he must have been mistaken.
    b. She comprehended that this would mean a big change in her lifestyle.
    c. ?She comprehended this would mean a big change in her lifestyle.

An illustrative sample of factive predicates is provided in (2).

(2) be significant, be tragic, be relevant, be odd, ignore, resent, know, realize, bear in mind, take into account, make clear, find out, etc.

What is common to them is that any simple assertion with a factive predicate, such as (3a), commits the speaker to the belief that the complement sentence, just by itself, is also true.

(3) a. It is odd that Bill is alone.
    b. Bill is alone.
    c. It is possible that Bill is alone.

It would be insincere for anyone to assert (3a) if he did not believe that (3b) is true. Intuitively, in uttering (3a) the speaker must take it for granted that Bill is alone; he is making a comment about that fact. The same relation holds between (4a) and (4b).

(4) a. Mary realized that it was raining.
   b. It was raining.
   c. Mary believed that it was raining.

Notice that these relations break down if we replace *odd* by *possible* and *realized* by *believed*. (3c) and (4c) do not carry a commitment to the truth of the complement sentence.

───────────────── B ─────────────────
(5) John regretted telling a lie.

Identify whether sentence (5) in <B> has a presupposition, and then explain why, stating the presupposed proposition of the sentence and what is the presupposition-triggering element in the sentence.

05 Read the passage and fill in each blank with ONE word from the passage. Write your answers in the correct order. [2 points]

The relation of logical entailment holds when the truth of one sentence requires the truth of another. More specifically, given two sentences p and q, p logically entails q if the truth of p requires the truth of q. In other words, if p is true, q cannot be false. Take the following two sentences:

(1) a. Arjun buttered the toast with a knife.
  b. Arjun buttered the toast.

The sentence in (1a) logically entails the one in (1b) because if (a) is true, then it must be the case that (b) is true as well. If Arjun buttered the toast with a knife, then it must be true that Arjun buttered the toast.

The entailment relation in (1) allows both (a) and (b) to be false, as in a situation where Arjun did not butter the toast with a knife, and he did not butter it at all. It is also consistent with a situation in which (a) is false, but (b) is ___①___: Arjun may have buttered the toast with a spoon rather than knife. What logical entailment rules out is a situation where (a) is true and (b) is false.

To test whether one sentence entails another, we can use the contradiction test: if we join sentence p with the negation of sentence q and the result is contradictory, then we know that p entails q. What happens when we apply this test for the sentences in (1)? (We use # to indicate that although the sentence is grammatical, it is semantically unacceptable.)

(2) #Arjun buttered the toast with a knife but he did not butter the toast.

This sentence is contradictory, which confirms that (1a) entails (1b): you cannot assert the truth of (1a) while asserting the falsity of (1b).
Consider another example of entailment:

(3) a. Snoopy is a beagle.
  b. Snoopy is a dog.

The sentence in (3a) logically ____②____ the one in (3b) because if (a) is true, then (b) must be true. Even though you may never have seen Snoopy, if you know what a beagle is and you know what a dog is, then you know that if Snoopy is a beagle, then Snoopy is also a dog. The contradiction test confirms this: sentence (4) is semantically unacceptable.

(4) #Snoopy is a beagle but he is not a dog.

06 Read the passage <A> and the sentences in <B>, and follow the directions. [4 points]

─────────────── A ───────────────

Factive predicates are verbs or adjectives that take a sentential complement that is presupposed to be true. For the purposes of our discussion, a sentential complement is simply a clause that functions as a direct object. Factive predicates include *know, discover, find out, regret,* and *be sorry*. In (1), the complement is designated by the square bracket.

(1) Lucy knows [that Charlie will try to kick the football].

The sentence in (1), with the main verb *know*, presupposes that it is true that Charlie will try to kick the football. No such presupposition is associated with the verb *believe*, as shown by the difference in the results of the contradiction test.

(2) a. Lucy believes that Charlie will try to kick the football but she is wrong about it.
   b. #Lucy knows that Charlie will try to kick the football but she is wrong about it.

The verb *know* requires that its complement be true.

So-called *aspectual* verbs like *stop* and *quit*, which help indicate that an action is ongoing or complete, also trigger presuppositions. This is why all the examples in (3) entail that Linus is or was waiting for the Great Pumpkin, regardless of whether the aspectual verb is negative.

(3) a. Linus quit waiting for the Great Pumpkin.
   b. Linus didn't quit waiting for the Great Pumpkin.

To sum up, different kinds of triggers give rise to various types of presuppositions. Factive predicates give rise to the presupposition that their complements are true, while aspectual verbs give rise to presuppositions about the temporal properties of the event described by the predicate.

─┤ B ├─

(a) It seems to me that she failed again.

(b) Snoopy is glad that Woodstock is his best friend.

(c) Linus didn't continue to wait for the Great Pumpkin.

(d) It is true that she failed again.

(e) I suppose that he is honest.

In <B>, identify TWO sentences that take a complement clause that is presupposed to be true, and state the presupposed proposition of each sentence, based on the passage in <A>.

07 Read the passage and fill in each blank with ONE word from the passage. Write your answers in the correct order. [2 points]

> If a sentence A entails a sentence B, sentence A cannot be true without B being true as well. For instance, the English sentence "Pat is a fluffy cat" entails the sentence "Pat is a cat" since one cannot be a fluffy cat without being a cat. On the other hand, this sentence does not entail "Pat chases mice" since it is possible (if unlikely) for a cat to not chase mice.
>
> Entailments also differ from presuppositions, whose truth is taken for granted. The classic example of a presupposition is the existence presupposition which arises from definite descriptions. For instance, the sentence "The king of France is bald" presupposes that there is a king of France. Unlike an entailment, presuppositions survive when the sentence is negated. For instance, "The king of France is not bald" likewise presupposes that there is a king of France.
>
> Implicatures are deductions that are not made strictly on the basis of the content expressed in the discourse. Rather, they are made in accordance with the conversational maxims, taking into account both the linguistic meaning of the utterance as well as the particular circumstances in which the utterance is made. Consider the following conversation:
>
> (1) Speaker A: Smith doesn't have any girlfriend these days.
>   Speaker B: He's been driving over to the West End a lot lately.
>
> The implicature is that Smith has a girlfriend in the West End. The reasoning is that B's answer would be irrelevant unless it contributed information related to A's question. We assume speakers try to be cooperative. So it is fair to conclude that B uttered the second sentence because the reason that Smith drives to the West End is that he has a girlfriend there.
>
> Because implicatures are derived on the basis of assumptions about the speaker that might turn out to be wrong, they can be easily cancelled. For this reason A could have responded as follows: *Speaker A: He goes to the West End to visit his mother who is ill.* Although B's utterance implies that the reason Smith goes to the West End is to visit his girlfriend, A's response cancels this implicature.

Therefore, implicatures are different than ___①___ which cannot be cancelled; it is logically necessary. Implicatures are also different than ___②___. They are the possible consequences of utterances in their context, whereas presuppositions are situations that must exist for utterances to be appropriate in context.

___
___

멘토영어학
문제은행

Part 06
Pragmatics

PART 06 Pragmatics

• Answer Key p.87

01 Read the passage and fill in each blank with ONE word from the passage. Write your answers in the correct order. [2 points]

> Philosophers use the term *speech acts* for things you can do with sentences of your language—things like making statements, asking questions, issuing commands, or uttering exclamations. Which of these you can do with a given sentence depends to a large extent on its syntactic form. The syntax of English distinguishes a set of clause types that are characteristically used to perform different kinds of speech acts. The major types are the five illustrated in (1):
>
> (1) a. declarative   You are very tactful.
>   b. closed interrogative Are you very tactful?
>   c. open interrogative   How tactful are you?
>   d. exclamative   How tactful you are!
>   e. imperative   Be very tactful.
>
> Although the correspondence between these clause types and the speech acts they can be used to perform is not one-to-one, speech acts do have a characteristic correlation with clause types. We show the default correlation in (2):
>
> (2) CLAUSE TYPE   CHARACTERISTIC SPEECH ACT
>   a. declarative   making a statement
>   b. closed interrogative asking a closed question
>   c. open interrogative   asking an open question
>   d. exclamative   making an exclamatory statement
>   e. imperative   issuing a directive

Now consider the following examples:

(3) a. Could you please open the door?
   b. <u>Turn up late</u> and you'll be fired.

Example (3a) would normally be used and understood as a directive (specifically, a polite request); but it is of closed interrogative form. It's not an imperative. The underlined clause of (3b) has ___①___ form, but would not be naturally interpreted as a/an ___②___: I'm not telling you to turn up late. The whole sentence is understood as if it had a conditional adjunct: it means "If you turn up late, you'll be fired". This of course implies that you should NOT turn up late, so the sentence does the opposite of telling you to turn up late!

02 Read the passage and fill in the blank with ONE word from the passage.
[2 points]

The assumptions that hearers make about a speaker's conduct seemed to Grice to be of several different types, giving rise to different types of inference, or, from the speaker's point of view, implicatures. In identifying these, Grice called them maxims. Grice's four main maxims are as follows:

(1) The Maxim of Quality:
   a. Do not say what you believe is false
   b. Do not say that for which you lack adequate evidence
(2) The Maxim of Quantity:
   a. Make your contribution as informative as is required
   b. Do not make your contribution more informative than is required
(3) The Maxim of Relevance:
   a. Make your contributions relevant
(4) The Maxim of Manner:
   a. Avoid ambiguity and obscurity
   b. Be brief and orderly

How considerations of relevance can help make sense of a conversational turn is illustrated in (5).

(5) A: (picking up a book from a display in a bookshop)
      "Have you read *Long Walk to Freedom*?"
    B: "I find autobiographies fascinating."

A asked about *Long Walk to Freedom*. B talks about autobiographies. A asked whether B had read the book. B talks about what she finds fascinating. One might think that B had ignored the question, but the conversation can be read as co-operative and coherent by trying to work out how B's contribution could be relevant to A's question. If the book is an autobiography, then B has not switched topics.

Now consider the following conversation:

(6) A: "Can anyone use this car park?"
    B: "It's for customers of the supermarket."

If the car park was for the use of everyone, then that would include the supermarket's customers and there would be no need to mention them; so B's utterance appears to offer superfluous information. An assumption that B is abiding by the maxim of _____—and therefore not giving more information than needed—invites an implicature that it is necessary to specify supermarket customers—it is for them and not for other motorists.

03 Read the passages and follow the directions. [4 points]

─┤ A ├─

Cooperative Principle, in turn, consists of four conversational maxims: Maxim of Quality, Maxim of Quantity, Maxim of Relevance, and Maxim of Manner. First, Maxim of Quality states that each participant's contribution should be truthful and based on sufficient evidence. Second, Maxim of Quantity states that each participant's contribution to a conversation should be no more or less informative than required. Third, Maxim of Relevance states that each participant's contribution should be relevant to the subject of the conversation. Finally, Maxim of Manner states that each participant's contribution should be expressed in a reasonably clear fashion; that is, it should not be vague, ambiguous, or excessively wordy. These are not prescriptive rules but rather part of a strategy used by the community of language users to enable the use of conversational implicature.

Implicatures can arise when a maxim is flouted. To flout a maxim is to choose not to follow that maxim in order to implicate something. Suppose an undergraduate in a geography class says the first utterance in (1), in response to a question from the instructor. The instructor, Mr. Barbados, then says the second utterance in (1).

(1) Student: Reno's the capital of Nevada.
　　Mr. Barbados: Yeah, and London's the capital of New Jersey.

The instructor's utterance raises an implicature. The student reasons (unconsciously) as follows: Mr. Barbados said that London is the capital of New Jersey; he knows that is not true. He appears to be flouting the Maxim of _____; there must be a reason for him saying something patently false. The inference (i.e., the implicature) is that the student's answer is false (i.e., Reno is not the capital of Nevada).

B

Now consider the following dialogue:

(2) Sally: I hope you brought the bread and the cheese.
    Peter: Ah, I brought the bread.

First, read the passage <A> and fill in the blank with ONE word from the passage. Second, in <B>, state which maxim Peter's utterance in (2) is flouting, and what Peter's utterance implicates, based on the description in <A>.

앤드류 채

멘토영어학
문제은행

초판인쇄 | 2025. 7. 1.   **초판발행** | 2025. 7. 7.
편저자 | 앤드류 채   **발행인** | 박 용   **발행처** | (주)박문각출판
표지디자인 | 박문각 디자인팀   **등록** | 2015년 4월 29일 제2019-000137호
주소 | 06654 서울특별시 서초구 효령로 283 서경 B/D   **팩스** | (02)584-2927
전화 | 교재 문의 (02)6466-7202, 동영상 문의 (02)6466-7201

저자와의
협의하에
인지생략

이 책의 무단 전재 또는 복제 행위는 저작권법 제136조에 의거, 5년 이하의 징역 또는 5,000만 원 이하의 벌금에 처하거나 이를 병과할 수 있습니다.

ISBN 979-11-7262-953-3
정가 31,000원

다음 카페_유희태 전공영어팀
http://cafe.daum.net/YHT2S2R

 네이버 블로그_유희태 전공영어팀
https://blog.naver.com/kmo7740

2026 교원임용시험 전공영어 대비
최신 기출문제 경향 반영

앤드류 채
멘토영어학 문제은행

모범답안

LSI 영어연구소 앤드류 채 편저

앤드류 채
멘토영어학
문제은행

2026 교원임용시험 전공영어 대비
최신 기출문제 경향 반영

MENTOR

앤드류 채
멘토영어학 문제은행

모범답안

LSI 영어연구소 앤드류 채 편저

박문각 임용 동영상강의 www.pmg.co.kr

박문각

Mentor Linguistics
CONTENTS

Part 01	Syntax	⋯ 3
Part 02	Grammar	⋯ 32
Part 03	Phonetics & Phonology	⋯ 49
Part 04	Morphology	⋯ 81
Part 05	Semantics	⋯ 83
Part 06	Pragmatics	⋯ 87

Part 01 Syntax

01 Raising

01

본책 p.008

하위내용영역	배점	예상정답률
영어학 (통사론) B형 기입형	2점	90%

모범답안

① two ② three

채점기준

2점: ①, ② 모두 답안과 일치하면 2점을 준다.

1점: ①, ② 중 하나만 답안과 일치하면 1점을 준다.

0점: ①, ② 모두 답안과 일치하지 않으면 0점을 준다.

02

본책 p.010

하위내용영역	배점	예상정답률
영어학 (통사론) A형 서술형	4점	65%

모범답안

Sentence (c) is ungrammatical. The adjective 'free' belongs to *ready*-type; thus, it cannot allow an extraposed construction. Sentence (e) is ungrammatical. The adjective 'frosty' belongs to *ready*-type; thus, it cannot allow the construction with an infinitive clause subject.

채점기준

내용학: 4점

(1) Sentence (c) is ungrammatical이 맞으면 1점을 준다.

(2) The adjective 'free' belongs to *ready*-type; thus, it cannot allow an extraposed construction의 내용이 맞으면 1점을 준다.

(3) Sentence (e) is ungrammatical이 맞으면 1점을 준다.

(4) The adjective 'frosty' belongs to *ready*-type; thus, it cannot allow the construction with an infinitive clause subject의 내용이 맞으면 1점을 준다.

03

본책 p.012

하위내용영역	배점	예상정답률
영어학 (통사론) B형 기입형	2점	90%

모범답안

① subject ② object

채점기준

2점 : ①, ② 모두 답안과 일치하면 2점을 준다.

1점 : ①, ② 중 하나만 답안과 일치하면 1점을 준다.

0점 : ①, ② 모두 답안과 일치하지 않으면 0점을 준다.

04

본책 p.014

하위내용영역	배점	예상정답률
영어학 (통사론) B형 기입형	2점	90%

모범답안

subject

채점기준

2점 : 답안과 일치하면 2점을 준다.

0점 : 답안과 일치하지 않으면 0점을 준다.

02 Complements & Adjuncts

01

하위내용영역	배점	예상정답률
영어학 (통사론) B형 기입형	2점	80%

모범답안

① longer ② so

채점기준

2점: ①, ② 모두 답안과 일치하면 2점을 준다.
1점: ①, ② 중 하나만 답안과 일치하면 1점을 준다.
0점: ①, ② 모두 답안과 일치하지 않으면 0점을 준다.

02

하위내용영역	배점	예상정답률
영어학 (통사론) A형 서술형	4점	50%

모범답안

Sentence (a) contains the PP which has the different function from the rest: the PP 'with a razor-blade' is an adjunct. Sentence (f) contains the PP which has the different function from the rest: the PP 'at the office' is an adjunct.

채점기준

내용학: 4점

(1) Sentence (a) contains the PP which has the different function from the rest이 맞으면 1점을 준다.
(2) the PP 'with a razor-blade' is an adjunct이 맞으면 1점을 준다.
(3) Sentence (f) contains the PP which has the different function from the rest이 맞으면 1점을 준다.
(4) the PP 'at the office' is an adjunct이 맞으면 1점을 준다.

03

하위내용영역	배점	예상정답률
영어학 (통사론) B형 기입형	2점	90%

모범답안

external complement

채점기준

2점: 답안과 일치하면 2점을 준다.
0점: 답안과 일치하지 않으면 0점을 준다.

04 본책 p.021

하위내용영역	배점	예상정답률
영어학 (통사론) A형 서술형	4점	45%

모범답안

Version 1

Sentence (b) is ambiguous. The clause 'when you are ready' can be interpreted as complement or adjunct. Sentence (f) is ambiguous. The phrase 'last night' can be interpreted as complement or adjunct.

Version 2

Sentences (b) and (f) are ambiguous. In (b), the clause 'when you are ready' can either be a complement or an adjunct. In (f), The phrase 'last night' can either be a complement or an adjunct.

채점기준

내용학: 4점
(1) Sentence (b) is ambiguous이 맞으면 1점을 준다.
(2) The clause 'when you are ready' can be interpreted as complement or adjunct의 내용이 맞으면 1점을 준다.
(3) Sentence (f) is ambiguous이 맞으면 1점을 준다.
(4) The phrase 'last night' can be interpreted as complement or adjunct의 내용이 맞으면 1점을 준다.

05 본책 p.023

하위내용영역	배점	예상정답률
영어학 (통사론) B형 기입형	2점	70%

모범답안

① from ② with

채점기준

2점: ①, ② 모두 답안과 일치하면 2점을 준다.
1점: ①, ② 중 하나만 답안과 일치하면 1점을 준다.
0점: ①, ② 모두 답안과 일치하지 않으면 0점을 준다.

06

하위내용영역	배점	예상정답률
영어학 (통사론) A형 서술형	4점	60%

모범답안

(b) is false. The correct statement is as follows: the underlined clause is the complement and is a sister of N. (e) is false: the underlined PP is the adjunct and is a sister of N' (N-bar).

채점기준

내용학 : 4점
(1) (b) is false이 맞으면 1점을 준다.
(2) the underlined clause is the complement and is a sister of N이 맞으면 1점을 준다.
(3) (e) is false이 맞으면 1점을 준다.
(4) the underlined PP is the adjunct and is a sister of N' (N-bar)이 맞으면 1점을 준다.

07

하위내용영역	배점	예상정답률
영어학 (통사론) A형 서술형	4점	60%

모범답안

Version 1

The phrase (e) is ungrammatical because the noun 'ignorance' cannot select a CP complement. The phrase (f) is ungrammatical because the noun 'article' cannot select a CP complement.

Version 2

(e) is ungrammatical. The noun 'ignorance' cannot combine with a CP complement, (indicating that they do not have CP in the value of COMPS). (f) is ungrammatical. The noun 'article' cannot combine with a CP complement, (indicating that they do not have CP in the value of COMPS).

채점기준

내용학 : 4점
(1) The phrase (e) is ungrammatical이 맞으면 1점을 준다.
(2) the noun 'ignorance' cannot select a CP complement의 내용이 맞으면 1점을 준다.
(3) The phrase (f) is ungrammatical이 맞으면 1점을 준다.
(4) the noun 'article' cannot select a CP complement의 내용이 맞으면 1점을 준다.

08

본책 p.029

하위내용영역	배점	예상정답률
영어학 (통사론) B형 기입형	2점	90%

모범답안

① adjacent   ② function

채점기준

2점: ①, ② 모두 답안과 일치하면 2점을 준다.
1점: ①, ② 중 하나만 답안과 일치하면 1점을 준다.
0점: ①, ② 모두 답안과 일치하지 않으면 0점을 준다.

09

본책 p.031

하위내용영역	배점	예상정답률
영어학 (통사론) A형 서술형	4점	60%

모범답안

(f) is ambiguous. (f) means 'a student who studies high moral principles' when the PP 'of high moral principles' is interpreted as a complement, and (f) also means 'a student who has high moral principles' when the PP 'of high moral principles' is used as an adjunct.

채점기준

내용학: 4점
(1) (f) is ambiguous이 맞으면 2점을 준다.
(2) (f) means 'a student who studies high moral principles' when the PP 'of high moral principles' is interpreted as a complement의 내용이 맞으면 1점을 준다.
(3) (f) also means 'a student who has high moral principles' when the PP 'of high moral principles' is used as an adjunct의 내용이 맞으면 1점을 준다.

03 Substitution

01

하위내용영역	배점	예상정답률
영어학 (통사론) A형 서술형	4점	60%

[모범답안]

Version 1

Sentence (d) is ungrammatical. The proform 'one' must replace an N' (N-bar), but 'one' in (d) is replacing the noun (N) 'claim'. A pro-N' 'one' cannot replace an N (by itself unless an N is the constituent of an N').

Version 2

Sentence (d) is ungrammatical. The proform 'one' in (d) is replacing the noun (N) 'claim'. A pro-N' 'one' cannot replace an N; it must replace an N' (N-bar).

[채점기준]

내용학 : 4점
(1) Sentence (d) is ungrammatical이 맞으면 2점을 준다.
(2) The proform 'one' in (d) is replacing the noun (N) 'claim'의 내용이 맞으면 1점을 준다.
(3) A pro-N' 'one' cannot replace an N; it must replace an N'의 내용이 맞으면 1점을 준다.

02

하위내용영역	배점	예상정답률
영어학 (문법/통사론) B형 서술형	4점	35%

[모범답안]

Version 1

Sentences (a) and (c) are ungrammatical. In (a) the antecedent for 'did so (do so)' is 'read all the reports'; we cannot add 'most of them' as another complement in the second clause. In (c) the antecedent for 'did so (do so)' is 'rode her bicycle'; we cannot add 'to school' as another complement (of the verb 'rode') in the second clause.

Version 2

Sentence (a) is ungrammatical because 'did so (do so)' must be interpreted as 'read all the reports'; thus, we can't add 'most of them' as another complement (object) in the second clause. Sentence (c) is ungrammatical. The antecedent for 'did so (do so)' is 'rode her bicycle'. The added phrase 'to school' can consist of another complement in the second clause; it cannot combine with *do so* (in the second clause).

MENTOR LINGUISTICS

채점기준

내용학 : 4점

(1) Sentence (a) is ungrammatical이 맞으면 1점을 준다.
(2) In (a) the antecedent for 'did so (do so)' is 'read all the reports'; we cannot add 'most of them' as another complement in the second clause의 내용이 맞으면 1점을 준다.
(3) Sentence (c) is ungrammatical이 맞으면 1점을 준다.
(4) In (c) the antecedent for 'did so (do so)' is 'rode her bicycle'; we cannot add 'to school' as another complement (of the verb 'rode') in the second clause의 내용이 맞으면 1점을 준다.
(5) (a)와 (c) 모두 답으로 선택하지 않은 경우나 그 외에 답을 추가 선택한 경우는 부분 점수 없이 0점을 준다.

03

본책 p.037

하위내용영역	배점	예상정답률
영어학 (통사론) A형 서술형	4점	60%

모범답안

Version 1

First, in (4b) the word 'French' is an AP adjunct, and in (5a) the word 'French' is an NP complement. Second, in (4c) 'French' is an adjective, and in (5c) 'French' is a noun.

Version 2

First, in (4b) 'French' functions as an adjunct and its form is an (prenominal) AP. In (5b) 'French' functions as a complement and its form is an (prenominal) NP. Second, in (4c) 'French' is an adjective, and in (5c) 'French' is a noun.

채점기준

내용학 : 4점

(1) in (4b) the word 'French' is an AP adjunct이 맞으면 1점을 준다.
(2) in (5a) the word 'French' is an NP complement이 맞으면 1점을 준다.
(3) in (4c) 'French' is an adjective이 맞으면 1점을 준다.
(4) in (5c) 'French' is a noun이 맞으면 1점을 준다.

04

본책 p.039

하위내용영역	배점	예상정답률
영어학 (통사론) B형 기입형	2점	85%

모범답안

① noun phrases ② teacher of language

채점기준

2점: ①, ② 모두 답안과 일치하면 2점을 준다.

1점: ①, ② 중 하나만 답안과 일치하면 1점을 준다.

0점: ①, ② 모두 답안과 일치하지 않으면 0점을 준다.

05

본책 p.041

하위내용영역	배점	예상정답률
영어학 (통사론) A형 서술형	4점	65%

모범답안

Sentence (a) is ungrammatical. In (a), 'did so' replaces the substring 'carried her'; it is not a V-bar (V') constituent. Sentence (c) is ungrammatical. In (c), 'did so' replaces just the verb 'drove'; it is not a V-bar (V') constituent.

채점기준

내용학: 4점

(1) Sentence (a) is ungrammatical이 맞으면 1점을 준다.

(2) In (a), 'did so' replaces the substring 'carried her'; it is not a V-bar (V') constituent의 내용이 맞으면 1점을 준다.

(3) Sentence (c) is ungrammatical이 맞으면 1점을 준다.

(4) In (c), 'did so' replaces just the verb 'drove'; it is not a V-bar (V') constituent의 내용이 맞으면 1점을 준다.

06

본책 p.043

하위내용영역	배점	예상정답률
영어학 (통사론) A형 서술형	4점	65%

모범답안

Sentence (e) is ungrammatical. The pronoun 'one' replaces the N 'student'; the pronoun 'one' can replace an N' but not an N. Sentence (f) is ungrammatical. The pronoun 'one' replaces the N 'king'; the pronoun 'one' can replace an N' but not an N.

채점기준

내용학: 4점

(1) Sentence (e) is ungrammatical이 맞으면 1점을 준다.

(2) The pronoun 'one' replaces the N 'student'; the pronoun 'one' can replace an N' but not an N의 내용이 맞으면 1점을 준다.

(3) Sentence (f) is ungrammatical이 맞으면 1점을 준다.

(4) The pronoun 'one' replaces the N 'king'; the pronoun 'one' can replace an N' but not an N의 내용이 맞으면 1점을 준다.

04 Case Theory

01

본책 p.045

하위내용영역	배점	예상정답률
영어학 (통사론) A형 서술형	4점	65%

모범답안

Version 1

Sentence (d) is ungrammatical. The adjective 'envious' is not a case assigner; the NP 'Mary' is the caseless NP. (It violates the case filter.) Sentence (e) is ungrammatical. The noun 'destruction' is not a case assigner; the NP 'the rainforests' is the caseless NP. (It violates the case filter.)

Version 2

Sentence (d) is ungrammatical because the NP 'Mary' cannot be (accusative) case-assigned by the adjective 'envious', (violating the case filter). Sentence (e) is ungrammatical because the NP 'the rainforests' cannot be (accusative) case-assigned by the noun 'destruction', (violating the case filter).

채점기준

내용학: 4점

(1) Sentence (d) is ungrammatical이 맞으면 1점을 준다.
(2) The adjective 'envious' is not a case assigner; the NP 'Mary' is the caseless NP의 내용이 맞으면 1점을 준다.
(3) Sentence (e) is ungrammatical이 맞으면 1점을 준다.
(4) The noun 'destruction' is not a case assigner; the NP 'the rainforests' is the caseless NP의 내용이 맞으면 1점을 준다.

02

본책 p.047

하위내용영역	배점	예상정답률
영어학 (통사론) B형 기입형	2점	90%

모범답안

① external   ② preposition

채점기준

2점: ①, ② 모두 답안과 일치하면 2점을 준다.
1점: ①, ② 중 하나만 답안과 일치하면 1점을 준다.
0점: ①, ② 모두 답안과 일치하지 않으면 0점을 준다.

05 Binding Theory

01

하위내용영역	배점	예상정답률
영어학 (통사론) A형 서술형	4점	60%

[모범답안]

Sentence (b) is ungrammatical because the anaphor 'himself' is not bound by its antecedent 'Frank' within its smallest binding domain 'to behave himself'. Sentence (d) is ungrammatical because the anaphor 'himself' is not bound by its antecedent 'Frank' within its smallest binding domain 'to gather evidence about himself'.

[채점기준]

내용학 : 4점

(1) Sentence (b) is ungrammatical이 맞으면 1점을 준다.
(2) the anaphor 'himself' is not bound by its antecedent 'Frank' within its smallest binding domain 'to behave himself'의 내용이 맞으면 1점을 준다.
(3) Sentence (d) is ungrammatical이 맞으면 1점을 준다.
(4) the anaphor 'himself' is not bound by its antecedent 'Frank' within its smallest binding domain 'to gather evidence about himself'의 내용이 맞으면 1점을 준다.

02

하위내용영역	배점	예상정답률
영어학 (통사론) A형 서술형	4점	60%

[모범답안]

Sentence (a) is ungrammatical. The anaphor 'himself' is not bound by the potential antecedent 'John' in its binding domain; (it violates Binding Principle A). Sentence (e) is ungrammatical. The anaphor 'himself' is not bound by the potential antecedent 'Bill' in its binding domain; (it violates Binding Principle A).

[채점기준]

내용학 : 4점

(1) Sentence (a) is ungrammatical이 맞으면 1점을 준다.
(2) The anaphor 'himself' is not bound by the potential antecedent 'John' in its binding domain의 내용이 맞으면 1점을 준다.
(3) Sentence (e) is ungrammatical이 맞으면 1점을 준다.
(4) The anaphor 'himself' is not bound by the potential antecedent 'Bill' in its binding domain의 내용이 맞으면 1점을 준다.

03

본책 p.053

하위내용영역	배점	예상정답률
영어학 (통사론) A형 서술형	4점	65%

모범답안

Sentence (d) is ungrammatical because the anaphor 'ourselves' cannot be bound by the c-commanding constituent 'We' within the closest clause 'to examine ourselves'. Sentence (f) is ungrammatical because the pronominal 'them' is bound by the c-commanding constituent 'patients' within the closest clause 'to examine them', violating Principle B.

채점기준

내용학: 4점

(1) Sentence (d) is ungrammatical이 맞으면 1점을 준다.
(2) the anaphor 'ourselves' cannot be bound by the c-commanding constituent 'We' within the closest clause 'to examine ourselves'의 내용이 맞으면 1점을 준다.
(3) Sentence (f) is ungrammatical이 맞으면 1점을 준다.
(4) the pronominal 'them' is bound by the c-commanding constituent 'patients' within the closest clause 'to examine them', violating Principle B의 내용이 맞으면 1점을 준다.

04

본책 p.055

하위내용영역	배점	예상정답률
영어학 (통사론) B형 기입형	2점	90%

모범답안

① antecedent ② reflexive

채점기준

2점: ①, ② 모두 답안과 일치하면 2점을 준다.
1점: ①, ② 중 하나만 답안과 일치하면 1점을 준다.
0점: ①, ② 모두 답안과 일치하지 않으면 0점을 준다.

06 Control Theory

01

하위내용영역	배점	예상정답률
영어학 (통사론) B형 기입형	2점	80%

모범답안

① object ② subject

채점기준

2점: ①, ② 모두 답안과 일치하면 2점을 준다.
1점: ①, ② 중 하나만 답안과 일치하면 1점을 준다.
0점: ①, ② 모두 답안과 일치하지 않으면 0점을 준다.

02

하위내용영역	배점	예상정답률
영어학 (통사론) A형 서술형	4점	60%

모범답안

Sentence (c) is ungrammatical. The control verb 'coax(ed)' assigns a semantic role to its subject; thus, the expletive 'there' cannot appear in the subject position.
Sentence (f) is ungrammatical. The control verb 'order(ed)' assigns a semantic role to its object; thus, the expletive 'there' cannot appear in the object position.

채점기준

내용학: 4점

(1) Sentence (c) is ungrammatical이 맞으면 1점을 준다.
(2) The control verb 'coax(ed)' assigns a semantic role to its subject; thus, the expletive 'there' cannot appear in the subject position의 내용이 맞으면 1점을 준다.
(3) Sentence (f) is ungrammatical이 맞으면 1점을 준다.
(4) The control verb 'order(ed)' assigns a semantic role to its object; thus, the expletive 'there' cannot appear in the object position의 내용이 맞으면 1점을 준다.

07 Theta Theory

01
본책 p.061

하위내용영역	배점	예상정답률
영어학 (통사론) B형 기입형	2점	80%

모범답안

① EXPERIENCER ② GOAL

채점기준

2점: ①, ② 모두 답안과 일치하면 2점을 준다.
1점: ①, ② 중 하나만 답안과 일치하면 1점을 준다.
0점: ①, ② 모두 답안과 일치하지 않으면 0점을 준다.

02
본책 p.063

하위내용영역	배점	예상정답률
영어학 (통사론) B형 기입형	2점	80%

모범답안

① Theme ② Experiencer

채점기준

2점: ①, ② 모두 답안과 일치하면 2점을 준다.
1점: ①, ② 중 하나만 답안과 일치하면 1점을 준다.
0점: ①, ② 모두 답안과 일치하지 않으면 0점을 준다.

08 Constituency

01

하위내용영역	배점	예상정답률
영어학 (통사론) A형 서술형	4점	60%

[모범답안]

Sentence (c) is ungrammatical. The different functions cannot be conjoined: the PP 'to the park' is a complement and the PP 'for health reasons' is an adjunct. Sentence (f) is ungrammatical. The different functions cannot be conjoined: the PP 'of the riots' is a complement and the PP 'in the bar' is an adjunct.

[채점기준]

내용학: 4점

(1) Sentence (c) is ungrammatical이 맞으면 1점을 준다.
(2) The different functions cannot be conjoined: the PP 'to the park' is a complement and the PP 'for health reasons' is an adjunct의 내용이 맞으면 1점을 준다.
(3) Sentence (f) is ungrammatical이 맞으면 1점을 준다.
(4) The different functions cannot be conjoined: the PP 'of the riots' is a complement and the PP 'in the bar' is an adjunct의 내용이 맞으면 1점을 준다.

02

하위내용영역	배점	예상정답률
영어학 (통사론) A형 서술형	4점	60%

[모범답안]

Version 1

Sentence (c) is ungrammatical. TP 'them to be conscientious' cannot be in the focus position of a *wh*-cleft sentence. Sentence (f) is ungrammatical. AP 'very pretty' cannot be in the focus position of a *it*-cleft sentence.

Version 2

Sentences (c) and (f) are ungrammatical. In (c) TP 'them to be conscientious' cannot be in the focus position of a Pseudocleft. In (f) AP 'very pretty' cannot be in the focus position of a Cleft.

[채점기준]

내용학: 4점

(1) Sentence (c) is ungrammatical이 맞으면 1점을 준다.
(2) TP 'them to be conscientious' cannot be in the focus position of a *wh*-cleft sentence의 내용이 맞으면 1점을 준다.

(3) Sentence (f) is ungrammatical이 맞으면 1점을 준다.
(4) AP 'very pretty' cannot be in the focus position of a *it*-cleft sentence의 내용이 맞으면 1점을 준다.

03

본책 p.068

하위내용영역	배점	예상정답률
영어학 (통사론) A형 서술형	4점	60%

[모범답안]

Sentence (d) is ungrammatical. The different categories cannot be coordinated (conjoined); (the clause) 'that John made a mistake' is the CP and 'him to be in great pain' is the TP. Sentence (e) is ungrammatical. The different categories cannot be coordinated (conjoined); 'there to be fried squid at the reception' is the TP and 'for John to stay' is the CP.

[채점기준]

내용학: 4점

(1) Sentence (d) is ungrammatical이 맞으면 1점을 준다.
(2) The different categories cannot be coordinated (conjoined); (the clause) 'that John made a mistake' is the CP and 'him to be in great pain' is the TP의 내용이 맞으면 1점을 준다.
(3) Sentence (e) is ungrammatical이 맞으면 1점을 준다.
(4) The different categories cannot be coordinated (conjoined); 'there to be fried squid at the reception' is the TP and 'for John to stay' is the CP의 내용이 맞으면 1점을 준다.

04

본책 p.070

하위내용영역	배점	예상정답률
영어학 (통사론) A형 서술형	4점	65%

[모범답안]

Version 1

Sentence (d) is ungrammatical. When the VP 'interrupt the speaker' is preposed, the VP-adverb 'politely' must be moved along with its VP. Sentence (f) is ungrammatical. When the VP 'clean his garage' is preposed, the VP-adverb 'meticulously' must be moved along with its VP.

Version 2

Sentences (d) and (f) are ungrammatical. In (d), the AdvP 'politely' must be moved along with the (main) verb 'interrupt' and its (Direct) Object 'the speaker'; leaving this VP-adverb 'politely' behind leads to an ungrammatical result. In (f), the VP-adverb 'meticulously' must be moved along with the whole VP 'clean his garage'. Leaving this VP-adverb behind leads to an ungrammatical result.

채점기준

내용학: 4점

(1) Sentence (d) is ungrammatical이 맞으면 1점을 준다.
(2) When the VP 'interrupt the speaker' is preposed, the VP-adverb 'politely' must be moved along with its VP의 내용이 맞으면 1점을 준다.
(3) Sentence (f) is ungrammatical이 맞으면 1점을 준다.
(4) When the VP 'clean his garage' is preposed, the VP-adverb 'meticulously' must be moved along with its VP의 내용이 맞으면 1점을 준다.

05

하위내용영역	배점	예상정답률
영어학 (통사론) A형 서술형	4점	60%

모범답안

Version 1

The underlined part in (c) qualifies as an NP constituent. It can move to the sentence-initial position: Those funny people who eat with their hands and sing at the dinner table I like. It can be replaced by a proform: I like them.

Version 2

The underlined part in (c) qualifies as an NP constituent. Movement Test: Those funny people who eat with their hands and sing at the dinner table I like. Substitution Test: I like them.

채점기준

내용학: 4점

(1) The underlined part in (c) qualifies as an NP constituent이 맞으면 2점을 준다.
(2) Those funny people who eat with their hands and sing at the dinner table I like이 맞으면 1점을 준다.
(3) I like them이 맞으면 1점을 준다.

06

하위내용영역	배점	예상정답률
영어학 (통사론) A형 서술형	4점	40%

모범답안

Sentence (7) is ungrammatical. 'Put off' is a phrasal verb. (Only full phrases can be preposed in this way), but the sequence 'off the customers' isn't a phrase; (it isn't even a constituent.)

> [채점기준]

내용학: 4점

(1) Sentence (7) is ungrammatical이 맞으면 2점을 준다.
(2) 'Put off' is a phrasal verb이 맞으면 1점을 준다.
(3) (Only full phrases can be preposed in this way), but the sequence 'off the customers' isn't a phrase; (it isn't even a constituent.)의 내용이 맞으면 1점을 준다.
(4) Sentence (7)번 외에 다른 번호를 추가로 선택한 경우 0점으로 한다.

07

하위내용영역	배점	예상정답률
영어학 (통사론) A형 서술형	4점	55%

> [모범답안]

Sentence (d) is ungrammatical. In the Gapping construction, all auxiliary verbs must be omitted, but the presence of 'has been' makes the whole sentence ungrammatical. Sentence (e) is ungrammatical. In the VP ellipsis construction, the auxiliary verb (cannot be elided but) must be left behind; there is no auxiliary verb (in the second clause) in (e).

> [채점기준]

내용학: 4점

(1) Sentence (d) is ungrammatical이 맞으면 1점을 준다.
(2) In the Gapping construction, all auxiliary verbs must be omitted, but the presence of 'has been' makes the whole sentence ungrammatical의 내용이 맞으면 1점을 준다.
(3) Sentence (e) is ungrammatical이 맞으면 1점을 준다.
(4) In the VP ellipsis construction, the auxiliary verb (cannot be elided but) must be left behind; there is no auxiliary verb (in the second clause) in (e)의 내용이 맞으면 1점을 준다.

09 Verbs

01

하위내용영역	배점	예상정답률
영어학 (통사론) A형 서술형	4점	45%

[모범답안]

Sentence (d) is ungrammatical. The subject 'the avalanche' is selected by the (matrix/main) verb 'tell (told)'; this sentence is semantically ill-formed. Sentence (f) is ungrammatical. The subject 'the key' is selected by the (matrix/main) verb 'ask (asked)'; this sentence is semantically ill-formed.

[채점기준]

내용학 : 4점
(1) Sentence (d) is ungrammatical이 맞으면 1점을 준다.
(2) The subject 'the avalanche' is selected by the (matrix/main) verb 'tell (told)'; this sentence is semantically ill-formed의 내용이 맞으면 1점을 준다.
(3) Sentence (f) is ungrammatical이 맞으면 1점을 준다.
(4) The subject 'the key' is selected by the (matrix/main) verb 'ask (asked)'; this sentence is semantically ill-formed의 내용이 맞으면 1점을 준다.

02

하위내용영역	배점	예상정답률
영어학 (통사론) B형 기입형	2점	90%

[모범답안]

subject

[채점기준]

2점 : 답안과 일치하면 2점을 준다.
0점 : 답안과 일치하지 않으면 0점을 준다.

03 본책 p.081

하위내용영역	배점	예상정답률
영어학 (통사론) A형 서술형	4점	60%

모범답안

Sentence (b) is ungrammatical. (The verb 'blamed' requires two complements: an NP and a PP.) The PP 'on humans' is a complement and thus the same type of PP 'on natural causes' cannot co-occur. Sentence (f) is ungrammatical. The PP 'on financial matters' is a complement; thus, the same type of PP 'on etiquette' cannot co-occur.

채점기준

내용학: 4점

(1) Sentence (b) is ungrammatical이 맞으면 1점을 준다.
(2) The PP 'on humans' is a complement and thus the same type of PP 'on natural causes' cannot co-occur의 내용이 맞으면 1점을 준다.
(3) Sentence (f) is ungrammatical이 맞으면 1점을 준다
(4) The PP 'on financial matters' is a complement; thus, the same type of PP 'on etiquette' cannot co-occur의 내용이 맞으면 1점을 준다.

04 본책 p.083

하위내용영역	배점	예상정답률
영어학 (통사론) A형 서술형	4점	65%

모범답안

Sentence (a) is ungrammatical. The verb 'claim(ed)' cannot combine with an indirect question; (only a finite CP can function as its complement). Sentence (d) is ungrammatical. The complement CP of the verb 'wonder(ed)' cannot be a canonical CP (or a finite CP); it must be an indirect question.

채점기준

내용학: 4점

(1) Sentence (a) is ungrammatical이 맞으면 1점을 준다.
(2) The verb 'claim(ed)' cannot combine with an indirect question; (only a finite CP can function as its complement)의 내용이 맞으면 1점을 준다.
(3) Sentence (d) is ungrammatical이 맞으면 1점을 준다.
(4) The complement CP of the verb 'wonder(ed)' cannot be a canonical CP (or a finite CP); it must be an indirect question의 내용이 맞으면 1점을 준다.

10 Syntactic Structures

01
본책 p.085

하위내용영역	배점	예상정답률
영어학 (통사론) B형 기입형	2점	80%

모범답안

① tense ② non-past

채점기준

2점: ①, ② 모두 답안과 일치하면 2점을 준다.
1점: ①, ② 중 하나만 답안과 일치하면 1점을 준다.
0점: ①, ② 모두 답안과 일치하지 않으면 0점을 준다.

02
본책 p.087

하위내용영역	배점	예상정답률
영어학 (통사론) B형 기입형	2점	90%

모범답안

modal auxiliary

채점기준

2점: 답안과 일치하면 2점을 준다.
0점: 답안과 일치하지 않으면 0점을 준다.

03
본책 p.088

하위내용영역	배점	예상정답률
영어학 (통사론) B형 기입형	2점	90%

모범답안

auxiliary

채점기준

2점: 답안과 일치하면 2점을 준다.
0점: 답안과 일치하지 않으면 0점을 준다.

04

본책 p.089

하위내용영역	배점	예상정답률
영어학 (통사론) B형 기입형	2점	90%

모범답안

Head-Complement

채점기준

2점: 답안과 일치하면 2점을 준다.
0점: 답안과 일치하지 않으면 0점을 준다.

05

본책 p.091

하위내용영역	배점	예상정답률
영어학 (통사론) A형 서술형	4점	60%

모범답안

The underlined parts in (e) are not the intermediate categories; the phrase 'speak French fluently' is a VP constituent, and 'which' functions as a pro-VP. The underlined parts in (f) are not the intermediate categories; the phrase 'finish the assignment' is a VP constituent, and 'so' functions as a pro-VP.

채점기준

내용학: 4점

(1) The underlined parts in (e) are not the intermediate categories이 맞으면 1점을 준다.
(2) the phrase 'speak French fluently' is a VP constituent, and 'which' functions as a pro-VP의 내용이 맞으면 1점을 준다.
(3) The underlined parts in (f) are not the intermediate categories이 맞으면 1점을 준다.
(4) the phrase 'finish the assignment' is a VP constituent, and 'so' functions as a pro-VP의 내용이 맞으면 1점을 준다.

06

본책 p.093

하위내용영역	배점	예상정답률
영어학 (통사론) B형 기입형	2점	95%

모범답안

head

채점기준

2점: 답안과 일치하면 2점을 준다.
0점: 답안과 일치하지 않으면 0점을 준다.

11 Additional Tests

01

본책 p.094

하위내용영역	배점	예상정답률
영어학 (통사론) B형 기입형	2점	90%

모범답안

① non-gradable ② gradable

채점기준

2점: ①, ② 모두 답안과 일치하면 2점을 준다.
1점: ①, ② 중 하나만 답안과 일치하면 1점을 준다.
0점: ①, ② 모두 답안과 일치하지 않으면 0점을 준다.

02

본책 p.096

하위내용영역	배점	예상정답률
영어학 (통사론) B형 기입형	2점	80%

모범답안

① verb ② prepositions

채점기준

2점: ①, ② 모두 답안과 일치하면 2점을 준다.
1점: ①, ② 중 하나만 답안과 일치하면 1점을 준다.
0점: ①, ② 모두 답안과 일치하지 않으면 0점을 준다.

03

본책 p.098

하위내용영역	배점	예상정답률
영어학 (통사론) B형 기입형	2점	90%

[모범답안]

① direct object ② predicative complement

[채점기준]

2점: ①, ② 모두 답안과 일치하면 2점을 준다.

1점: ①, ② 중 하나만 답안과 일치하면 1점을 준다.

0점: ①, ② 모두 답안과 일치하지 않으면 0점을 준다.

04

본책 p.100

하위내용영역	배점	예상정답률
영어학 (통사론) B형 기입형	2점	80%

[모범답안]

① adjunct ② predicative

[채점기준]

2점: ①, ② 모두 답안과 일치하면 2점을 준다.

1점: ①, ② 중 하나만 답안과 일치하면 1점을 준다.

0점: ①, ② 모두 답안과 일치하지 않으면 0점을 준다.

05

본책 p.102

하위내용영역	배점	예상정답률
영어학 (통사론) A형 서술형	4점	50%

[모범답안]

Version 1

Sentence (a) is ungrammatical because no constituent can be moved out of a sentential subject 'for Mary to kiss (whom)'; it violates a subject condition. Sentence (e) is ungrammatical because once you move the *wh*-phrase 'what' into the specifier of the embedded CP, then that CP becomes an island for further extraction, the other *wh*-phrase 'who' into the main CP specifier; it violates a *wh*-island.

Version 2

Sentences (a) and (e) are ungrammatical. In (a), in the sentential subject 'for Mary to kiss whom', the *wh*-phrase 'whom' cannot be moved into the main CP specifier because no constituent can be moved out of a sentential subject; it violates a subject condition. In (e), when the *wh*-phrase 'what' is moved into the embedded specifier, the other *wh*-phrase 'who' cannot be moved into the main CP specifier; it violates a *wh*-island.

[채점기준]

내용학: 4점

(1) Sentence (a) is ungrammatical이 맞으면 1점을 준다.
(2) because no constituent can be moved out of a sentential subject 'for Mary to kiss (whom)'; it violates a subject condition의 내용이 맞으면 1점을 준다.
(3) Sentence (e) is ungrammatical이 맞으면 1점을 준다.
(4) because once you move the *wh*-phrase 'what' into the specifier of the embedded CP, then that CP becomes an island for further extraction, the other *wh*-phrase 'who' into the main CP specifier; it violates a *wh*-island의 내용이 맞으면 1점을 준다.

06   본책 p.104

하위내용영역	배점	예상정답률
영어학 (통사론) B형 기입형	2점	80%

[모범답안]

① adverb   ② adjective

[채점기준]

2점: ①, ② 모두 답안과 일치하면 2점을 준다.
1점: ①, ② 중 하나만 답안과 일치하면 1점을 준다.
0점: ①, ② 모두 답안과 일치하지 않으면 0점을 준다.

07   본책 p.106

하위내용영역	배점	예상정답률
영어학 (통사론) B형 기입형	2점	90%

[모범답안]

① verb   ② noun

채점기준

2점: ①, ② 모두 답안과 일치하면 2점을 준다.
1점: ①, ② 중 하나만 답안과 일치하면 1점을 준다.
0점: ①, ② 모두 답안과 일치하지 않으면 0점을 준다.

08

본책 p.108

하위내용영역	배점	예상정답률
영어학 (통사론) B형 기입형	2점	90%

모범답안

head

채점기준

2점: 답안과 일치하면 2점을 준다.
0점: 답안과 일치하지 않으면 0점을 준다.

09

본책 p.110

하위내용영역	배점	예상정답률
영어학 (통사론) A형 서술형	4점	60%

모범답안

Sentence (a) is ungrammatical. The element 'what' from the subject is not extractable. Sentence (d) is ungrammatical. The element 'who' from the subject is not extractable.

채점기준

내용학: 4점
(1) Sentence (a) is ungrammatical이 맞으면 1점을 준다.
(2) The element 'what' from the subject is not extractable의 내용이 맞으면 1점을 준다.
(3) Sentence (d) is ungrammatical이 맞으면 1점을 준다.
(4) The element 'who' from the subject is not extractable의 내용이 맞으면 1점을 준다.

10

본책 p.112

하위내용영역	배점	예상정답률
영어학 (통사론) A형 서술형	4점	60%

모범답안

Sentence (b) is ungrammatical because the verb 'rumor' can be used only in passive forms. Sentence (d) is ungrammatical because the verb 'repute' can be used only in passive forms.

채점기준

내용학: 4점
(1) Sentence (b) is ungrammatical이 맞으면 1점을 준다.
(2) the verb 'rumor' can be used only in passive forms의 내용이 맞으면 1점을 준다.
(3) Sentence (d) is ungrammatical이 맞으면 1점을 준다.
(4) the verb 'repute' can be used only in passive forms의 내용이 맞으면 1점을 준다.

11

본책 p.114

하위내용영역	배점	예상정답률
영어학 (통사론) B형 기입형	2점	90%

모범답안

① determiner ② countable

채점기준

2점: ①, ② 모두 답안과 일치하면 2점을 준다.
1점: ①, ② 중 하나만 답안과 일치하면 1점을 준다.
0점: ①, ② 모두 답안과 일치하지 않으면 0점을 준다.

12

본책 p.116

하위내용영역	배점	예상정답률
영어학 (통사론) A형 서술형	4점	65%

모범답안

Sentence (b) is ungrammatical. The adjective 'key' cannot be used predicatively; it is only used attributively. Sentence (d) is ungrammatical. The postnominal PP 'in the doorway' cannot modify the proper noun 'John' which is the complete NP.

채점기준

내용학: 4점

(1) Sentence (b) is ungrammatical이 맞으면 1점을 준다.
(2) The adjective 'key' cannot be used predicatively; it is only used attributively의 내용이 맞으면 1점을 준다.
(3) Sentence (d) is ungrammatical이 맞으면 1점을 준다.
(4) The PP 'in the doorway' cannot modify the proper noun 'John' which is the complete NP의 내용이 맞으면 1점을 준다.

13

본책 p.118

하위내용영역	배점	예상정답률
영어학 (통사론) B형 기입형	2점	90%

모범답안

[− INV]

채점기준

2점: 답안과 일치하면 2점을 준다.
0점: 답안과 일치하지 않으면 0점을 준다.

14

본책 p.120

하위내용영역	배점	예상정답률
영어학 (통사론) B형 기입형	2점	90%

모범답안

numeral specifier

채점기준

2점: 답안과 일치하면 2점을 준다.
0점: 답안과 일치하지 않으면 0점을 준다.

15
본책 p.121

하위내용영역	배점	예상정답률
영어학 (통사론) B형 기입형	2점	90%

모범답안

① object ② syntactic category

채점기준

2점: ①, ② 모두 답안과 일치하면 2점을 준다.
1점: ①, ② 중 하나만 답안과 일치하면 1점을 준다.
0점: ①, ② 모두 답안과 일치하지 않으면 0점을 준다.

Part 02 Grammar

01

본책 p.126

하위내용영역	배점	예상정답률
영어학 (문법) B형 서술형	4점	60%

모범답안

Version 1

In (a), (the NP) 'a fool' functions as a predicative complement. There is only a single person involved, the one referred to by the subject NP 'I'. In (b) 'a fool' functions as an object. There are two people involved, the subject NP 'I' and the object NP 'a fool'.

Version 2

In (a), (the NP) 'a fool' functions as a predicative complement, and in (b) 'a fool' functions as an object. In (a) there is only a single person involved, the one referred to by the subject NP 'I'. Sentence (b) refers to two people: me, and the fool I could feel pushing in front of me on the platform.

채점기준

내용학: 4점

(1) In (a), (the NP) 'a fool' functions as a predicative complement이 맞으면 1점을 준다.
(2) There is only a single person involved, the one referred to by the subject NP 'I'의 내용이 맞으면 1점을 준다.
(3) In (b) 'a fool' functions as an object이 맞으면 1점을 준다.
(4) There are two people involved, the subject NP 'I' and the object NP 'a fool'의 내용이 맞으면 1점을 준다.

02

본책 p.128

하위내용영역	배점	예상정답률
영어학 (문법) B형 서술형	4점	60%

모범답안

Version 1

Sentence (b) is unambiguous and indicates the segregatory meaning (interpretation). Phrase (c) is unambiguous and indicates the segregatory meaning.

Version 2

Sentence (b) is unambiguous and has only the segregatory interpretation (meaning). Phrase (c) is unambiguous and has only the segregatory interpretation.

[참고]
Only the segregatory meaning is ordinarily possible when the coordinated modifiers denote mutually exclusive properties.

채점기준

내용학: 4점

(1) Sentence (b) is unambiguous and indicates the segregatory meaning (interpretation)이 맞으면 2점을 준다. (각 1점)
(2) Phrase (c) is unambiguous and indicates the segregatory meaning이 맞으면 2점을 준다. (각 1점)

03

본책 p.130

하위내용영역	배점	예상정답률
영어학 (문법) B형 서술형	4점	70%

모범답안

Version 1

Sentence (c) is ungrammatical. After a positive clause ('He was unkind'), we cannot add a constituent introduced by 'not even'. Sentence (e) is ungrammatical. The negative tag (didn't they?) cannot attach to the negative clause ('Few of them realised it was a hoax'); (the positive tag (did they?) can attach to the negative clause.)

Version 2

Sentence (c) is ungrammatical. We cannot add a constituent introduced by 'not even' to the positive clause ('He was unkind'). Sentence (e) is ungrammatical. The main clause ('Few of them realised it was a hoax') is the negative clause; thus, it cannot have the negative tag (didn't they?).

채점기준

내용학: 4점

(1) Sentence (c) is ungrammatical이 맞으면 1점을 준다.
(2) After a positive clause ('He was unkind'), we cannot add a constituent introduced by 'not even'의 내용이 맞으면 1점을 준다.
(3) Sentence (e) is ungrammatical이 맞으면 1점을 준다.
(4) The negative tag (didn't they?) cannot attach to the negative clause ('Few of them realised it was a hoax')의 내용이 맞으면 1점을 준다.

04

본책 p.132

하위내용영역	배점	예상정답률
영어학 (문법) B형 서술형	4점	50%

모범답안

Version 1

Sentence (c) is ungrammatical. The nonrestrictive relative clause 'which doesn't surprise me at all' modifies the entire main clause; thus, it must be set off from the main clause by a comma. Sentence (d) is ungrammatical. The two clauses, 'whose books have sold well' and 'who everyone likes', are nonrestrictive relative clauses; they cannot be stacked.

Version 2

Sentence (c) is ungrammatical. The nonrestrictive relative clause 'which doesn't surprise me at all', which modifies the entire main clause (the main clause), must be set off from it by a comma. Sentence (d) is ungrammatical. The nonrestrictive relative clauses, ('whose books have sold well, who everyone likes',) cannot be stacked.

채점기준

내용학: 4점

(1) Sentence (c) is ungrammatical이 맞으면 1점을 준다.
(2) The nonrestrictive relative clause 'which doesn't surprise me at all' modifies the entire main clause; thus, it must be set off from the main clause by a comma의 내용이 맞으면 1점을 준다.
(3) Sentence (d) is ungrammatical이 맞으면 1점을 준다.
(4) The two clauses, 'whose books have sold well' and 'who everyone likes', are nonrestrictive relative clauses; they cannot be stacked의 내용이 맞으면 1점을 준다.

05

본책 p.134

하위내용영역	배점	예상정답률
영어학 (문법) B형 서술형	4점	50%

모범답안

Version 1

Sentence (a) is ungrammatical. The PP 'under what circumstances' is in adjunct function; the stranding construction to be avoided in adjuncts. Sentence (b) is ungrammatical. The clause (containing the preposition) 'for which grant we should apply' is (a subordinate interrogative clause) functioning as complement to a preposition 'on'; fronting is impossible (or stranding is obligatory).

Version 2

Sentence (a) is ungrammatical because with the adjunct PP 'under what circumstances' stranding is prohibited. Sentence (b) is ungrammatical. The (interrogative) clause 'for which grant we should apply' is complement of 'on'; fronting is impossible.

채점기준

내용학: 4점

(1) Sentence (a) is ungrammatical이 맞으면 1점을 준다.
(2) The PP 'under what circumstances' is in adjunct function; the stranding construction to be avoided in adjuncts의 내용이 맞으면 1점을 준다.
(3) Sentence (b) is ungrammatical이 맞으면 1점을 준다.
(4) The clause (containing the preposition) 'for which grant we should apply' is (a subordinate interrogative clause) functioning as complement to a preposition 'on'; fronting is impossible의 내용이 맞으면 1점을 준다.

06

본책 p.136

하위내용영역	배점	예상정답률
영어학 (문법) B형 서술형	4점	65%

모범답안

Sentence (d) is ungrammatical. The verb 'insist' cannot license (or accept) interrogatives. Sentence (e) is ungrammatical. The verb 'inquire' cannot license declaratives.

채점기준

내용학: 4점

(1) Sentence (d) is ungrammatical이 맞으면 1점을 준다.
(2) The verb 'insist' cannot license (or accept) interrogatives의 내용이 맞으면 1점을 준다.
(3) Sentence (e) is ungrammatical이 맞으면 1점을 준다.
(4) The verb 'inquire' cannot license declaratives의 내용이 맞으면 1점을 준다.

07

본책 p.138

하위내용영역	배점	예상정답률
영어학 (문법) B형 서술형	4점	65%

모범답안

Version 1

Sentence (a) is ungrammatical. The degree adverb 'nearly' cannot occur sentence finally. Sentence (e) is ungrammatical. The negative frequency adverb 'seldom' in sentence-initial position requires subject-aux inversion.

Version 2

Sentence (a) is ungrammatical. <u>Degree adverbs like 'nearly' appear before but not after verbs</u>. Sentence (e) is ungrammatical. <u>When the negative frequency adverb 'seldom' appears sentence initially, the rule of subject-aux inversion must be applied</u>.

채점기준

내용학: 4점

(1) Sentence (a) is ungrammatical이 맞으면 1점을 준다.
(2) The degree adverb 'nearly' cannot occur sentence finally의 내용이 맞으면 1점을 준다.
(3) Sentence (e) is ungrammatical이 맞으면 1점을 준다.
(4) The negative frequency adverb 'seldom' in sentence-initial position requires subject-aux inversion의 내용이 맞으면 1점을 준다.

08

하위내용영역	배점	예상정답률
영어학 (문법) B형 서술형	4점	50%

모범답안

Version 1

The underlined word (owing) in (4) belongs to the verb category. The word 'owing' is predicator (in a gerund-participial clause); this clause itself has no overt subject, but an understood subject is retrievable from the subject of the main clause 'farmers'. The underlined word (owing) in (5) belongs to the preposition category. This word does not have a predicational relationship to the subject 'many farms'.

Version 2

The underlined word (owing) in (4) is a verb. 'Owing' is interpreted as follows: we understand that it is farmers who owe so much to the bank. The understood subject is retrievable from the subject of the main clause 'farmers'. The underlined word (owing) in (5) is a preposition. This word does not have a predicational relationship to the subject 'many farms'; 'owing to X' means 'because of X'.

채점기준

내용학: 4점

(1) The underlined word (owing) in (4) belongs to the verb category이 맞으면 1점을 준다.
(2) The word 'owing' is predicator (in a gerund-participial clause); this clause itself has no overt subject, but an understood subject is retrievable from the subject of the main clause 'farmers'의 내용이 맞으면 1점을 준다.
(3) The underlined word (owing) in (5) belongs to the preposition category이 맞으면 1점을 준다.
(4) This word does not have a predicational relationship to the subject 'many farms'의 내용이 맞으면 1점을 준다.

09

하위내용영역	배점	예상정답률
영어학 (문법) B형 서술형	4점	55%

[모범답안]

Version 1

Sentence (b) is ungrammatical because the adjective 'lawful' cannot be used predicatively. The phrase (d) is ungrammatical because the adjective 'content' cannot be used attributively.

Version 2

Sentence (b) is ungrammatical. The adjective 'lawful' is attributive-only. The phrase (d) is ungrammatical because the adjective 'content' is a never-attributive adjective.

[채점기준]

내용학 : 4점
(1) Sentence (b) is ungrammatical이 맞으면 1점을 준다.
(2) the adjective 'lawful' cannot be used predicatively의 내용이 맞으면 1점을 준다.
(3) The phrase (d) is ungrammatical이 맞으면 1점을 준다.
(4) the adjective 'content' cannot be used attributively의 내용이 맞으면 1점을 준다.

10

하위내용영역	배점	예상정답률
영어학 (문법) B형 서술형	4점	65%

[모범답안]

Discourse (a) is inappropriate. In the clause 'John had saved a seat for her', the new information 'a seat' comes before the old information '(for) her'; it should put the old information 'her' before the new information 'a seat'. Sentence (d) is inappropriate. The heavy direct object NP 'an alternative solution~the dispute' in the middle of the sentence is inappropriate; (it should move the heavy direct object NP to the end of the sentence.)

[채점기준]

내용학 : 4점
(1) Discourse (a) is inappropriate이 맞으면 1점을 준다.
(2) In the clause 'John had saved a seat for her', the new information 'a seat' comes before the old information '(for) her'; it should put the old information 'her' before the new information 'a seat'의 내용이 맞으면 1점을 준다.
(3) Sentence (d) is inappropriate이 맞으면 1점을 준다.
(4) The heavy direct object NP 'an alternative solution~the dispute' in the middle of the sentence is inappropriate의 내용이 맞으면 1점을 준다.

11

하위내용영역	배점	예상정답률
영어학 (문법) B형 서술형	4점	60%

모범답안

Version 1

First, in (i), sentence (d) is ungrammatical. This sentence has a semantic affinity with negation because of the adjective 'unaware'; 'some', which has positive orientation, cannot occur in (d). Second, verbal negation forms are as follows: (iia) We didn't know either of them, and (iib) He doesn't ever apologise (apologize).

Version 2

In (i) sentence (d) is ungrammatical. 'Some' is a positive polarity item and cannot occur in the sentence which has a negative meaning (due to the adjective 'unaware').
(iia) We didn't know either of them.
(iib) He doesn't ever apologise (apologize).

채점기준

내용학: 4점
(1) in (i), sentence (d) is ungrammatical이 맞으면 1점을 준다.
(2) This sentence has a semantic affinity with negation because of the adjective 'unaware'; 'some', which has positive orientation, cannot occur in (d)의 내용이 맞으면 1점을 준다.
(3) (iia) We didn't know either of them이 맞으면 1점을 준다.
(4) (iib) He doesn't ever apologise (apologize)이 맞으면 1점을 준다.

12

하위내용영역	배점	예상정답률
영어학 (문법) B형 서술형	4점	65%

모범답안

Version 1

Sentence (d) is inappropriate. When it is natural to expect change to occur (i.e., physical laws seem to be involved), the ergative sentence is needed. Sentence (f) is inappropriate. The verb 'broke' used ergatively does not permit an agent; thus, it cannot be used with a by-phrase.

Version 2

Sentence (d) is inappropriate because it is natural to expect change to occur; thus, the verb 'melt(ed)' used with a passive form is inappropriate. Sentence (f) is inappropriate. The verb 'broke' used ergatively cannot be used with a by-phrase.

채점기준

내용학 : 4점

(1) Sentence (d) is inappropriate이 맞으면 1점을 준다.
(2) When it is natural to expect change to occur (i.e., physical laws seem to be involved), the ergative sentence is needed의 내용이 맞으면 1점을 준다.
(3) Sentence (f) is inappropriate이 맞으면 1점을 준다.
(4) The verb 'broke' used ergatively does not permit an agent; thus, it cannot be used with a by-phrase의 내용이 맞으면 1점을 준다.

13

본책 p.150

하위내용영역	배점	예상정답률
영어학 (문법) B형 서술형	4점	65%

모범답안

Version 1

The phrase (iic) is ungrammatical. In the fronted preposition construction, fossilisation doesn't allow any departure from the fixed order of verb + preposition 'let + off'.

Version 2

(iic) is ungrammatical. The fronted preposition construction is not permitted in (iic) because 'let + off' is fossilised in that the preposition must follow the verb, with only the object intervening.

채점기준

내용학 : 4점

(1) The phrase (iic) is ungrammatical이 맞으면 2점을 준다.
(2) fossilisation doesn't allow any departure from the fixed order of verb + preposition 'let + off'의 내용이 맞으면 2점을 준다.

14

본책 p.152

하위내용영역	배점	예상정답률
영어학 (문법) B형 서술형	4점	55%

모범답안

First, in (ia), (the phrase or word) 'dead' is used as a predicative complement (Predicative Complement), and in (ib), 'long' is used as a adverb phrase complement (ADVP Complement). Second, the phrase 'two weeks ago' is the prepositional phrase. In (iia), the phrase 'two weeks ago' functions as predicative complement to the verb 'was (be)'. In (iib), 'two weeks ago' modifies the noun phrase 'his behaviour'.

채점기준

내용학 : 4점

(1) in (ia), (the phrase or word) 'dead' is used as a predicative complement (Predicative Complement)이 맞으면 1점을 준다.
(2) in (ib), 'long' is used as a adverb phrase complement (ADVP Complement)이 맞으면 1점을 준다.
(3) the phrase 'two weeks ago' is the prepositional phrase이 맞으면 1점을 준다.
(4) In (iia), the phrase 'two weeks ago' functions as predicative complement to the verb 'was (be)'. In (iib), 'two weeks ago' modifies the noun phrase 'his behaviour'의 내용이 맞으면 1점을 준다.

15   본책 p.154

하위내용영역	배점	예상정답률
영어학 (문법) B형 서술형	4점	65%

모범답안

Version 1

The sentences in (c) and (e) have Item Subjuncts and can be paraphrased as follows: (c) He was very proud when he accepted the award, and (e) He was bitter when he buried his child.

Version 2

The two sentences with *Item Subjuncts* are (c) and (e). These can be paraphrased as follows: (c) He was very proud when he accepted the award, and (e) He was bitter when he buried his child.

채점기준

내용학 : 4점

(1) The sentences in (c) and (e) have Item Subjuncts이 맞으면 2점을 준다. (각 1점)
(2) He was very proud when he accepted the award이 맞으면 1점을 준다.
(3) He was bitter when he buried his child이 맞으면 1점을 준다.

16   본책 p.156

하위내용영역	배점	예상정답률
영어학 (문법) B형 서술형	4점	65%

모범답안

Sentence (a) is ungrammatical. In (a) 'stood by' is an inseparable phrasal verb; it does not allow for the particle movement. Sentence (b) is ungrammatical. In (b) 'commented on' is a prepositional verb; the separation of the verb and preposition will produce an ungrammatical sentence.

채점기준

내용학: 4점

(1) Sentence (a) is ungrammatical이 맞으면 1점을 준다.
(2) In (a) 'stood by' is an inseparable phrasal verb; it does not allow for the particle movement의 내용이 맞으면 1점을 준다.
(3) Sentence (b) is ungrammatical이 맞으면 1점을 준다.
(4) In (b) 'commented on' is a prepositional verb; the separation of the verb and preposition will produce an ungrammatical sentence의 내용이 맞으면 1점을 준다.

17

본책 p.158

하위내용영역	배점	예상정답률
영어학 (문법) B형 서술형	4점	70%

모범답안

Version 1

Sentence (c) is ungrammatical. In the passive, the object NP 'Bill' must be absent; (it must not appear right after the passive verb). Sentence (e) is ungrammatical. In the active, the (active) transitive verb 'take(n)' must have its object, but it doesn't have the object.

Version 2

Sentence (c) is ungrammatical. It is the passive sentence, and the object NP 'Bill' must be absent; (it must not appear right after the passive verb). Sentence (e) is ungrammatical. It is the active sentence, and the (active) transitive verb 'take(n)' must have its object, but it doesn't have the object.

채점기준

내용학: 4점

(1) Sentence (c) is ungrammatical이 맞으면 1점을 준다.
(2) In the passive, the object NP 'Bill' must be absent; (it must not appear right after the passive verb)의 내용이 맞으면 1점을 준다.
(3) Sentence (e) is ungrammatical이 맞으면 1점을 준다.
(4) In the active, the (active) transitive verb 'take(n)' must have its object, but it doesn't have the object의 내용이 맞으면 1점을 준다.

18

본책 p.160

하위내용영역	배점	예상정답률
영어학 (문법) B형 서술형	4점	50%

모범답안

Sentence (4) is ambiguous. When the adjunct 'all the time' lies outside the scope of the negation, it means 'I listened none of the time'. When the adjunct 'all the time' lies inside the scope of the negation, it says that 'I listened some of the time'.

[참고]

When an adjunct is final, it may or may not lie outside the scope:

(4) a. I wasn't LISTENING all the time.   [i.e. I listened none of the time.]
    b. I wasn't listening all the TIME.   [i.e. I listened some of the time.]

채점기준

내용학: 4점

(1) Sentence (4) is ambiguous이 맞으면 2점을 준다.
(2) When the adjunct 'all the time' lies outside the scope of the negation, it means 'I listened none of the time'의 내용이 맞으면 1점을 준다.
(3) When the adjunct 'all the time' lies inside the scope of the negation, it says that 'I listened some of the time'의 내용이 맞으면 1점을 준다.

19

본책 p.162

하위내용영역	배점	예상정답률
영어학 (문법) B형 서술형	4점	45%

모범답안

Version 1

Phrase (c) is ungrammatical. (The lower NP in partitive phrases must be definite;) and in the of-phrase, no quantificational NP 'many problems' is allowed. Sentence (f) is ungrammatical. The mass (non-count) quantifier 'little' serving as a determiner cannot directly precede a singular count noun 'speech'.

Version 2

Phrase (c) is ungrammatical. In partitive phrases, no quantificational NP 'many problems' is allowed in the of-phrase. Sentence (f) is ungrammatical. The partitive constructions in (f) allow a mass (non-count) quantifier such as 'little' to cooccur with a lower of-NP containing a singular count noun. But in (f), the same element 'little' serving as a determiner cannot directly precede such nouns.

채점기준

내용학 : 4점

(1) Phrase (c) is ungrammatical이 맞으면 1점을 준다.
(2) (The lower NP in partitive phrases must be definite;) and in the *of*-phrase, no quantificational NP 'many problems' is allowed의 내용이 맞으면 1점을 준다.
(3) Sentence (f) is ungrammatical이 맞으면 1점을 준다.
(4) The mass (non-count) quantifier 'little' serving as a determiner cannot directly precede a singular count noun 'speech'의 내용이 맞으면 1점을 준다.

20

본책 p.164

하위내용영역	배점	예상정답률
영어학 (문법) B형 서술형	4점	55%

모범답안

Version 1

The one word for the blank is 'on'.
Sentence (6) is grammatical and sentence (7) is ungrammatical. The adjective 'clear' in (6) allows indirect questions as subjects, whereas the verb 'go' in (7) does not.

Version 2

The one word for the blank is 'on'.
Sentence (6) is grammatical. The adjective 'clear' allows indirect questions as subjects. Sentence (7) is ungrammatical. The verb 'go' does not allow indirect questions as subjects.

채점기준

내용학 : 4점

(1) The one word for the blank is 'on'이 맞으면 2점을 준다.
(2) Sentence (6) is grammatical. The adjective 'clear' allows indirect questions as subjects의 내용이 맞으면 1점을 준다.
(3) Sentence (7) is ungrammatical. The verb 'go' does not allow indirect questions as subjects의 내용이 맞으면 1점을 준다.

21

본책 p.166

하위내용영역	배점	예상정답률
영어학 (문법) B형 서술형	4점	55%

모범답안

Version 1

Sentences (e) and (f) are ungrammatical. The determiner 'these' and the head noun 'government' do not agree each other in terms of the morphosyntactic agreement number value whereas the index value of the subject can be anchored either to a singular or to plural kind of entity.

Version 2

Sentences (e) and (f) are ungrammatical. In terms of the morphosyntactic agreement number value, the head noun 'government' has to be singular so that it can combine with a singular determiner, but in (e) and (f) the head noun 'government' combines with the plural determiner. However, the index value of the subject can be anchored either to a singular or to plural kind of entity.

채점기준

내용학: 4점

(1) Sentences (e) and (f) are ungrammatical이 맞으면 2점을 준다. (각 1점)
(2) The determiner 'these' and the head noun 'government' do not agree each other in terms of the morphosyntactic agreement number value의 내용이 맞으면 1점을 준다.
(3) whereas the index value of the subject can be anchored either to a singular or to plural kind of entity의 내용이 맞으면 1점을 준다.

22

하위내용영역	배점	예상정답률
영어학 (문법) B형 서술형	4점	65%

모범답안

Version 1

Sentence (a) is ungrammatical: They won't finish it at all.
Sentence (d) is ungrammatical: Her mother is not coming, either.

Version 2

Sentences (a) and (d) are ungrammatical. The correct sentences are as follows: (a) They won't finish it at all, and (d) Her mother is not coming, either.

채점기준

내용학: 4점

(1) Sentence (a) is ungrammatical이 맞으면 1점을 준다.
(2) They won't finish it at all이 맞으면 1점을 준다.
(3) Sentence (d) is ungrammatical이 맞으면 1점을 준다.
(4) Her mother is not coming, either이 맞으면 1점을 준다.

23

하위내용영역	배점	예상정답률
영어학 (문법) B형 서술형	4점	55%

모범답안

Sentence (a) is ungrammatical. The verb 'hit' cannot be used in the form of middle voice. Sentence (d) is ungrammatical. (Middle voices in general describe permanent properties of the subject); the (middle) verb 'wash(ed)' cannot be compatible with the duration adverb 'yesterday morning'.

채점기준

내용학: 4점

(1) Sentence (a) is ungrammatical이 맞으면 1점을 준다.
(2) The verb 'hit' cannot be used in the form of middle voice의 내용이 맞으면 1점을 준다.
(3) Sentence (d) is ungrammatical이 맞으면 1점을 준다.
(4) (Middle voices in general describe permanent properties of the subject); the (middle) verb 'wash(ed)' cannot be compatible with the duration adverb 'yesterday morning'의 내용이 맞으면 1점을 준다.

24

하위내용영역	배점	예상정답률
영어학 (문법) B형 서술형	4점	55%

모범답안

Sentence (b) is ungrammatical. The adjective 'fraught' requires the PP complement, and the head of PP needs 'with'. Sentence (d) is ungrammatical. The adjective 'amazed' requires the PP complement, and the head of PP needs 'at'.

채점기준

내용학: 4점

(1) Sentence (b) is ungrammatical이 맞으면 1점을 준다.
(2) The adjective 'fraught' requires the PP complement, and the head of PP needs 'with'의 내용이 맞으면 1점을 준다.
(3) Sentence (d) is ungrammatical이 맞으면 1점을 준다.
(4) The adjective 'amazed' requires the PP complement, and the head of PP needs 'at'의 내용이 맞으면 1점을 준다.

25

하위내용영역	배점	예상정답률
영어학 (문법) B형 서술형	4점	55%

모범답안

Sentence (a) is ambiguous. The underlined adjective 'open' has two interpretations: one is an obligatory resultative interpretation; ("Its state changed from closed to open"), and the other is an optional depictive interpretation; ("It was already open when it arrived").

채점기준

내용학: 4점

(1) Sentence (a) is ambiguous이 맞으면 2점을 준다.
(2) one is an obligatory resultative interpretation; ("Its state changed from closed to open")의 내용이 맞으면 1점을 준다.
(3) the other is an optional depictive interpretation; ("It was already open when it arrived")의 내용이 맞으면 1점을 준다.

26

하위내용영역	배점	예상정답률
영어학 (문법) B형 서술형	4점	55%

모범답안

First, sentence (ic) is ungrammatical. The negator 'not' (can modify a nonfinite VP, but) cannot modify a finite VP 'left the town'. Second, (iia) is Sentential Negation, and (iib) is Constituent Negation.

채점기준

내용학: 4점

(1) sentence (ic) is ungrammatical이 맞으면 1점을 준다.
(2) The negator 'not' (can modify a nonfinite VP, but) cannot modify a finite VP 'left the town'의 내용이 맞으면 1점을 준다.
(3) (iia) is Sentential Negation이 맞으면 1점을 준다.
(4) (iib) is Constituent Negation이 맞으면 1점을 준다.

27

하위내용영역	배점	예상정답률
영어학 (문법) B형 서술형	4점	60%

모범답안

Sentence (a) is ungrammatical. The partitive phrase 'None of these men' belongs to Type I. The number value of the partitive phrase is singular; the main verb 'want' must be singular ('wants'). Sentence (e) is ungrammatical. The phrase 'One of the story' belongs to Type I which selects a plural *of*-NP phrase, but it is not a plural *of*-NP phrase.

채점기준

내용학: 4점

(1) Sentence (a) is ungrammatical이 맞으면 1점을 준다.
(2) The partitive phrase 'None of these men' belongs to Type I. The number value of the partitive phrase is singular; the main verb 'want' must be singular ('wants')의 내용이 맞으면 1점을 준다.
(3) Sentence (e) is ungrammatical이 맞으면 1점을 준다.
(4) The phrase 'One of the story' belongs to Type I which selects a plural *of*-NP phrase, but it is not a plural *of*-NP phrase의 내용이 맞으면 1점을 준다.

28

하위내용영역	배점	예상정답률
영어학 (문법) B형 서술형	4점	60%

모범답안

Version 1

Sentence (b) is ungrammatical. The passive subject 'A pound' is not influenced (or affected) by the action denoted by the main verb 'weigh'. Sentence (d) is ungrammatical. The passive subject 'Four' is not influenced (or affected) by the action denoted by the main verb 'equal'.

Version 2

Sentence (b) is ungrammatical. 'A pound' cannot be affected by the action performed by the agent. Sentence (d) is ungrammatical. 'Four' cannot be affected by the action performed by the agent.

채점기준

내용학: 4점

(1) Sentence (b) is ungrammatical이 맞으면 1점을 준다.
(2) The passive subject 'A pound' is not influenced (or affected) by the action denoted by the main verb 'weigh'의 내용이 맞으면 1점을 준다.
(3) Sentence (d) is ungrammatical이 맞으면 1점을 준다.
(4) The passive subject 'Four' is not influenced (or affected) by the action denoted by the main verb 'equal'의 내용이 맞으면 1점을 준다.

29

본책 p.182

하위내용영역	배점	예상정답률
영어학 (문법) B형 서술형	4점	60%

모범답안

Sentence (b) is ungrammatical. The (semi-)passive verb (with an adjectival feature) 'concerned' cannot occur with the verb-modifying adverb 'much'. Sentence (f) is ungrammatical. The *get* passive cannot occur with the verb 'understood' that describes cognition.

채점기준

내용학: 4점

(1) Sentence (b) is ungrammatical이 맞으면 1점을 준다.
(2) The (semi-)passive verb (with an adjectival feature) 'concerned' cannot occur with the verb-modifying adverb 'much'의 내용이 맞으면 1점을 준다.
(3) Sentence (f) is ungrammatical이 맞으면 1점을 준다.
(4) The *get* passive cannot occur with the verb 'understood' that describes cognition의 내용이 맞으면 1점을 준다.

Part 03 Phonetics & Phonology

01

본책 p.186

하위내용영역	배점	예상정답률
영어학 (음운론) A형 기입형	2점	80%

모범답안

① consonants   ② − continuant

채점기준

2점: ①, ② 모두 답안과 일치하면 2점을 준다.
1점: ①, ② 중 하나만 답안과 일치하면 1점을 준다.
0점: ①, ② 모두 답안과 일치하지 않으면 0점을 준다.

02

본책 p.188

하위내용영역	배점	예상정답률
영어학 (음운론) A형 서술형	4점	65%

모범답안

Version 1

First, Iambic Reversal occurs in the phrase 'champagne cocktails'. Second, it occurs to avoid clashes. The clashing sequences of WSSW change into the sequences of SWSW (i.e., the sequence of two trochaic feet).

Version 2

First, Iambic Reversal occurs in the phrase 'champagne cocktails' to avoid clashes. Second, the clashing sequences of WSSW change into the sequences of SWSW (, the sequence of two trochaic feet).

채점기준

내용학: 4점
(1) Iambic Reversal occurs in the phrase 'champagne cocktails'이 맞으면 1점을 준다.
(2) it occurs to avoid clashes의 내용이 맞으면 1점을 준다.
(3) The clashing sequences of WSSW change into the sequences of SWSW의 내용이 맞으면 2점을 준다.
   (각 1점)

03

본책 p.190

하위내용영역	배점	예상정답률
영어학 (음운론) B형 서술형	4점	50%

모범답안

Version 1
Vowel Nasalization occurs only if a nasal sound is in the same stem.

Version 2
Vowels are nasalized before a nasal consonant if it is in the same stem (or within the same stem).

Version 3
Vowel nasalization is stem-bounded.

채점기준

내용학: 4점

Vowel Nasalization occurs only if a nasal sound is in the same stem의 내용이 맞으면 4점을 준다.

04

본책 p.192

하위내용영역	배점	예상정답률
영어학 (음운론) A형 기입형	2점	90%

모범답안

① bearing ② heavy

채점기준

2점: ①, ② 모두 답안과 일치하면 2점을 준다.
1점: ①, ② 중 하나만 답안과 일치하면 1점을 준다.
0점: ①, ② 모두 답안과 일치하지 않으면 0점을 준다.

05

본책 p.193

하위내용영역	배점	예상정답률
영어학 (음운론) A형 서술형	4점	65%

모범답안

Version 1
First, the phonological form of a word 'notable' is [norəbəl]. It is eligible for Tapping. Second, the phonological form of a word 'notation' is [noutʰeʃən]. Aspiration rule is applied (in this word).

Version 2

First, the phonological form of a word 'notable' is [nóɾəbəl]. It is eligible for Tapping. Second, the phonological form of a word 'notation' is [notʰéʃən]. Aspiration rule is applied (in this word).

채점기준

내용학: 4점
(1) the phonological form of a word 'notable' is ['noɾəbəl]이 맞으면 1점을 준다.
(2) It is eligible for Tapping의 내용이 맞으면 1점을 준다.
(3) the phonological form of a word 'notation' is [no'tʰeʃən]의 내용이 맞으면 1점을 준다.
(4) Aspiration rule is applied의 내용이 맞으면 1점을 준다.

06

본책 p.195

하위내용영역	배점	예상정답률
영어학 (음운론) B형 서술형	4점	20%

모범답안

(a) and (b) show the same internal structure. The internal structure of this group is (1e) ([A['BC]D]). (c) and (d) are the other pair. They belong to (1d) ([[AB] ['CD]]).

채점기준

내용학: 4점
(1) (a) and (b) show the same internal structure이 맞으면 1점을 준다.
(2) The internal structure of this group is (1e)의 내용이 맞으면 1점을 준다.
(3) (c) and (d) are the other pair이 맞으면 1점을 준다.
(4) They belong to (1d)의 내용이 맞으면 1점을 준다.

07

본책 p.197

하위내용영역	배점	예상정답률
영어학 (음운론) A형 기입형	2점	80%

모범답안

① [− anterior] ② [− lateral]

채점기준

2점: ①, ② 모두 답안과 일치하면 2점을 준다.
1점: ①, ② 중 하나만 답안과 일치하면 1점을 준다.
0점: ①, ② 모두 답안과 일치하지 않으면 0점을 준다.

| 08 | | | 본책 p.198 |

하위내용영역	배점	예상정답률
영어학 (음운론) B형 서술형	4점	60%

모범답안

First, (/t/ is deleted when) it occurs between /n/ and a stressless (or unstressed) vowel. Second, the two interpretations are as follows: 'They are planting a garden' or 'They are planning a garden'.

채점기준

내용학 : 4점
(1) (/t/ is deleted when) it occurs between /n/ and a stressless vowel이 맞으면 2점을 준다.
(2) 'They are planting a garden' or 'They are planning a garden'이 맞으면 2점을 준다. (각 1점)

| 09 | | | 본책 p.200 |

하위내용영역	배점	예상정답률
영어학 (음운론) A형 기입형	2점	80%

모범답안

① different ② same

채점기준

2점: ①, ② 모두 답안과 일치하면 2점을 준다.
1점: ①, ② 중 하나만 답안과 일치하면 1점을 준다.
0점: ①, ② 모두 답안과 일치하지 않으면 0점을 준다.

| 10 | | | 본책 p.201 |

하위내용영역	배점	예상정답률
영어학 (음운론) A형 서술형	4점	60%

모범답안

First, the word 'envelope' is an example of phonological doublets: one word has two different phonemic forms (, either [ˈɛnvəˌloʊp] or [ˈɑnvəˌloʊp]). Second, the word 'ban' is a case of free variation: a single phonemic representation /bæn/ gives rise to two phonetic forms (of [bɛ̃æ̃n] and [bæ̃n]).

[채점기준]

내용학: 4점
(1) the word 'envelope' is an example of phonological doublets이 맞으면 1점을 준다.
(2) one word has two different phonemic forms (, either [ˈɛnvəˌloʊp] or [ˈɑnvəˌloʊp])의 내용이 맞으면 1점을 준다.
(3) the word 'ban' is a case of free variation이 맞으면 1점을 준다.
(4) a single phonemic representation /bæn/ gives rise to two phonetic forms (of [bẽ͠n] and [bæ͠n])의 내용이 맞으면 1점을 준다.

11

본책 p.203

하위내용영역	배점	예상정답률
영어학 (음운론) B형 서술형	4점	45%

[모범답안]

First, the two words are 'logician' and 'presidential'. In (the word) 'logician', /k/ changes to /ʃ/ before a suffix which begins with /ɪ/, followed immediately by a vowel. In 'presidential', /t/ changes to /ʃ/ before a suffix which begins with /ɪ/, followed immediately by a vowel.

[채점기준]

내용학: 4점
(1) the two words are 'logician' and 'presidential'이 맞으면 2점을 준다. (각 1점)
(2) In 'logician', /k/ changes to /ʃ/ before a suffix which begins with /ɪ/, followed immediately by a vowel의 내용이 맞으면 1점을 준다.
(3) In 'presidential', /t/ changes to /ʃ/ before a suffix which begins with /ɪ/, followed immediately by a vowel의 내용이 맞으면 1점을 준다.

12

본책 p.205

하위내용영역	배점	예상정답률
영어학 (음운론) A형 기입형	2점	80%

[모범답안]

① place ② manner

[채점기준]

2점: ①, ② 모두 답안과 일치하면 2점을 준다.
1점: ①, ② 중 하나만 답안과 일치하면 1점을 준다.
0점: ①, ② 모두 답안과 일치하지 않으면 0점을 준다.

| 13 | | | 본책 p.206 |

하위내용영역	배점	예상정답률
영어학 (음운론) A형 서술형	4점	65%

모범답안

First, the blank ① is 'word', and the blank ② is 'morphological'. Second, tense-vowel phonemes are realised as long before voiced fricatives.

채점기준

내용학: 4점
(1) the blank ① is 'word', and the blank ② is 'morphological'이 맞으면 2점을 준다. (각 1점)
(2) tense-vowel phonemes are realised as long before voiced fricatives의 내용이 맞으면 2점을 준다.

| 14 | | | 본책 p.208 |

하위내용영역	배점	예상정답률
영어학 (음운론) B형 서술형	4점	45%

모범답안

First, the two words are 'camomile' and 'convoy'. Second, secondary stress occurs on the first syllable in (1) only where that syllable is heavy.

채점기준

내용학: 4점
(1) the two words are 'camomile' and 'convoy'가 맞으면 2점을 준다. (각 1점)
(2) secondary stress occurs on the first syllable in (1) only where that syllable is heavy의 내용이 맞으면 2점을 준다.

| 15 | | | 본책 p.210 |

하위내용영역	배점	예상정답률
영어학 (음운론) A형 기입형	2점	70%

모범답안

① antepenultimate ② penultimate

채점기준

2점: ①, ② 모두 답안과 일치하면 2점을 준다.
1점: ①, ② 중 하나만 답안과 일치하면 1점을 준다.
0점: ①, ② 모두 답안과 일치하지 않으면 0점을 준다.

16

하위내용영역	배점	예상정답률
영어학 (음운론) B형 서술형	4점	55%

모범답안

First, the one word for the blank is 'plural'. Second, nasal assimilation optionally occurs across morpheme boundaries in (2) and across word boundaries in (3).

채점기준

내용학 : 4점

(1) the one word for the blank is 'plural'이 맞으면 2점을 준다.
(2) nasal assimilation optionally occurs across morpheme boundaries in (2) and across word boundaries in (3) 의 내용이 맞으면 2점을 준다. (각 1점)

17

하위내용영역	배점	예상정답률
영어학 (음운론) A형 서술형	4점	50%

모범답안

Version 1

First, nasal stops belong to (fit into) (3a) and oral stops belong to (3b). Second, the feature combination (3d) refers to approximants.

Version 2

First, the feature combination of [− continuant] and [+ sonorant] in (3a) belongs to nasal stops, and oral stops have the feature combination of [− continuant] and [− sonorant] in (3b). Second, the feature combination (3d) refers to approximants.

채점기준

내용학 : 4점

(1) nasal stops belong to (3a) and oral stops belong to (3b)이 맞으면 2점을 준다. (각 1점)
(2) the feature combination (3d) refers to approximants의 내용이 맞으면 2점을 준다.

18

하위내용영역	배점	예상정답률
영어학 (음운론) B형 서술형	4점	60%

> **모범답안**

First, while /ɛlm/ is well-formed, /silm/ is not well-formed. Well-formed syllables should contain no more than three X-positions in the rhyme. /ɛlm/ has three X-positions in the rhyme. However, /silm/ has four X-positions in the rhyme.

> **채점기준**

내용학: 4점

(1) while /ɛlm/ is well-formed, /silm/ is not well-formed이 맞으면 1점을 준다.
(2) Well-formed syllables should contain no more than three X-positions in the rhyme의 내용이 맞으면 1점을 준다.
(3) /ɛlm/ has three X-positions in the rhyme의 내용이 맞으면 1점을 준다.
(4) /silm/ has four X-positions in the rhyme의 내용이 맞으면 1점을 준다.

19
본책 p.218

하위내용영역	배점	예상정답률
영어학 (음운론) A형 기입형	2점	70%

> **모범답안**

Alveolar obstruents

> **채점기준**

2점: 답안과 일치하면 2점을 준다.
0점: 답안과 일치하지 않으면 0점을 준다.

20
본책 p.219

하위내용영역	배점	예상정답률
영어학 (음운론) B형 서술형	4점	45%

> **모범답안**

Version 1
First, the words are 'globes' and 'coax'. Second, coronal obstruents can be appended to the core syllable.

Version 2
First, the words, 'globes' and 'coax', violate both of the two constraints, Three-X exceeded and Sonority violated. Second, coronal obstruents can be appended to the core syllable.

채점기준

내용학: 4점
(1) the words are 'globes' and 'coax'이 맞으면 2점을 준다. 정답 단어 2개 중 하나만 쓴 경우나 그 외에 단어를 추가로 선택한 경우 0점을 준다.
(2) coronal obstruents can be appended to the core syllable의 내용이 맞으면 2점을 준다.

21

하위내용영역	배점	예상정답률
영어학 (음운론) A형 기입형	2점	70%

모범답안

① + consonantal ② − continuant

채점기준

2점: ①, ② 모두 답안과 일치하면 2점을 준다.
1점: ①, ② 중 하나만 답안과 일치하면 1점을 준다.
0점: ①, ② 모두 답안과 일치하지 않으면 0점을 준다.

22

하위내용영역	배점	예상정답률
영어학 (음운론) A형 서술형	4점	60%

모범답안

First, derivational suffixes in (1b) are stress-neutral whereas those in (1c) are stress-shifting. Second, the stress-shifting suffixes in (2) are '-ette', '-ese', and '-esque'.

채점기준

내용학: 4점
(1) derivational suffixes in (1b) are stress-neutral whereas those in (1c) are stress-shifting이 맞으면 2점을 준다. (각 1점)
(2) the stress-shifting suffixes in (2) are '-ette', '-ese', and '-esque'의 내용이 맞으면 2점을 준다. (정답과 다른 접미사를 쓰거나 정답 중 일부만 쓴 경우는 0점을 준다.)

23

본책 p.224

하위내용영역	배점	예상정답률
영어학 (음운론) B형 서술형	4점	50%

모범답안

First, in (5), the word 'students' is the strongest stress of the noun phrase and the word 'regularly' is the strongest stress in the higher verb phrase. Second, the word 'regularly' is the strongest stress of the whole construction in (5).

채점기준

내용학: 4점

(1) in (5), the word 'students' is the strongest stress of the noun phrase and the word 'regularly' is the strongest stress in the higher verb phrase이 맞으면 2점을 준다. (각 1점)
(2) the word 'regularly' is the strongest stress of the whole construction in (5)의 내용이 맞으면 2점을 준다.

24

본책 p.226

하위내용영역	배점	예상정답률
영어학 (음운론) A형 기입형	2점	90%

모범답안

① unrounded ② rounded

채점기준

2점: ①, ② 모두 답안과 일치하면 2점을 준다.
1점: ①, ② 중 하나만 답안과 일치하면 1점을 준다.
0점: ①, ② 모두 답안과 일치하지 않으면 0점을 준다.

25

본책 p.228

하위내용영역	배점	예상정답률
영어학 (음운론) B형 서술형	4점	50%

모범답안

The feature for the blank ① is '− continuant', and the blank ② is '+ consonantal'.
The redundancy statement for liquids is as follows: If [+ sonorant, + consonantal, + continuant], then [− syllabic].

채점기준

내용학 : 4점
(1) The feature for the blank ① is '−continuant', and the blank ② is '+consonantal'이 맞으면 2점을 준다. (각 1점)
(2) If [+sonorant, +consonantal, +continuant], then [−syllabic]이 맞으면 2점을 준다.

26

본책 p.230

하위내용영역	배점	예상정답률
영어학 (음운론) A형 서술형	4점	65%

모범답안

First, (aspiration also occurs in) unstressed syllables. Second, the two data sets are (6a) and (6c).

채점기준

내용학 : 4점
(1) unstressed syllables의 내용이 맞으면 2점을 준다.
(2) the two data sets are (6a) and (6c)이 맞으면 2점을 준다. (각 1점)

27

본책 p.232

하위내용영역	배점	예상정답률
영어학 (음운론) B형 서술형	4점	60%

모범답안

First, the one word for the blank is 'obstruents'. Second, (English words can end in two stops when) the second consonant is an alveolar stop.

채점기준

내용학 : 4점
(1) the one word for the blank is 'obstruents'이 맞으면 2점을 준다.
(2) the second consonant is an alveolar stop의 내용이 맞으면 2점을 준다.

28

본책 p.234

하위내용영역	배점	예상정답률
영어학 (음운론) A형 기입형	2점	80%

[모범답안]

① stressed   ② place

[채점기준]

2점: ①, ② 모두 답안과 일치하면 2점을 준다.

1점: ①, ② 중 하나만 답안과 일치하면 1점을 준다.

0점: ①, ② 모두 답안과 일치하지 않으면 0점을 준다.

29
본책 p.236

하위내용영역	배점	예상정답률
영어학 (음운론) A형 서술형	4점	50%

[모범답안]

First, in the word 'corrosion', three rules are as follows: Rule 1 (Velar softening), Rule 2 (Palatalization) and Rule 4 (Vowel lengthening). Second, in the word 'corroded', three rules are as follows: Rule 4 (Vowel lengthening), Rule 5 (Past tense) and Rule 6 (Flapping).

[채점기준]

내용학: 4점

(1) in the word 'corrosion', three rules are as follows: Rule 1 (Velar softening), Rule 2 (Palatalization) and Rule 4 (Vowel lengthening)이 맞으면 2점을 준다.

(2) in the word 'corroded', three rules are as follows: Rule 4 (Vowel lengthening), Rule 5 (Past tense) and Rule 6 (Flapping)이 맞으면 2점을 준다.

30
본책 p.238

하위내용영역	배점	예상정답률
영어학 (음운론) B형 서술형	4점	65%

[모범답안]

Version 1

In (3), in 'hand', the final /d/ of *hand* is elided, and then the /n/ assimilates to the following /k/.

Version 2

In (3), in 'hand', 'hand' loses its final /d/, and then the /n/ assimilates to the following /k/.

[채점기준]

내용학: 4점

the final /d/ of *hand* is elided, and then the /n/ assimilates to the following /k/의 내용이 맞으면 4점을 준다.

31

본책 p.240

하위내용영역	배점	예상정답률
영어학 (음운론) A형 기입형	2점	90%

모범답안

① regressive ② voiceless stops

채점기준

2점: ①, ② 모두 답안과 일치하면 2점을 준다.
1점: ①, ② 중 하나만 답안과 일치하면 1점을 준다.
0점: ①, ② 모두 답안과 일치하지 않으면 0점을 준다.

32

본책 p.241

하위내용영역	배점	예상정답률
영어학 (음운론) A형 서술형	4점	60%

모범답안

First, the word 'canoe' ([knu]) violates phonotactic constraints. Second, consonant cluster simplification occurs when there are sequences of identical ('geminate') consonants (at word or morpheme boundaries in connected speech).

채점기준

내용학: 4점
(1) the word 'canoe' ([knu]) violates phonotactic constraints이 맞으면 2점을 준다.
(2) there are sequences of identical ('geminate') consonants의 내용이 맞으면 2점을 준다.

33

본책 p.243

하위내용영역	배점	예상정답률
영어학 (음운론) B형 서술형	4점	55%

모범답안

First, the one word is 'onset'. Second, the first C in a CC cluster in (2c) is the (sonority) trough (or the trough in sonority).

채점기준

내용학: 4점

(1) the one word is 'onset'이 맞으면 2점을 준다.
(2) the first C in a CC cluster in (2c) is the (sonority) trough (or the trough in sonority)의 내용이 맞으면 2점을 준다.

34

하위내용영역	배점	예상정답률
영어학 (음운론) A형 기입형	2점	80%

모범답안

① unrounded ② monosyllabic

채점기준

2점: ①, ② 모두 답안과 일치하면 2점을 준다.
1점: ①, ② 중 하나만 답안과 일치하면 1점을 준다.
0점: ①, ② 모두 답안과 일치하지 않으면 0점을 준다.

35

하위내용영역	배점	예상정답률
영어학 (음운론) B형 서술형	4점	60%

모범답안

Version 1

First, the one word for the blank is 'voiceless'. Second, Tapping is ordered before /aɪ/ Raising (in the dialect in which 'writing' and 'riding' are pronounced the same).

Version 2

First, the one word is 'voiceless'. Second, Tapping is applied before /aɪ/ Raising (in the dialect in which 'writing' and 'riding' are pronounced the same).

채점기준

내용학: 4점

(1) the one word for the blank is 'voiceless'이 맞으면 2점을 준다.
(2) Tapping is ordered before /aɪ/ Raising의 내용이 맞으면 2점을 준다.

36

본책 p.249

하위내용영역	배점	예상정답률
영어학 (음운론) A형 서술형	4점	60%

모범답안

First, (velars become fronted) before front vowels. Second, the three feature values are [− sonorant], [+ continuant], and [+ voice].

채점기준

내용학 : 4점
(1) before front vowels이 맞으면 1점을 준다.
(2) the three feature values are [− sonorant], [+ continuant], and [+ voice]이 맞으면 3점을 준다. (각 1점)

37

본책 p.251

하위내용영역	배점	예상정답률
영어학 (음운론) B형 서술형	4점	55%

모범답안

First, the two words are (c) 'poison' and (d) 'ransom'. In (c) 'poison', the noun is basic, and in (d) 'ransom', the noun is basic.

채점기준

내용학 : 4점
(1) the two words are (c) 'poison' and (d) 'ransom'이 맞으면 2점을 준다. (각 1점)
(2) In (c) 'poison', the noun is basic, and in (d) 'ransom', the noun is basic의 내용이 맞으면 2점을 준다. (각 1점)

38

본책 p.253

하위내용영역	배점	예상정답률
영어학 (음운론) A형 기입형	2점	90%

모범답안

① falling ② rising

채점기준

2점 : ①, ② 모두 답안과 일치하면 2점을 준다.
1점 : ①, ② 중 하나만 답안과 일치하면 1점을 준다.
0점 : ①, ② 모두 답안과 일치하지 않으면 0점을 준다.

39

하위내용영역	배점	예상정답률
영어학 (음운론) A형 서술형	4점	70%

모범답안

In (2), velar nasal [ŋ] occurs immediately after lax vowels in monosyllabic words.

채점기준

내용학: 4점

(1) velar nasal [ŋ] occurs immediately after lax vowels in monosyllabic words의 내용이 맞으면 4점을 준다.

40

하위내용영역	배점	예상정답률
영어학 (음운론) B형 서술형	4점	50%

모범답안

First, the two sets of data are (5a) and (6a). Second, (the stress falls on the syllable immediately before the suffix) when that syllable is heavy.

채점기준

내용학: 4점

(1) the two sets of data are (5a) and (6a)이 맞으면 2점을 준다. (각 1점)
(2) (the stress falls on the syllable immediately before the suffix) when that syllable is heavy의 내용이 맞으면 2점을 준다.

41

하위내용영역	배점	예상정답률
영어학 (음운론) A형 기입형	2점	80%

모범답안

voiced obstruents

채점기준

2점: 답안과 일치하면 2점을 준다.
0점: 답안과 일치하지 않으면 0점을 준다.

42

하위내용영역	배점	예상정답률
영어학 (음운론) A형 서술형	4점	50%

[모범답안]

Version 1

First, the one word is 'alveolar'. Second, (4b) is less acceptable. It violates the restriction on non-alveolar clusters after long vowels (including diphthongs).

Version 2

First, the one word is 'alveolar'. Second, (4b) is less acceptable because long vowels (including diphthongs) are never followed by non-alveolar clusters.

[채점기준]

내용학 : 4점

(1) the one word is 'alveolar'가 맞으면 2점을 준다.
(2) (4b) is less acceptable의 내용이 맞으면 1점을 준다.
(3) It violates the restriction on non-alveolar clusters after long vowels (including diphthongs)의 내용이 맞으면 1점을 준다.

43

하위내용영역	배점	예상정답률
영어학 (음운론) B형 서술형	4점	60%

[모범답안]

First, stress reversal does not occur in (4b) and (4e). In (4b) and (4e), the initial syllables (of the first words) are unstressed: unstressed initial syllables are not part of the word's structure but extensions of the preceding foot.

[채점기준]

내용학 : 4점

(1) stress reversal does not occur in (4b) and (4e)이 맞으면 2점을 준다. (각 1점)
(2) the initial syllables (of the first words) are unstressed의 내용이 맞으면 2점을 준다.

44

하위내용영역	배점	예상정답률
영어학 (음운론) A형 기입형	2점	80%

모범답안

① distinctive ② liquids

채점기준

2점: ①, ② 모두 답안과 일치하면 2점을 준다.
1점: ①, ② 중 하나만 답안과 일치하면 1점을 준다.
0점: ①, ② 모두 답안과 일치하지 않으면 0점을 준다.

45

하위내용영역	배점	예상정답률
영어학 (음운론) A형 서술형	4점	65%

모범답안

First, the schwa articulation is related to (a) assimilation. Second, vowel lengthening occurs before (one of the following) voiced fricatives: (/v/, /ð/, /z/).

채점기준

내용학: 4점

(1) the schwa articulation is related to (a) assimilation이 맞으면 2점을 준다.
(2) vowel lengthening occurs before (one of the following) voiced fricatives의 내용이 맞으면 2점을 준다.

46

하위내용영역	배점	예상정답률
영어학 (음운론) B형 서술형	4점	45%

모범답안

Version 1

First, the one word for the blank is 'final'. Second, the group (1b) has the same stress pattern with the word 'cadet'. In (1b), the words (including 'cadet') have the final stressed syllables, and the rhyme consists of a short (lax) vowel and at least one coda in their final syllables.

Version 2

First, the one word for the blank is 'final'. Second, the word 'cadet' should belong to the group (1b). In (1b), the words (such as 'cadet') have the final stressed syllables. Also, the rhyme consists of a short (lax) vowel and at least one coda in their final syllables.

[채점기준]

내용학 : 4점

(1) the one word for the blank is 'final'이 맞으면 1점을 준다.
(2) the group (1b) has the same stress pattern with the word 'cadet'이 맞으면 1점을 준다.
(3) In (1b), the words (including 'cadet') have the final stressed syllables의 내용이 맞으면 1점을 준다.
(4) the rhyme consists of a short (lax) vowel and at least one coda in their final syllables의 내용이 맞으면 1점을 준다.

47
본책 p.270

하위내용영역	배점	예상정답률
영어학 (음운론) A형 기입형	2점	90%

[모범답안]

① dissimilation ② stressed

[채점기준]

2점 : ①, ② 모두 답안과 일치하면 2점을 준다.
1점 : ①, ② 중 하나만 답안과 일치하면 1점을 준다.
0점 : ①, ② 모두 답안과 일치하지 않으면 0점을 준다.

48
본책 p.271

하위내용영역	배점	예상정답률
영어학 (음운론) A형 서술형	4점	55%

[모범답안]

Version 1

First, a function word receives a nonemphatic stress when it is surrounded by unstressed syllables on both sides. Second, the ambiguity is resolved as follows: (i) "'old 'men ∧ and 'women" means "old men, and women of unspecified age", and (ii) "'old ∧ 'men and 'women" means "men and women, all of whom are old".

MENTOR LINGUISTICS

Version 2

First, a function word receives a nonemphatic stress when it is surrounded by unstressed syllables on both sides. Second, the ambiguity is resolved as follows: (i) "'old 'men ∧ and 'women" means "<u>old men and women of any age (or women and old men)</u>", and (ii) "'old ∧ 'men and 'women" means "<u>old men and old women</u>".

채점기준

내용학: 4점

(1) a function word receives a nonemphatic stress when it is surrounded by unstressed syllables on both sides의 내용이 맞으면 2점을 준다.
(2) "'old 'men ∧ and 'women" means "old men, and women of unspecified age"의 내용이 맞으면 1점을 준다.
(3) "'old ∧ 'men and 'women" means "men and women, all of whom are old"의 내용이 맞으면 1점을 준다.

49
본책 p.273

하위내용영역	배점	예상정답률
영어학 (음운론) B형 서술형	4점	50%

모범답안

The two words are 'cylinder' and 'confetti'. The word 'cylinder' has the heavy penultimate syllable; nevertheless, the stress falls on the antepenult. The word 'confetti' ought to have antepenultimate stress because it has the light penultimate syllable; instead, it stresses the penult and resort to ambisyllabicity to make that syllable heavy.

채점기준

내용학: 4점

(1) The two words are 'cylinder' and 'confetti'이 맞으면 2점을 준다. (각 1점)
(2) The word 'cylinder' has the heavy penultimate syllable; nevertheless, the stress falls on the antepenult의 내용이 맞으면 1점을 준다.
(3) The word 'confetti' ought to have antepenultimate stress because it has the light penultimate syllable; instead, it stresses the penult and resort to ambisyllabicity to make that syllable heavy의 내용이 맞으면 1점을 준다.

50
본책 p.275

하위내용영역	배점	예상정답률
영어학 (음운론) A형 기입형	2점	85%

모범답안

① rounded   ② phonemic

채점기준

2점: ①, ② 모두 답안과 일치하면 2점을 준다.

1점: ①, ② 중 하나만 답안과 일치하면 1점을 준다.

0점: ①, ② 모두 답안과 일치하지 않으면 0점을 준다.

51

하위내용영역	배점	예상정답률
영어학 (음운론) A형 서술형	4점	65%

모범답안

First, the one word for the blank is 'place'. Second, in (4), /æ/ Diphthongization rule comes before /n/ Assimilation rule.

채점기준

내용학: 4점

(1) the one word for the blank is 'place'가 맞으면 2점을 준다.

(2) /æ/ Diphthongization rule comes before /n/ Assimilation rule의 내용이 맞으면 2점을 준다.

52

하위내용영역	배점	예상정답률
영어학 (음운론) B형 서술형	4점	55%

모범답안

First, the one word for the blank is 'onset'. Second, intrusive /r/ does not occur when it is preceded by vowels or second elements of diphthongs which are [+high].

채점기준

내용학: 4점

(1) the one word for the blank is 'onset'이 맞으면 2점을 준다.

(2) intrusive /r/ does not occur when it is preceded by vowels or second elements of diphthongs which are [+high]의 내용이 맞으면 2점을 준다.

53

하위내용영역	배점	예상정답률
영어학 (음운론) A형 기입형	2점	85%

모범답안

same

채점기준

2점: 답안과 일치하면 2점을 준다.
0점: 답안과 일치하지 않으면 0점을 준다.

54

하위내용영역	배점	예상정답률
영어학 (음운론) A형 서술형	4점	65%

모범답안

First, the one word for the blank is 'phonemes'. Second, [ɱ] occurs when the preceding consonant is voiceless.

채점기준

내용학: 4점
(1) the one word for the blank is 'phonemes'가 맞으면 2점을 준다.
(2) [ɱ] occurs when the preceding consonant is voiceless의 내용이 맞으면 2점을 준다.

55

하위내용영역	배점	예상정답률
영어학 (음운론) B형 서술형	4점	30%

모범답안

First, the counterexample is 'yellow'. Second, the generalisation should be revised as follows: /l/ is realised as (clear) [l] in (syllable) onsets and as (dark) [ɫ] elsewhere.
[참고]
/l/ is realised, in RP, as [l] whenever it occurs in a syllable onset; and it is realised as [ɫ] elsewhere. Note that it would be wrong to state this rule the other way round, as '/l/ is realised as [ɫ] in rhymes and as [l] elsewhere': this would falsely predict /l/ in ambisyllabic position (yellow) to be dark.

채점기준

내용학 : 4점
(1) the counterexample is 'yellow'가 맞으면 2점을 준다.
(2) /l/ is realised as (clear) [l] in (syllable) onsets and as (dark) [ɫ] elsewhere의 내용이 맞으면 2점을 준다.

56

본책 p.286

하위내용영역	배점	예상정답률
영어학 (음운론) A형 기입형	2점	85%

모범답안

① overlapping   ② phonemic

채점기준

2점 : ①, ② 모두 답안과 일치하면 2점을 준다.
1점 : ①, ② 중 하나만 답안과 일치하면 1점을 준다.
0점 : ①, ② 모두 답안과 일치하지 않으면 0점을 준다.

57

본책 p.288

하위내용영역	배점	예상정답률
영어학 (음운론) B형 서술형	4점	60%

모범답안

Version 1

(4a) represents [aɪ] which precedes a voiceless consonant /p/ in the next word. Hence the word-bounded rule of /aɪ/ Raising is blocked. In contrast, (4b) represents [ʌɪ] which precedes a voiceless consonant /p/ within the same word. Hence the word-bounded rule of /aɪ/ Raising can apply.

Version 2

First, (4a) represents [aɪ] and that of (4b) represents [ʌɪ]. Second, (4a) has an /aɪ/ that precedes a voiceless consonant /p/ in the next word. Hence the word-bounded rule of /aɪ/ Raising is blocked. In contrast, (4b) has an /aɪ/ that precedes a voiceless consonant /p/ within the same word. Hence the word-bounded rule of /aɪ/ Raising can apply.

> **채점기준**

내용학 : 4점

(1) (4a) represents [aɪ] and that of (4b) represents [ʌɪ]이 맞으면 2점을 준다. (각 1점)
(2) (4a) has an /aɪ/ that precedes a voiceless consonant /p/ in the next word. Hence the word-bounded rule of /aɪ/ Raising is blocked의 내용이 맞으면 1점을 준다.
(3) (4b) has an /aɪ/ that precedes a voiceless consonant /p/ within the same word. Hence the word-bounded rule of /aɪ/ Raising can apply의 내용이 맞으면 1점을 준다.

58
본책 p.290

하위내용영역	배점	예상정답률
영어학 (음운론) A형 기입형	2점	85%

> **모범답안**

① onset ② labials

> **채점기준**

2점 : ①, ② 모두 답안과 일치하면 2점을 준다.
1점 : ①, ② 중 하나만 답안과 일치하면 1점을 준다.
0점 : ①, ② 모두 답안과 일치하지 않으면 0점을 준다.

59
본책 p.292

하위내용영역	배점	예상정답률
영어학 (음운론) A형 서술형	4점	55%

> **모범답안**

First, the one word for the blank is 'non-homorganic'. Second, in (2a), weak aspiration occurs when voiceless stops are in an unstressed syllable. In (2b), voiceless stops are produced with weak aspiration before syllabic consonants.

> **채점기준**

내용학 : 4점

(1) the one word for the blank is 'non-homorganic'이 맞으면 2점을 준다.
(2) in (2a), weak aspiration occurs when voiceless stops are in an unstressed syllable의 내용이 맞으면 1점을 준다.
(3) In (2b), voiceless stops are produced with weak aspiration before syllabic consonants의 내용이 맞으면 1점을 준다.

60

하위내용영역	배점	예상정답률
영어학 (음운론) B형 서술형	4점	50%

모범답안

First, the two sets are (4a) and (4f). Second, in (4a), the vowel in 'mouth (verb)' is longer before the voiced consonant /ð/ than before its voiceless counterpart /θ/ in 'mouth (noun)'. In (4f), the vowel in 'lose' is longer before the voiced consonant /z/ than before its voiceless counterpart /s/ in 'loose'.

채점기준

내용학: 4점
(1) the two sets are (4a) and (4f)가 맞으면 2점을 준다. (각 1점)
(2) in (4a), the vowel in 'mouth (verb)' is longer before the voiced consonant /ð/ than before its voiceless counterpart /θ/ in 'mouth (noun)'의 내용이 맞으면 1점을 준다.
(3) In (4f), the vowel in 'lose' is longer before the voiced consonant /z/ than before its voiceless counterpart /s/ in 'loose'의 내용이 맞으면 1점을 준다.

61

하위내용영역	배점	예상정답률
영어학 (음운론) A형 기입형	2점	90%

모범답안

① unstressed ② antepenultimate

채점기준

2점: ①, ② 모두 답안과 일치하면 2점을 준다.
1점: ①, ② 중 하나만 답안과 일치하면 1점을 준다.
0점: ①, ② 모두 답안과 일치하지 않으면 0점을 준다.

62

하위내용영역	배점	예상정답률
영어학 (음운론) A형 서술형	4점	65%

모범답안

Version 1

First, the two constructions are (3a) and (4b). The reason for the preference is eurhythmic: (3a) and (4b) have the optimal rhythmic alternation (in which strong and weak syllables alternate in an S-W-S-W pattern and the others do not).

Version 2

First, the two constructions are (3a) 'bleak and lonely' and (4b) 'crisp and crunchy'. Speakers favour the constructions (3a) and (4b) that have the optimal rhythmic alternation over the alternative ones that are less eurhythmic.

채점기준

내용학: 4점

(1) the two constructions are (3a) and (4b)이 맞으면 2점을 준다. (각 1점)
(2) The reason for the preference is eurhythmic: (3a) and (4b) have the optimal rhythmic alternation (in which strong and weak syllables alternate in an S-W-S-W pattern and the others do not)의 내용이 맞으면 2점을 준다.

63

하위내용영역	배점	예상정답률
영어학 (음운론) B형 서술형	4점	60%

모범답안

First, (c) and (e) do not have the same pattern as (5). In (c), the /t/ targets in both 'detest' and 'detestable' do not undergo flapping (because the (underlined) /t/ in each word occurs (is) in a stressed syllable). In (e), the /t/ targets in both 'retard' and 'retardant' do not undergo flapping (because the (underlined) /t/ in each word occurs (is) in a stressed syllable).

채점기준

내용학: 4점

(1) (c) and (e) do not have the same pattern as (5)이 맞으면 2점을 준다. (각 1점)
(2) In (c), the /t/ targets in both 'detest' and 'detestable' do not undergo flapping (because the (underlined) /t/ in each word occurs (is) in a stressed syllable)의 내용이 맞으면 1점을 준다.
(3) In (e), the /t/ targets in both 'retard' and 'retardant' do not undergo flapping (because the (underlined) /t/ in each word occurs (is) in a stressed syllable)의 내용이 맞으면 1점을 준다.

64

하위내용영역	배점	예상정답률
영어학 (음운론) A형 기입형	2점	90%

모범답안

① vowel ② complementary

채점기준

2점: ①, ② 모두 답안과 일치하면 2점을 준다.
1점: ①, ② 중 하나만 답안과 일치하면 1점을 준다.
0점: ①, ② 모두 답안과 일치하지 않으면 0점을 준다.

65

하위내용영역	배점	예상정답률
영어학 (음운론) B형 서술형	4점	65%

모범답안

(7a) and (7c) have the same stress pattern because both (7a) and (7c) have antepenultimate primary stress (whereas the group (7b) takes primary stress on the '‐ate').

채점기준

내용학: 4점
(1) (7a) and (7c) have the same stress pattern이 맞으면 2점을 준다.
(2) because both (7a) and (7c) have antepenultimate primary stress (whereas the group (7b) takes primary stress on the '‐ate')의 내용이 맞으면 2점을 준다.

66

하위내용영역	배점	예상정답률
영어학 (음운론) A형 기입형	2점	85%

모범답안

① onset ② aspirated

채점기준

2점: ①, ② 모두 답안과 일치하면 2점을 준다.
1점: ①, ② 중 하나만 답안과 일치하면 1점을 준다.
0점: ①, ② 모두 답안과 일치하지 않으면 0점을 준다.

67

본책 p.305

하위내용영역	배점	예상정답률
영어학 (음운론) B형 서술형	4점	60%

모범답안

First, the word for the blank is 'palato-alveolars (or alveo-palatals)'. Second, [ɪ] in 'topic' is likely to change to an [ə] in 'topical' because the velar [k] in 'topical' is the onset of the following syllable.

채점기준

내용학: 4점
(1) the word for the blank is 'palato-alveolars (or alveo-palatals)'가 맞으면 2점을 준다.
(2) the velar [k] in 'topical' is the onset of the following syllable의 내용이 맞으면 2점을 준다.

68

본책 p.307

하위내용영역	배점	예상정답률
영어학 (음운론) A형 서술형	4점	65%

모범답안

First, the one word for the blank is 'nucleus'. Second, C_1 is deleted in (3c) because it provides a higher jump in sonority from the single onset to the nucleus: (a CV sequence is more natural when the contrast between the C and the V is greater.)

채점기준

내용학: 4점
(1) the one word for the blank is 'nucleus'가 맞으면 2점을 준다.
(2) it provides a higher jump in sonority from the single onset to the nucleus의 내용이 맞으면 2점을 준다.

69

하위내용영역	배점	예상정답률
영어학 (음운론) B형 서술형	4점	65%

모범답안

Version 1

First, the word for the blank is 'labial'. Second, in (1b), stop + nasal sequences are not in the same syllable; (they are not tautosyllabic). (Likewise,) in (2b), non-homorganic nasal + stop sequences are found across syllables.

Version 2

The word for the blank is 'labial'. In (1b), stop + nasal sequences are in the different syllable; (they are heterosyllabic), and in (2b), we can get such non-homorganic sequences across syllables.

채점기준

내용학 : 4점

(1) the word for the blank is 'labial'이 맞으면 2점을 준다.
(2) in (1b), stop + nasal sequences are not in the same syllable의 내용이 맞으면 1점을 준다.
(3) in (2b), non-homorganic nasal + stop sequences are found across syllables의 내용이 맞으면 1점을 준다.

70

하위내용영역	배점	예상정답률
영어학 (음운론) A형 기입형	2점	65%

모범답안

① [− anterior]   ② [+ lateral]

채점기준

2점 : ①, ② 모두 답안과 일치하면 2점을 준다.
1점 : ①, ② 중 하나만 답안과 일치하면 1점을 준다.
0점 : ①, ② 모두 답안과 일치하지 않으면 0점을 준다.

71

하위내용영역	배점	예상정답률
영어학 (음운론) A형 서술형	4점	65%

모범답안

First, the word for the blank ① is 'phonemes' and the word for the blank ② is 'allophones'. Second, (in (2) and (3)), [p] occurs word-finally whereas [b] occurs intervocalically.

채점기준

내용학 : 4점

(1) the word for the blank ① is 'phonemes' and the word for the blank ② is 'allophones'가 맞으면 2점을 준다. (각 1점)
(2) (in (2) and (3)), [p] occurs word-finally whereas [b] occurs intervocalically의 내용이 맞으면 2점을 준다. (각 1점)

72

하위내용영역	배점	예상정답률
영어학 (음운론) B형 서술형	4점	60%

모범답안

The unstressed [ə] deletion occurs when [ə] is before a sonorant whereas [ə] is not deleted when it is followed by an obstruent.

채점기준

내용학 : 4점

(1) The unstressed [ə] deletion occurs when it is before a sonorant의 내용이 맞으면 2점을 준다.
(2) [ə] is not deleted when it is followed by an obstruent의 내용이 맞으면 2점을 준다.

73

하위내용영역	배점	예상정답률
영어학 (음운론) A형 기입형	2점	90%

모범답안

① distinctive ② − continuant

[채점기준]

2점 : ①, ② 모두 답안과 일치하면 2점을 준다.
1점 : ①, ② 중 하나만 답안과 일치하면 1점을 준다.
0점 : ①, ② 모두 답안과 일치하지 않으면 0점을 준다.

74

본책 p.318

하위내용영역	배점	예상정답률
영어학 (음운론) B형 서술형	4점	60%

[모범답안]

First, the blank ① is 'onset', and the blank ② is 'different (or following)'. Second, (English vowels are lengthened when followed by a voiced obstruent in) the coda position of the same syllable.

[채점기준]

내용학 : 4점

(1) the blank ① is 'onset', and the blank ② is 'different (or following)'이 맞으면 2점을 준다. (각 1점)
(2) (English vowels are lengthened when followed by a voiced obstruent in) the coda position of the same syllable의 내용이 맞으면 2점을 준다.

75

본책 p.320

하위내용영역	배점	예상정답률
영어학 (음운론) A형 서술형	4점	65%

[모범답안]

First, the word for the blank is 'voiced'. Second, voiceless fricatives [ç], [ɬ], and [ɹ̥] occur after voiceless stops (plosives).

[채점기준]

내용학 : 4점

(1) the word for the blank is 'voiced'가 맞으면 2점을 준다.
(2) voiceless fricatives [ç], [ɬ], and [ɹ̥] occur after voiceless stops (plosives)의 내용이 맞으면 2점을 준다.

76

본책 p.322

하위내용영역	배점	예상정답률
영어학 (음운론) B형 서술형	4점	65%

모범답안

First, the word for the blank is 'voicing'. Second, a fricative becomes is voiceless when it is followed by a voiceless obstruent in the following word.

채점기준

내용학: 4점

(1) 'voicing'이 맞으면 2점을 준다.
(2) a fricative become voiceless when it is followed by a voiceless obstruent in the following word의 내용이 맞으면 2점을 준다.

Part 04 Morphology

01

하위내용영역	배점	예상정답률
영어학 (형태론) A형 서술형	4점	40%

모범답안

Version 1

The root is 'act', a verb, to which we add the suffix '-ive', resulting in an adjective, 'active'. To this adjective, we add the suffix '-ate' forming a verb 'activate'. Finally, the suffix '-ion' attaches to this verb and converts it into the noun 'activation'.

Version 2

First, the suffix (the affix) '-ive' attaches to the verbal base 'act' to give an adjective 'active'. Second, the suffix '-ate' attaches to this adjective and converts it into a verb 'activate'. Finally, the suffix '-ion' is added, converting the verb into the noun 'activation'.

Version 3

First, the suffix '-ive' attaches to the verb 'act' to form the adjective 'active'. Second, the suffix '-ate' attaches to the adjective 'active' to form the verb 'activate'. Lastly, the suffix '-ion' attaches to the verb 'activate' to form the noun 'activation'.

채점기준

내용학 : 4점

(1) The root is 'act', a verb, to which we add the suffix '-ive', resulting in an adjective, 'active'의 내용이 맞으면 1점을 준다.
(2) To this adjective, we add the suffix '-ate' forming a verb 'activate'의 내용이 맞으면 2점을 준다.
(3) the suffix '-ion' attaches to this verb and converts it into the noun 'activation'의 내용이 맞으면 1점을 준다.

02

하위내용영역	배점	예상정답률
영어학 (형태론) A형 서술형	4점	65%

모범답안

Version 1

First, (ic) is ungrammatical. In 'dropped kick', the tense marker '-ed' cannot be attached to the first element. Second, (iia) is Non-compound Expression, and (iib) is Compound Word.

Version 2

First, (ic) is ungrammatical because in the phrase 'dropped kick', the compound verb with internal tense is not possible. Second, in (iia) 'wet suit' belongs to Non-compound Expression, and in (iib) 'wet suit' belongs to Compound Word.

[채점기준]

내용학: 4점
(1) (ic) is ungrammatical이 맞으면 1점을 준다.
(2) In 'dropped kick', the tense marker '-ed' cannot be attached to the first element의 내용이 맞으면 1점을 준다.
(3) (iia) is Non-compound Expression이 맞으면 1점을 준다.
(4) (iib) is Compound Word이 맞으면 1점을 준다.

03 본책 p.330

하위내용영역	배점	예상정답률
영어학 (형태론) A형 기입형	2점	80%

[모범답안]

① cook ② obstruent

[채점기준]

2점: ①, ② 모두 답안과 일치하면 2점을 준다.
1점: ①, ② 중 하나만 답안과 일치하면 1점을 준다.
0점: ①, ② 모두 답안과 일치하지 않으면 0점을 준다.

04 본책 p.331

하위내용영역	배점	예상정답률
영어학 (형태론) A형 서술형	4점	65%

[모범답안]

The formation rules are applied as follows: (i) mind + ful → mindful (Noun + fəl → Adjective), (ii) un + mindful → unmindful (ʌn + Adjective → Adjective), and (iii) unmindful + ness → unmindfulness (Adjective + nəs → Noun)

[채점기준]

내용학: 4점
(1) (i) mind + ful → mindful (Noun + fəl → Adjective)이 맞으면 2점을 준다.
(2) (ii) un + mindful → unmindful (ʌn + Adjective → Adjective)이 맞으면 1점을 준다.
(3) (iii) unmindful + ness → unmindfulness (Adjective + nəs → Noun)이 맞으면 1점을 준다.

Part 05 Semantics

01

하위내용영역	배점	예상정답률
영어학 (의미론) A형 서술형	4점	70%

[모범답안]

Version 1

A pair of sentences in (iii) shows the semantic relation of entailment. If we negate (iiia) 'John hasn't arrived in Edinburgh', then it no longer entails (iiib) 'John is in Edinburgh'. (Negating an entailing sentence destroys the entailment / If we negate an entailing sentence, then the entailment fails.)

Version 2

A pair of sentences in (iii) shows the semantic relation of entailment. If we negate (iiia) 'John hasn't arrived in Edinburgh', then it no longer entails (iiib) 'John is in Edinburgh'. (If we negate an entailing sentence 'John hasn't arrived in Edinburgh', we don't know about whether John is in Edinburgh.)

[채점기준]

내용학 : 4점

(1) A pair of sentences in (iii) shows the semantic relation of entailment이 맞으면 2점을 준다.
(2) If we negate (iiia), then it no longer entails (iiib)의 내용이 맞으면 2점을 준다.

02

하위내용영역	배점	예상정답률
영어학 (의미론) A형 서술형	4점	65%

[모범답안]

Sentence (b) does not produce presupposition. The non-factive predicate 'is true' does not presuppose the truth of the complement clause ('Jill had lent Ed her key'). Sentence (e) does not produce presupposition because a *yes-no* question doesn't serve as a presupposition trigger.

[채점기준]

내용학 : 4점

(1) Sentence (b) does not produce presupposition이 맞으면 1점을 준다.
(2) The non-factive predicate 'is true' does not presuppose the truth of the complement clause의 내용이 맞으면 1점을 준다.
(3) Sentence (e) does not produce presupposition이 맞으면 1점을 준다.
(4) a *yes-no* question doesn't serve as a presupposition trigger의 내용이 맞으면 1점을 준다.

03

하위내용영역	배점	예상정답률
영어학 (의미론) A형 서술형	4점	70%

모범답안

Version 1

The blank ① is 'Hyponymy' and the blank ② is 'meronymy'.

The sentence (e) is wrong: house is a hyponym of building. The sentence (f) is wrong: saw is a hyponym of tool.

Version 2

① Hyponymy   ② meronymy

The sentences (e) and (f) are wrong. The correct forms are as follows: (e) house is a hyponym of building and (f) saw is a hyponym of tool.

채점기준

내용학: 4점

(1) The blank ① is 'Hyponymy' and the blank ② is 'meronymy'이 맞으면 2점을 준다. (각 1점)
(2) The sentence (e) is wrong: house is a hyponym of building이 맞으면 1점을 준다.
(3) The sentence (f) is wrong: saw is a hyponym of tool이 맞으면 1점을 준다.

04

하위내용영역	배점	예상정답률
영어학 (의미론) A형 서술형	4점	60%

모범답안

Sentence (5) has a presupposed proposition (in it). The presupposed proposition of the sentence is that John told a lie, and the presupposition-triggering element of the sentence is the (factive) verb 'regret'. (Therefore, the verb 'regret' is a factive predicate and induces the factive proposition from its embedded clause.)

채점기준

내용학: 4점

(1) Sentence (5) has a presupposed proposition (in it)이 맞으면 2점을 준다.
(2) The presupposed proposition of the sentence is that John told a lie이 맞으면 1점을 준다.
(3) the presupposition-triggering element of the sentence is the (factive) verb 'regret'이 맞으면 1점을 준다.

05

하위내용영역	배점	예상정답률
영어학 (의미론) A형 기입형	2점	90%

모범답안

① true ② entails

채점기준

2점 : ①, ② 모두 답안과 일치하면 2점을 준다.
1점 : ①, ② 중 하나만 답안과 일치하면 1점을 준다.
0점 : ①, ② 모두 답안과 일치하지 않으면 0점을 준다.

06

하위내용영역	배점	예상정답률
영어학 (의미론) A형 서술형	4점	60%

모범답안

Sentence (b) takes a complement clause that is presupposed to be true. The presupposed proposition of the sentence is that Woodstock is his best friend. Sentence (c) has a presupposition (or a presupposed proposition in it). The presupposed proposition of the sentence is that Linus was waiting for the Great Pumpkin.

채점기준

내용학 : 4점

(1) Sentence (b) takes a complement clause that is presupposed to be true이 맞으면 1점을 준다.
(2) The presupposed proposition of the sentence is that Woodstock is his best friend이 맞으면 1점을 준다.
(3) Sentence (c) has a presupposition이 맞으면 1점을 준다.
(4) The presupposed proposition of the sentence is that Linus was waiting for the Great Pumpkin이 맞으면 1점을 준다.

07

본책 p.348

하위내용영역	배점	예상정답률
영어학 (의미론/화용론) A형 기입형	2점	85%

모범답안

① entailments ② presuppositions

채점기준

2점: ①, ② 모두 답안과 일치하면 2점을 준다.

1점: ①, ② 중 하나만 답안과 일치하면 1점을 준다.

0점: ①, ② 모두 답안과 일치하지 않으면 0점을 준다.

Part 06 Pragmatics

01

본책 p.352

하위내용영역	배점	예상정답률
영어학 (화용론) A형 기입형	2점	80%

모범답안

① imperative ② directive

채점기준

2점: ①, ② 모두 답안과 일치하면 2점을 준다.
1점: ①, ② 중 하나만 답안과 일치하면 1점을 준다.
0점: ①, ② 모두 답안과 일치하지 않으면 0점을 준다.

02

본책 p.354

하위내용영역	배점	예상정답률
영어학 (화용론) A형 기입형	2점	90%

모범답안

quantity (Quantity)

채점기준

2점: 답안과 일치하면 2점을 준다.
0점: 답안과 일치하지 않으면 0점을 준다.

03

본책 p.356

하위내용영역	배점	예상정답률
영어학 (화용론) A형 서술형	4점	60%

모범답안

First, the word for the blank is 'Quality'. Second, Peter's utterance in (2) flouts the Maxim of Quantity. Peter's utterance means that he did not bring the cheese.

채점기준

내용학: 4점

(1) the word for the blank is 'Quality'이 맞으면 1점을 준다.
(2) Peter's utterance in (2) flouts the Maxim of Quantity이 맞으면 1점을 준다.
(3) Peter's utterance means that he did not bring the cheese의 내용이 맞으면 2점을 준다.

앤드류 채

멘토영어학 문제은행

| 모범답안 |

초판인쇄 | 2025. 7. 1.   **초판발행** | 2025. 7. 7.
편저자 | 앤드류 채   **발행인** | 박 용   **발행처** | (주)박문각출판
표지디자인 | 박문각 디자인팀   **등록** | 2015년 4월 29일 제2019-000137호
주소 | 06654 서울특별시 서초구 효령로 283 서경 B/D   **팩스** | (02)584-2927
전화 | 교재 문의 (02)6466-7202, 동영상 문의 (02)6466-7201

저자와의
협의하에
인지생략

이 책의 무단 전재 또는 복제 행위는 저작권법 제136조에 의거, 5년 이하의 징역 또는 5,000만 원 이하의 벌금에 처하거나 이를 병과할 수 있습니다.

ISBN 979-11-7262-953-3

Mentor Linguistics Series

전공영어 멘토영어학   멘토영어학 기출분석   멘토영어학 문제은행

2024 고객선호브랜드지수 1위
교육(교육서비스) 부문

 2021 조선일보 국가브랜드 대상
에듀테크 부문 수상

 2019 한국 우수브랜드평가 대상
교육브랜드 부문 수상

 2023 고객선호브랜드지수 1위
교육(교육서비스) 부문

 2021 대한민국 소비자 선호도 1위
교육 부문 1위

 2018 대한민국 교육산업 대상
교육서비스 부문 수상

 2022 한국 브랜드 만족지수 1위
교육(교육서비스) 부문 1위

 2020 한국 산업의 1등
브랜드 대상 수상

brandstock BSTI
브랜드 가치평가 1위

앤드류 채 2026 멘토영어학 문제은행

MENTOR

ISBN 979-11-7262-953-3

교재관련 문의 02-6466-7202
학원관련 문의 02-816-2030
온라인강의 문의 02-6466-7201

www.pmg.co.kr 박문각

2026 교원임용시험 전공영어 대비

앤드류 채
멘토영어학
문제은행